THE UNMAKING OF A CONSERVATIVE
AFRICA
ANYTHING IS POSSIBLE

PETER JAMES CANNON

AuthorHouse™ LLC
1663 Liberty Drive
Bloomington, IN 47403
www.authorhouse.com
Phone: 1-800-839-8640

Published by AuthorHouse 06/2/2014

ISBN: 978-1-4969-2158-1 (sc)
ISBN: 978-1-4969-2214-4 (e)

Library of Congress Control Number: 2014911434

To the past, as represented by, my deceased former colleague Benedict Edherue, and the future, as represented by, my granddaughter Laila Isobel Cannon.

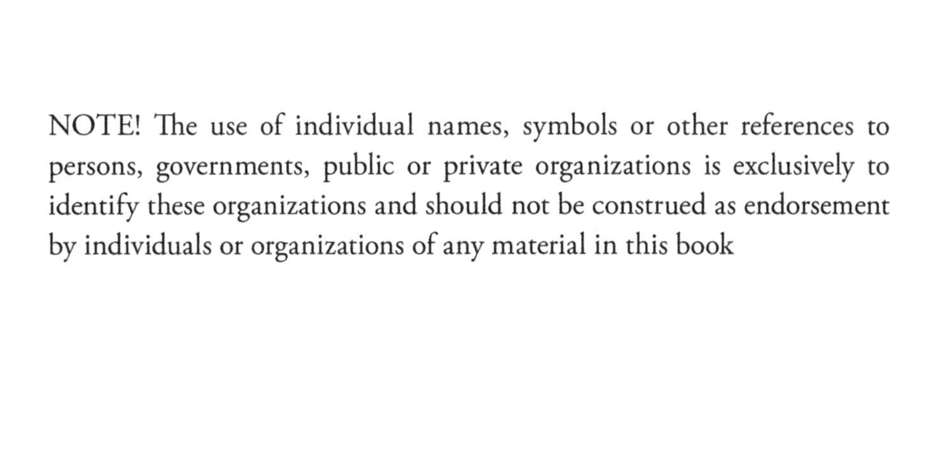

NOTE! The use of individual names, symbols or other references to persons, governments, public or private organizations is exclusively to identify these organizations and should not be construed as endorsement by individuals or organizations of any material in this book

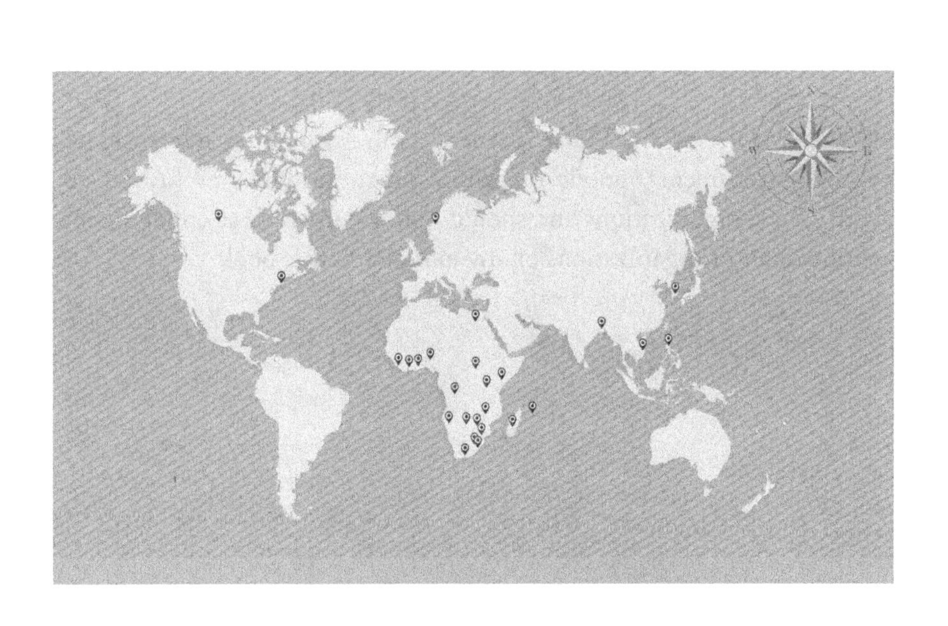

Contents

Acknowledgements

The writing of this book lasted more than a decade. I would have never completed it without the support of family and the support of those I encountered on this sojourn. Those I'm unable to mention by name, please accept my deep esteem. I would like to thank the numerous individuals who gave me encouragement and too numerous to name individually.

I would especially like to thank my wife Gudrun Cannon for encouragement; my daughter Chandra Cannon for her love and editorial work evident throughout this book, my granddaughter Laila Isobel Cannon for her laughter, my son Marc, for designing the books cover jacket and back cover, and my cousin Vinnie Cannon's son Alex Cannon for his editorial suggestions.

I'm profoundly grateful for the friendship of my late colleague Benedict Edherue. His humor kept all the good and bad in a realistic perspective. Enjoy the Ancestors Brother Ben.

Foreword

Peter James Cannon was the sole offspring of a catholic Irish-Italian first generation family. He grew up in insular, Providence, Rhode Island, smallest of all US states, in the years following World War II. His working class parents were socially conservative but strong supporters of the Democratic political party.

Cannon's education was completed in sequestered environments, of very strict old fashioned Catholic institutions, from primary school to graduate school. Upon graduation from Providence College in 1963, at age twenty-three, Cannon was a conservative, as were most men who came from similar backgrounds.

Who could have imagined decades later, Cannon would have worked in twenty-three countries outside of the United States: eighteen of these were in Africa.

It was unimaginable in 1963 to conceive Cannon's metamorphosis into a leftist leaning individual. If he learned only one belief after years of working and living in Africa, that was **anything is possible in Africa**.

Prologue

Easter time in West Africa: a time in which city dwellers try to get back to their home village. Cannon thought he would stay in Lagos for the holiday. Instead he was invited to accompany Ben Edherue to his Isoko village in the Niger delta. Ben, as he preferred to be called by ex-pats, was Cannon's colleague in his trade union days who had become a friend. Cannon later learned he was the only ex-pat Ben had ever invited to visit his home village. Cannon was told to bring a few changes of clothes and nothing else. Cannon was to be treated like any other villager, except for drinking water. He should be ready to leave by early morning as the drive to Benin City could take a while due to the horrible condition of the highway.

How in the world could it be possible that a white guy from Providence, Rhode Island in the United States of America would be travelling down the same highway in Nigeria that he had driven on numerous times during the civil war in 1968? Isokoland, was a very long way from Providence, Rhode Island Cannon's place of birth. Two places couldn't be more different: the only point of commonality was they both knew about corruption first hand.

The highway connecting Lagos to Benin City was a disaster in 2002, whereas in 1968 it was a highway comparable to that of a county road in the western world. About half way, we stopped at an area which sold food and drink for travelers. In no way did the eating establishments resemble western styled fast food eateries but by the number of patrons at tables, you knew the food had to be good. After washing one's hands, it was time to select what to eat. Cannon was told that this particular establishment was well known for its fresh fish grown in a pond in back. Cannon was given the head-a choice part-to go along with pounded yam. All washed down by a cold Star beer. What a feast!

Eventually in late afternoon we arrived in Benin City and checked into a local hotel which was used often by Ben in his work as a trade union educator. After washing up, it was time to find one of his "brothers" from his days of working on behalf of the Nigerian Labor Congress. We finally found Sylvester at home with his wife. After exchanging pleasantries we departed the home, stopped to pick-up Sylvester's girlfriend and headed down to the watering hole with the best pepper soup in Benin. After being in Nigeria for a while, a foreigner soon learned that Nigerians loved pepper soup. The hotter it tasted the better it was liked. It helped though, if it was washed down by a few cold beers.

Just before noon the following day, we departed Benin heading south to Ben's place of birth Ikori located in the oil producing region in the Delta State. We would be staying in Irri, a nearby town. Ben always referred to his Isoko tribe as if it was a separate country not part of Nigeria.

We stopped a few times to inspect bush meat sold on the roadside. Bush meat was any kind of a four legged creature that roamed the countryside. Ben selected a choice specimen that was placed in the trunk of the car, hair-and-all. He said it wasn't proper for him to return home empty handed.

Sunset in Isoko country comes quickly. The battered 1989 used vehicle, courtesy of some German who probably thought the vehicle was to be sold for scrap, had made good time from Lagos in spite of its being cobbled together by various bush mechanics. Instead of going direct to the village where the family was waiting with "chop" as food was known in West Africa, Ben turned off the two lane main highway, on to a dirt path, which led into a small compound in the village of Adah.

The square-shaped compound housed numerous families, but at this time of night was unusually still. The vehicle stopped in front of a semi-opened door. Inside was a small sitting room with two chairs and a table under a loosely hanging light bulb. From another room out came one of Ben's cousins who pulled on a shirt as he entered the sitting room. Isoko greetings were passed as the African crossed armed handshake was exchanged before both parties embraced. Cannon was introduced as brother who happened to be white.

The men moved outdoors where it was much cooler than being inside. Chairs materialized along with a bottle of Isoko gin. The bottle contained a brownish liquid with various objects, which were later identified as herbs. A glass for the visitor and small empty glass jars, formerly food containers, were brought out from inside. Glasses were filled, the following words were spoken:

"Esemo, Udi oro'me obo, Eke rai ona! Uno anwa z'eho Wha gbe bru obe ruru omai ehru emeje ma emo ra je re emu Ododo ore kpo ho eha eso ha Esemo wha da! Hoooo- the drinkers.

(Our ancestors, behold in my hands is the drink, this is your portion, as the drink is poured from drinking container to the ground. Ancients please continue to protect us continue to prosper us as your beautiful flowers. May we not suffer disgrace? Our ancestors drink! I am drinking. Hoooo- the drinkers).

A small portion of each drink was poured onto the dirt ground to honor the ancestors. At this moment Cannon knew he was "home". Isn't it true that the first human being was originally from Africa? Since this has yet to be proven otherwise, wouldn't it also be true that all human beings are "brothers and sisters"?

1

The Start of an Unlikely Journey

Little did a first generation Irish catholic male and a first generation Italian catholic female ever dream in their wildest imagination that their son would end up traveling to many parts of the world. Cannon's parents were the product of the European immigration to the United States in the middle 1800's. Both families journey, from two very different cultures, ended up in Providence. Cannon never found out why!

At the turn of the 20th century, the city of Providence was divided into neighborhoods reflecting the ethnicity of the inhabitants. Most resided in two or three family dwellings. Cannon's Irish catholic family resided in a section of Providence that was known locally as Beer Hill. Who could ever wonder why since it was almost totally Irish who were known to hoist a beer or two on a daily basis?

My father's family lost its breadwinner before the children had completed their teenage years. It was said grandpa Cannon's passing placed the family in dire financial straits. The loss of the breadwinner forced the eldest child, my father John, to drop out of high school to support the family. My father never got over his formal education lost opportunities.

Fortunately there were textile mills nearby where one could get employment fairly easily but at a very low starting wage. Little did people realize that before they reached middle age, the textile mills would be a thing of the past? Most mills moved south either just before World War II or shortly thereafter.

They moved south where wages were substantially lower and workers' unions did not exist. How ironic years later, this same industry fled the southern shores of the USA for greener pastures overseas where the wages were even cheaper and unions were not a factor?

Bordering the Beer Hill section of Providence was the neighborhood called Mount Pleasant which was predominately Italian. Here Cannon's catholic Italian side of the family, the DiMaio's operated a bakery which provided a very good living. They would be considered upper middle class using the modern day's economist classification of families. The Italians were as different as chalk and cheese in comparison to the Irish.

How in the world did a marriage ever occur? Prior to the start of World War II it was highly unusual that a marriage took place between Irish and Italian. Rumor had it Cannon's parents had to elope to get married out of Rhode Island. Cannon came into the world in 1939, a few months prior to the start of the second major war of the 20th century. When Cannon raised this subject with his Parents, he was told it wasn't important. Blending two opposite cultures into a Marriage deserved a better answer than Cannon was ever given.

The Italian side of the family were terrific cooks with one exception Cannons' mother Lena. The Italians considered her the worst cook out of the four daughters. The Irish thought Lena was a terrific cook especially when she made meatballs and spaghetti for them. It is possible she was smart to let her older sisters do all the cooking? Her culinary skills didn't improve too much when she married an Irish husband. The Italians loved to eat, while the Irish loved to drink.

Cannons father John really did not like Italian food. If Lena and son wanted Italian food she would have to cook a separate meal for John. His favorite food was hotdogs. Most of Cannons friends grew up eating meat and potatoes. Some had spaghetti covered with ketchup: is there anything worse than that? Cannon preferred pasta over potatoes but grew up eating whatever was on his plate.

Originally the Cannon family of three resided in a third floor walk-up flat on Hope Street which was located on the east side of the city of Providence: then and still considered to be where the wealthy resided except for those living in 3rd floor apartments. After a few years, the family moved into the Elmhurst section, more of a working class neighborhood, where they rented the bottom floor of a two story house: the owners lived in the upstairs section of the house.

As a child Cannon had friendly eyes with a twinkle. Often when Cannon behaved outrageous like emptying his Italian grandfather's wine barrels, the Italian's thought it was because he was half Irish. Cannon's physical make-up, included a full head of curly black hair and swarthy skin color, was more associated with his Italian rather than his Irish ethnicity.

Prior to enrolling in grammar school, Cannon was required to attend kindergarten in a nearby public school. It was while in kindergarten that Cannon's uniqueness first appeared: he was expelled for throwing all the play balls over the fence during recess. There's no need to dwell on the beating he received except to note it was delivered by his Italian Mother. In later years when physical punishment was in the cards, his Irish Father was fond of saying: "**Lena you better whack him because if I do, I'll kill him**".

The Catholic grammar school, St. Pius, was located next to the only Dominican college in the United States: Providence College. During those days, all the kids walked to school except for those few who came from neighborhoods that didn't have a catholic grammar school. They arrived in cars. There was a dress code: white shirt, blue tie and blue pants for the boys and white blouse and blue dresses for the girls. Seating in the classrooms, which usually held around twenty-five, was arranged by the alphabet: unless you were pegged as a problem child-then you were seated in the front row close to the sisters' desk. This made it easier for her to whack you. The Dominican Sisters were fair, but very strong on discipline. Cannon was on the receiving end of the good Sisters' discipline throughout his grammar school years more often than not.

The Dominican sisters thought the twinkle in Cannon's eyes was a sign of the devil especially when he was in trouble. An example of this occurred in the 3rd grade. While out riding a bicycle with a neighbor who was also in the 3rd grade, the neighbor fell off the bike and Cannon ran over his ear. The next day when the Sister pulled Eddy's ear blood gushed all over the place. What did the Sister do but whack Cannon because he had the devil in him. Make any sense? That was Catholic grammar school in the early 1950's.

Little time nor interest was devoted to international affairs except for one area: God-Less Communism. The good Sisters kept donation jars in classrooms to collect pennies or nickels for the poor starving children in China. It was only years later that Cannon realized the Sisters really meant Taiwan, not mainland China since after 1949, western Catholic missionaries were throw out after the Communists were victorious in the civil war. For the good Sisters it really didn't matter since the collection boxes were to be used to overcome the Communists. Nobody bothered to question the Sisters as to what was "communism"? Nor did Cannon's parents bother to discuss communism. It was a given that the US was the greatest while communists countries were bad.

The word communism didn't have too much meaning for Cannon until the 6th grade. It was then when Cannon's first basketball coach Joe Hassett was drafted into the US Marines to fight against the communists in Korea. Later in the 7th grade his new basketball coach Armand Batastini was drafted into the US Navy. There after the word communism took on a different meaning. Cannon can still remember picking up the evening Providence paper in 1954 and seeing the blearing headlines that Dien Bien Phu, in Vietnam, had fallen to the bad guys.

Fortunately both coaches returned to Providence safely after their military obligations were completed. Joe later became a very successful basketball coach in Rhode Island: one of his sons later went on to play in the professional National Basketball Association. Armand became a very successful local politician and continued coaching grammar school basketball for over 50 years.

Nearby the grammar school was a convent school run for rich girls: Elmhurst Academy. Some of the neighborhood boys were altar boys at the weekday daily mass, which the bordering girls had to attend. To become an altar boy, you had to study and memorize the Latin responses during low and high masses. If you were selected, one benefit was you were given a bread roll and cup of hot milk after mass.

Cannon got used to rising at an early hour so he could walk to the convent school before walking up the hill to his nearby grammar school. Free breakfast: it made life easier for Cannon's parents. They both worked which was a rarity back in the early 1950's. Most of the mothers of the neighborhood kids were stay at home moms'.

Knowing how to serve mass before reaching a double-digit age was very helpful in order to play sports on either the grammar school basketball or baseball teams. You see, one had to be an altar boy first before you could try out for either sport teams. While in the 6th grade, Cannon was able to get an evening paper route, too which covered the neighborhood: his first paying job.

It was the start of many, many various jobs in his life. Catholic grammar school education used the "rote memory" method of teaching: very unlike education today. Yet in those days, every kid could read and write fairly well and perform basic math before completing grammar school unlike the present time in the United States. Could it be not having television made it easier to learn the basics or different teaching methods or both?

Life's playing field was established early in Cannon's life: especially referring to status, family, religion and economics, which was reflected in the start of the early 1950's. Status was reflected by the type of housing one lived: family owned or rented housing. Hardly any families had only one child in the neighborhood. Everyone who Cannon played with was a Catholic. Did your family own a car or the new fad: a television? What did your Grandparents work at? What was their neighborhood like? Did they speak English?

Prior to finishing grammar school, Cannon's family moved into their own home. It was in a different neighborhood which, at the time did not have its own catholic school. After completing grammar school, Cannon was accepted at the nearby catholic high school that was within walking distance from his home.

Cannon secured his first job at age 14 working part-time in an ice cream parlor in Cranston. It required two bus trips to reach the parlor. The owner of the parlor was Cannon's mothers brother nick-named Uncle Tubby. He received his nick-name because of his girth. Uncle Tubby could eat enough for three people. He made terrific homemade ice cream. It wasn't until Cannon answered the phone in the ice cream parlor that he learned Uncle Tubby was possibility a bookie which was illegal. Needless to say, Cannon was instructed never to answer the telephone again.

The ice cream parlor job was followed with a local neighborhood supermarket job which was closer to home only approximately a 40 minute walk away. It was with the Atlantic & Pacific (A&P) chain. A&P was one of the first to wrap cut meat in see through plastic which was just catching on in the US. If your hot iron, which bonded the plastic together touched the meat it smelled badly.

During the summer between Cannon's junior and senior year of high school he got into some trouble with the law. He had accompanied a distant third cousin, who was car crazy, on a jaunt to acquire some new car tires: sort of taking from the rich to help the poor. Sad to say, the new tires were already on a car when the Police were driving by. To simplify matters, the juvenile court judge allowed Cannon to attend a very strict Catholic boarding school outside of Providence. At the time, the boarding school was a little like a mini jail. It even had bars on some of its windows. In retrospect, it helped Cannon get his head together and forget about cars.

Cannon wasn't the brightest light in the classroom. His interests were in sports not books. Upon completion of high school, Cannon at age 17 joined the US military for two years instead of proceeding to university like some of his friends he grew up with.

Cannon's military service was in-between the end of the Korean conflict and the start of the conflict in Vietnam. After completing US Coast Guard boot camp, he was stationed on a non-mobile light ship off the New Jersey coast. In today's world, the lightship is a thing of the past, replaced by a beacon. To reach the light ship one rode on a buoy tender out of Staten Island which provided water, food and other supplies.

Cannon was the youngest member of the crew which meant he got the bad jobs like cleaning the head (toilets). In those days brushes were not provided. Another job was washing dishes after meals. One also stood watch (four hours on each watch) with an eight hour break when one worked or spent sleeping. One spent two weeks on-board the vessel followed by one week off. Frequently Cannon used to hitch rides back to Providence during his week off since his monthly pay totaled some $ 77 per month. It was cheaper to hitch to Providence than trying to live in New York City for a week.

The light ship normally was permanently anchored off the New Jersey shore. It moved under its mechanical power once during Cannon's time aboard. It had to go into dry-dock Jersey City, New Jersey. While in dry dock there Cannon got the job of crawling into the water tanks in the ship's belly: they had to be cleaned, wire brushed, and painted in very tight quarters. In those days very little thought was given to safety equipment like masks, eye protectors, etc. As an (18) year old Cannon never thought anything about these duties- you did what you were told. One joy of being in dry dock was the absence of senior petty officers at night. Hence at night; one could go to the local gin mill to drink a few beers even if you were underage.

Cannon's other assignment was at a life boat station along the New Jersey coast which was located in the middle of the State. Cannon was a year older but still the junior person on station. Here he was made the substitute cook when the regular cook was on leave. Before going on leave the regular cook forgot to tell Cannon he needed to take the beef roast out of the freezer the night before it was to be cooked.

Cannon cooked the roast according to cooking book directions. It looked great but it couldn't be sliced since it was still frozen internally. Cannon caught hell for his mistake: the mashed potatoes were good though! Other than that disaster, Cannon did well as a substitute cook because he learned to cook from his Italian mother when he was still a boy.

Other tasks were standing watch in a tower located on the beach looking into the Atlantic Ocean. The watches took place 24 hours each day: a log was kept where one recorded various indices such as types of clouds, wind velocity, boat sightings, etc. Another task was to monitor a short wave radio band used by fishing boats in distress.

One rescue stands out in Cannon's mind. It was spring time on a weekend when the tower received a distress call from a boat carrying sport fishermen. It lost a rudder. Cannon was the seamen on the boat crew sent out to rescue the distress vessel. The other crew members consisted of a mechanic and a boson-mate who was the pilot of the rescue boat. The seas were very rough that day. The party boat people were all drunk.

Cannon had to crawl into the rescue boats forward hatch in order to throw a life line to the distressed vessel: his feet were being held by the mechanic. It took numerous tries to finally get someone aboard the distressed vessel to catch the life line which had a towing rope attached to it. After returning to the port of the distressed vessel, our rescue crew was given three cases of beer as an appreciation for our efforts.

Cannon completed his active duty in 1959 at age 19. Cannon had reached the enlisted rank of Seamen-not too high on the military pecking order. After four years on inactive reserve, Cannon received his honorable discharge from the United States Coast Guard in 1963.

Prior to the completion of active duty, Cannon took the college boards and he was accepted into the freshman class at Providence College. The college was within walking distance from his parents' home. The same Providence College, which was across the street from St. Pius grammar school. What a small world, Just like Rhode Island.

Cannon's life was to follow dual paths. One path consisted of attending day time classes. The other path was working full-time 40 hour a week jobs. The jobs during the school year were usually on the 4 PM to 12 shifts or the midnight to 8 AM shift which allowed Cannon to attend normal daytime classes. Cannon was able to pay for his education as a result but didn't enjoy much of college's social life. Some of these jobs included: gas station attendant, department store package wrapper, locked ward attendant in a city mental hospital, construction laborer, and a laborer loading 18 wheel tractor-trailers. The later was the best, since it required membership in the Teamsters Union. That job paid very well.

It was in Cannon's last year in college, that he was to experience an event that would change his life completely. Cannon majored in education at Providence College. His primary aim was to secure a high school teaching job in Providence and coach basketball. During his final year in college, Cannon was the junior varsity basketball coach at one of Providence's four public high schools. Even in those days it wasn't easy to secure a job without a "political" reference. It always helped to get the backing of a local city councilman to ensure employment in the city school system. Cannon found it incongruent that he needed to get a semi-literate councilman's approval to get a teaching job. The councilman was a local construction contractor whose company is still in the concrete business many years later. Cannon wasn't going to kiss anyone's backside to get a job he thought he was well qualified for: how dumb was that?

At this time, while having a few beers after work with some older guys from the neighborhood, he heard about the Peace Corps from a brew master at the Narragansett Brewery in Cranston, RI. Gerry McGettrick was much older than Cannon and was well respected in the neighborhood.

It was Gerry who suggested Cannon look into joining the Peace Corps since trying to get a teaching job in Providence without patronage was impossible. Gerry would eventually leave the brewery and join the Peace Corps himself. In those days, a college/university degree was not as important as it became in later years to become a member of the Peace Corps. Cannon applied and was accepted to train for a possible assignment in the Philippines after completing his bachelor degree from Providence College in 1963.

2

The Philippines- Where?

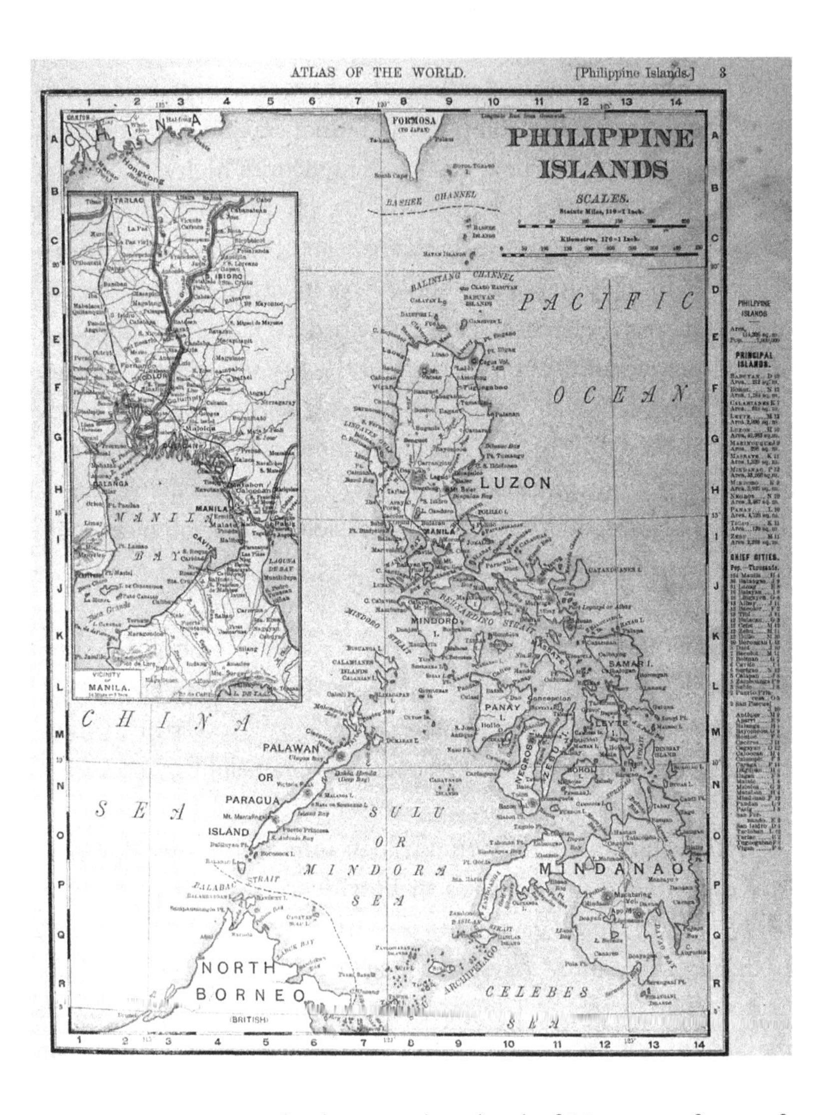

Peace Corps training took place on the island of Hawaii: a far cry from Providence. If you looked for a place that was the complete opposite of Providence, Rhode Island it was Hilo, Hawaii. How lucky could a recent college graduate get? Peace Corps training in Hawaii- a city kids dream.

Cannon was in awe of the numerous trainees who were graduates from some of the premier colleges and universities in the US. The training program under the auspices of the University of Hawaii was still in its development stages. An old unused hospital was the residential training center just on the outskirts of Hilo, which back in 1963 wasn't a tourist haven.

The curriculum for the training program was: World Affairs and Communism-25 hours, Physical Education and Recreation- 40 hours, Health and Medical Training- 40 hours, Area Studies-100 hours, Technical Studies (theory and practice of teaching English in the Philippines)-100 hours, Linguistics-36 hours, American Studies- 50 hours, Physical Education and Recreation-40 hours, Language Training- 85 hours, Peace Corps Orientation- 20 hours. The training program commenced on the 15th of June 1963 and ended on the 28th of August 1963.

More emphasis was placed on physical fitness. Indigenous speakers provided language training from the various major ethnic groups in the Philippines. Cannon struggled. Coming from a home in which any small bit of spoken Italian was looked upon as "old country" there was no basis for foreign languages. The study of language in high school and college was focused on the conjugation of verbs, the translation of sentences. Not on the oral aspect of the language.

Interestingly one of the subjects taught in training was World Affairs and Communism. Communism was to be fought on the international stage by Peace Corps volunteers. The Peace Corps was another forum to win hearts and minds for the United States in its cold war with Russia.

When Senator John F. Kennedy spoke to students at the University of Michigan in 1960, he challenged them to serve their country in the cause of peace by living and working in developing countries. After being elected President, Kennedy established the Peace Corps on March 1, 1961. Peace Corps afforded Americans' the opportunity to promote international understanding. It also would help combat the spread of communism in the developing world.

It must be remembered that prior to the election of John F. Kennedy as President of the United States, the USSR had put the first human being in space. Both countries were doing their best to influence and win the support of developing countries in Latin America, Asia and Africa. Communism was competing with democracy for influence throughout the world. It was almost axiomatic that some Catholic educated persons would tend towards a conservative view of the world and would become part of an organization that was opposing communism.

The volunteers-to-be were constantly being observed by various residential physiologists and psychiatrists throughout the entire training period. It was never clear as to how these observations were an indication on how well a person would perform in the field upon the completion of training. Would eating rice, the staple in the Philippines, make a trainee a better volunteer? Periodically people left on their own free will or were "de-selected out" meaning they were told they would not be going to the Philippines.

The training was so intense that it was just about impossible to get to enjoy the beauty of the Big Island and likewise impossible to get to know the local island residents. In retrospect, it seems the Peace Corps were trying out various training methodologies before adapting a standard core training program: which could be modified and adapted for each respective country which would have a program with the Peace Corps.

Upon completion of the training one final de-selection was in store. The trainees received various inoculations and then were sent out to climb Mount Mauna Loa or was it Mount Mauna Kea? They were told the next day to check their individual mail pigeonholes. Inside was a note stating a meeting room to report to nothing else. Hence one wondered whether one were going onwards to the Philippines or headed back to the US mainland.

Cannon was the last person to walk into the room for those going to the Philippines. He was suffering from a hangover after being out with a fellow Female trainee who found out she was de-selected. Cannon thought he was being de-selected, hence, was surprised to hear applause from those in the room.

The selected volunteers had a week to wind down in a hotel just off the beach in Honolulu prior to departing Hawaii for the Philippines. The highlight of the week was a visit by the Peace Corps Director Sargent Shriver who was the brother-in-law of President Kennedy. The Director administered the swearing-in oath before the selected volunteers deplaned for the Philippines.

After a very long trans-pacific flight, the volunteers arrived in Manila. Here the volunteers met their respective Peace Corps staff whom they would be serving under once they arrived in their assigned areas. The staff would be assisted by Volunteer Leaders, who were themselves former volunteers, who would be acting as regional supervisors together with the host country education officials.

Cannon was told he would be going to an area in the middle of the archipelago. This didn't bother him. What did was learning the area of his assignment didn't speak the language that was taught him in training. Cannon had a difficult time in training trying to gasp Ilongo-the Philippine dialect spoken in the Visayas. After three months, he couldn't even speak Ilongo that good. How was he to get along in a dialect that was completely new to him? Another surprise was the complete different life change. No training could prepare one for a world that had no relationship to life in the US.

Cannon and his group departed by plane to the island of Panay, the site of the Peace Corps Regional Office for the Visayas area where they participated in a brief orientation program at the Philippine Women's College. A few days after the training program was completed, Cannon departed the city of Iloilo for the province of Aklan which was at the northern tip of the island of Panay.

The flight to Kalibo was on a DC-3 twin engine plane a workhorse in World War II. The airport was tiny in comparison to the airport of Iloilo. The same was true for the city itself. The tallest building back in 1963 was two stories high. It wasn't much to look at but it later became a retreat place for Cannon. Kalibo was where he could get a cold ice cream or beer once in a while.

There in the city of Kalibo, he was met by his host family: Casinao and Louisa Inamac who both were teachers in the school where Cannon would be teaching. He also would be living in the Inamac home. Fortunately for Cannon many teachers in the Philippines spoke English hence the different dialect was not too much cause for dismay.

Then it was off on a jitney (a converted World War II jeep whose frame was elongated) for a two hour ride on a dirt road to the municipality (town) of Malinao. Upon disembarking, there was an hour's walk, also on a dirt pathway, to the barrio (village) of Liloan. Throughout the walk, one had to cross the Malinao River three times. During the rainy season, it was four times. At each crossing one had to remove ones shoes.

Even before arriving at the destination that was to be Cannon's home, Cannon wondered whether he was going to make it living in such a remote area. It seemed like the end of the modern world totally different than Providence, Rhode Island.

Cannon knew he would need to draw on the self-discipline acquired in the US military back in 1957 to 1959 to make the adjustment. Cannon's Catholic religion also was a big help in adjusting to this new way of life. The entire barrio was Catholic. The Catholic religion was the one cultural thing we all had in common.

For a kid who grew up in a city, the location he found himself in was totally rural: no electricity, no running water; no roads; no bars to get a cold beer in; no stores-just a few grass houses surrounding a basketball court. What a life change. Peace Corps training did not remotely reflect the reality of Cannon's new location.

The primary school where Cannon was to teach in was built from bamboo and grass. He was to teach English as a second language for grades one to eight. Next to the school was a Roman Catholic chapel, built out of the same materials as the school, which was periodically visited by the priest who lived some three to four miles away in the municipality of Malinao.

Cannon was to live with the Inamac family in barrio Liloan while the people were constructing his hut. The wooden house, a sign of prosperity in the barrio, was built on stilts so the families' chickens could sleep at night well protected. The house interior consisted of three rooms for sleeping, a dining/reception area and a kitchen/washing/toilet area. He was given a room of his own, while the teacher's four children were crammed into one room. The accommodation was to last until Cannon's one-bedroom bamboo and grass hut was finished some eight weeks after his arrival.

Cannon settled into a rhythm: up at dawn; morning ablutions, including teeth brushing, a bath out of a 10 gallon old kerosene tin full of water drawn from a nearby barrio well. Breakfast consisted of a banana, cold rice (from the previous night's meal), and a fried egg. Getting to work daily was easy enough: a walk across the plaza/basketball court to the school. A day consisted of teaching kids basic oral English and classes in second language techniques for the entire teaching staff except for the principal. Cannon sometimes wondered what the purpose was of teaching English in such a remote area. Upon completion of school, he would shoot a few baskets before retiring to spend a couple of hours trying to learn the local Aklanin dialect. The usual evening meal of rice and fish was consumed before sunset. Then it was bed time. Cannon avoided canned food trying to restrict his eating to foods grown in the Philippines.

A few weeks after re-locating to his new hut, the Peace Corps hospitality kit arrived. It consisted of a Coleman lantern, a portable long-range radio and a set of books.

The books were a mixture of various subjects: suitable for learning and relaxing. The radio was high tech for that period: it could draw- in various international stations including Voice of America's various programs. The arrival of the kit made Cannon a big hit in the barrio. People came to hear music or borrow a book to read.

It wasn't too long before the hosts were romantically scheming to see whether Cannon could get interested in one of the barrio maidens. Cannon decided it was best to remain celibate while in the barrio to avoid offending the barrio's Catholic customs.

Early in Cannon's stay, his host family took him to a fiesta in a nearby barrio. A Philippine fiesta is opened with a mass. Thereafter it becomes a big party: plenty of food, drink, music, etc. Being basically a Catholic country, each barrio had a patron saint which they would honor by hosting a fiesta. One of the biggest fiestas took place each January in Kalibo, the capital of Aklan province. It was called Sto. Nino Ati-Atihan (the name is supposedly derived from the first island Settlers called Aetas). The fiesta honored infant Jesus.

The host Barrio was only a short walking distance from Liloan. The Inamac family knew just about everyone. Cannon was a novelty in every home they visited. In one of the houses, he was given a big plate of food which he duly consumed. It was only later he learned not to clean his plate like he did in the USA. A clean plate in the Philippines showed the host you wanted more food.

After consuming two plates of food, Cannon's host started laughing. When he asked why, they said that Cannon had just eaten dog. Cannon ran to the open window and vomited. Later I asked the Inamac family never to tell me what I was eating. If it tasted decent, I would eat it. Cannon followed a similar eating pattern throughout his career working overseas.

A vehicle could reach the barrio if it had four-wheel drive, especially in the rainy season. It was a rarity to see a vehicle in the barrio rain or no rain. Weekly Cannon would join others from the barrio to trek into the municipality to attend Sunday Mass. While in the municipality, one shopped for provisions for the week local vegetables, rice, eggs, meat, fish and instant coffee. The fish and meat were later sun dried on the roof of the hut to avoid spoilage.

The barrio folks didn't think it was good for Cannon to live alone. Cannon never saw another individual living alone in the barrio. Individual living might be fine in the western world but not in Liloan. A male companion was found who would cook, clean house and eventually shop for him.

Jacinto was the person who introduced Cannon to fermented coconut wine called tuba. It was excellent if it was drunk fresh. If it was allowed to sit too long it turned into vinegar. If one drank enough of it, one could get a buzz. Later when Cannon was more familiar with life in the barrio, a Chinese bottle drink "shuktun" became available which was basically rot gut. Great Filipino beer was consumed on rare occasions in the barrio because it had to be purchased and trucked from the municipality mainly during the dry season when the river water level was low.

Barrio living didn't show poverty in the way city living in a developing country would. Except for the absentee landowners who resided in Manila and were wealthy by local standards, just about all barrio residents appeared to be on the same poverty plane.

Cannon wasn't able to discern economic difference until months later when he was more familiar with the families and their circumstances. Clothing worn, food consumed, kids away in Manila attending school, reverence shown by other barrio residents were some of the indicators that helped Cannon come to grips with the barrio pecking order and status.

By the time November 1963 rolled around, Cannon had adjusted to life in the barrio. On the 23rd of November, Cannon had walked into the municipality to buy food. While passing the church rectory, the priest stuck his head out his 2nd story window yelling that President Kennedy had been killed the previous day in the US. Cannon thought it was a joke since the priest's voice had a musical tone to it. This often happened when local Filipinos had bad news to convey. It was their way to put one at ease for what was to follow.

After being reassured by Peace Corps staff that the Peace Corps would continue in its mission by redoubling its efforts in honor of its founder the late John F. Kennedy, Cannon returned to Liloan to finish out the school year. Peace Corps decided Liloan was far too remote a location after Cannon fell ill and required medical treatment in Manila. He was transferred to a municipality in Iloilo province upon recuperation where he finished out the rest of his two year Peace Corps assignment.

Cannon's second assignment was in a municipality of Tigbauan that was located by the sea of Iloilo not too far from Iloilo city. It was easy to reach unlike Liloan since it was located along a paved road. Being a municipality, it had running water and electricity until 8 PM nightly. While there Cannon became very good friends with the local pharmacy owner- the Bellezia family who had a tiny "drug" store in the central market. It also sold cold beer and was a gathering place for a few of the locals. Cannon was a teacher of English as a second language in the municipality grammar school and surrounding barrios. To reach the barrios, Cannon would walk unless he got lucky and caught a ride on a jeepney.

Prior to Cannon's completion of service, some citizens decided to get the Municipal council to write a letter to President Lyndon Johnson saying the Municipality adopted Cannon as an honorary citizen on 19 May 1965. See Appendages. When Cannon returned to the USA, he received a letter on White House stationary from President Johnson congratulating him on his Peace Corps service.

Throughout his two teaching assignments, Cannon met wonderful people. They inevitably took him into their homes to feed him delicious local dishes (never mentioning what the dishes consisted of) and at times to offer him a San Miguel -one of the best beers in the world. It was even good when it was warm.

Likewise, Cannon met some terrific Peace Corps volunteers from other islands while working as a summer counselor at Camp Brotherhood located on the island of Negros Occidental-next to Panay. Bacolod, the capital, was also a center for growing sugar cane. There were a few very wealthy families who jointly made available the land which the camp was built on. The camp participants were drawn from the families of the sugar cane workers.

One of Cannon's favorite visiting places was Cebu. It was the oldest city in the Philippines and the second largest city in the country after Manila. It was centrally located in the archipelago. Unlike Manila, the city center was quite small and easy to get around on foot. There were a few inexpensive hotels which served as gathering points for visiting volunteers. The Peace Corps established a medical team in Cebu who serviced volunteers stationed in the Visayas and Mindanao.

During Cannon's first visit to Cebu, he met Leroy Miles an African-American volunteer. Leroy was stationed on the island of Leyte in Tacloban city. He was also visiting Cebu. Leroy introduced Cannon to an African-American who stayed in Cebu after World War II ended. There were a few other Americans who also stayed in Cebu. One ran a restaurant in the city and a night club in the hills overlooking the city. Cebu became Cannon's 2nd home in the Philippines when he had time off from teaching.

Gabe ran the Cebu Steam Laundry. It was located close to the port area. There was a small night club attached to the laundry building. Gabe and his family lived in a small house across the street from the laundry. He allowed selected volunteers to sleep in his residence. Cannon being Leroy's friend, was always One of those volunteers who could sleep in Gabe's place. Accommodations were basic: a place on the floor with a sleeping mat and a mosquito net. Gabe had a fantastic collection of blues and jazz records from the USA for his night club. He was a terrific person if he liked you: if not, Gabe was a very hard man.

After finishing up ones two year field commitment to the Peace Corps, the entire group was brought to Manila to undergo a "de-briefing" before departing the country. The Peace Corps brought in some of the folks who were involved in the training in Hawaii for the debriefing. When one of the de-briefers asked how many of the people in ones' barrio were communists or had tendencies towards communism: some of us decided to leave the de-briefing before it was over. Sometimes things are not as they appear to be? Could this question have been the main purpose for the Peace Corps-identifying communists or potential communists?

This was Cannon's first exposure to life outside the United States and to masses of people who were often too poor to eat twice a day. Poor people in Providence, Rhode Island and the United States in general were not the same as the poor in the Philippines. International politics was still an area of simplistic views: when you do well, you avoid evil. Anything that contributed towards fighting communism was good. In retrospect it's almost beyond belief that a person could be so naïve, but what more could you expect from a cradle Catholic from Providence?

Throughout Cannon's time in the Peace Corps, he practiced his Catholic faith with weekly attendance at mass regardless of wherever he found himself. The Catholic education Cannon received, from the sisters at St. Pius grammar school, stayed an integral part of his life thereafter.

The idea of returning to life in Providence, Rhode Island was daunting. Cannon's basic values were no longer confined to coaching basketball teaching in a high school in Providence.

Cannon wanted to return to overseas work as soon as he could secure employment if this was possible. Cannon returned to the US in the autumn of 1965 after spending a couple of months traveling in south Asia, the middle-East and Europe. This travel experience never would have occurred if it wasn't due to his joining the Peace Corps.

After returning to Providence, Cannon again came into contact with Gerry McGettrick who had finished a Peace Corps tour of duty in St. Lucia. Gerry told Cannon the domestic equivalent of the Peace Corps- the Job Corps, was recruiting staff and likely would be interested in an ex-Peace Corps volunteer. Cannon was offered a teaching position with a new residential camp being built in Arcadia National Park on Mount Desert Island in the state of Maine. The camp was to offer accommodations and training for mainly high school drop-outs from the inner cities. While Cannon was employed by the Job Corps, the center in Acadia wasn't operational, it was still being constructed.

Fortunately before the 1965 winter was completed, Cannon was able to land an overseas position with one of the major non-government organizations Catholic Relief Services (CRS) even though it meant he might have to go to South Vietnam. It seemed Catholic Relief Services (CRS) would be a natural for South Vietnam since it was the overseas arm of the US Catholic Bishops who were major supporters of the US governments' effort in the fight against communists. Throughout Cannon's education, he was taught about the evils of communism, especially its anti-religious nature. Going to Vietnam to oppose the spread of communism would be as natural to Cannon as eating apple pie is to most Americans.

The years which were to follow would see the life paths of Cannon and Ben Edherue go in vastly different directions. The former would follow a right wing political bent while the latter would move further along the Marxist path.

3

Isoko Beginning

Across the Atlantic, Ben's family was evolving in a setting very different from Providence. According to Isoko tradition, the first human being Ododo, was from the Isoko nation. This belief helped foster a deep respect for one's ancestors. Ben was fond of saying: **If you have no respect for your ancestors, how can you have respect for another human being**". The inhabitants of Isoko land were either fishermen or small time farmers eking out a subsistence living under the harsh administration of the British colonial masters. The odds of the Edherue family and the Cannon family crossing paths in the late 20th century was remote to say the least.

Numerous creeks as well as the River Niger crisscross the swampy region of what was to become Nigeria. Ethnic groups besides the Isoko, inhabited the villages in the area now referred to as the Niger Delta. Geographic boundaries determined trading and the goods traded. The Isoko grew subsistent crops and fished. The fish were dried for local consumption. What was left was delivered to local markets for trading. The traders were either those from the nearly Ibo group or in later years Muslim traders from the North.

The Edherue family was one of the first Isoko who started to experiment with seawater. They treated it with local grown indigenous herbs to make fermented liquor for their own consumption. As the years passed, the family became proficient in its liquor production, which was eagerly sought after by neighbors. The family recipe was held so secret that even distant relatives were not informed of its ingredients.

The production of alcohol from seawater placed the Edherue family in an envied position amongst his people. Additionally, it was the medium which provided the financial wherewithal for Ben's father to travel to Lagos in the early 20th century. It was common for African men from distant places to find their way to Lagos, but without their immediate families who remained in the villages. The prime reason why the entire family didn't migrate to Lagos was to ensure the children learned their Isoko language and traditions. Ben's father was able to obtain a white-collar job in Lagos due to his mathematical skills and ability to work in English.

Missionaries, some from the Republic of Ireland, were attracted to the Delta because of the people's openness towards their proselytizing. Along with the proselytizing, came schools and limited medical facilities. These services were used to the utmost by families eager to get ahead. They used the colonial system of the English instead of getting used by the same system.

Ben's family became involved in the underground trade union movement in Lagos. The colonial government promoted the above ground trade union movement as a means to help pacify the restless industrial workforce. The move to independence was brewing among the Nigerian people. Needless to say the more radical, non- government supported trade union movement was more influenced by Marxism ideology than by capitalism which was more focused on materialism. Even back in the early 1960's shortly before independence, Lagos was a teaming lively city drawing inhabitants from the tribes and villages throughout the country.

Shortly after Ben's birth, Nigeria became independent on October 1, 1960. Out went the British. In came the start of tribal differences. As was the case in many ex-colonies of the British (Ghana, Kenya, etc.) they ruled colonial Nigeria by using elites from various tribes overtly or covertly to compete against each other. It wasn't too long after independence that the system left by the British imploded into civil war in 1967. Some believe that the issue of ownership of petroleum rights was one of the prime factors in the supply of arms to both sides in the civil war. Western oil companies were the source of funds for both sides at the onset of the war.

Thus, when Ben moved from the village at age ten into Lagos, he moved into a household which placed emphasis on people not commercialism. It is not surprising that Marxism had an attraction since it more closely resembled Isoko village life and tradition than did the English capital orientated materialistic system

The members of the Edherue family found living in the capital city required a cunning way beyond that required in Isokoland. Not only were different dialects spoken, but also very different family values were the norm in the city. Schooling was the immediate venue where there were cultural and dialectic confrontations. The Isoko were a tiny tribe in comparison to the others inhabiting Lagos. Following Isoko customs, young Ben's lodgings were in a neighborhood inhabited by fellow Isokoians.

Ben's family was able to secure properties in a few neighborhoods that became decent sources of supplemental income. More and more young African males were migrating to Lagos either in search of employment or to enjoy life in the Bright Lights. Life in the rural village was harsh and very circumspect. Hence, the newly purchased properties were always full of renters

The Yoruba, who were from the region in which Lagos was located, were the main ethnic group. Hence the Edherue offspring's were forced to become fluent in languages other than English for their daily survival. Language skills were to be a major strength in Ben's forthcoming trade union career.

Ben's elementary schooling in Nigeria after independence was derived from the English. It wasn't tailored to the needs of the emerging Nigeria economic and political landscape. It was tailored to furthering the growth of materialism. Unfortunately, Ben soon became bored with school and started to look outside the formal school system for his inspiration. Trade unions were a natural draw.

Life in Lagos was vibrant and offered a young intelligent person many opportunities outside the mainstream. One of these areas, which produced young leaders, was the trade union movement. It offered persons from smaller tribes the opportunity to become involved in national issues, especially if they were multi-lingual. The union movement involved persons from various tribes in the country. It was one of the few institutions, besides government and religious, which cut across tribal lines.

Even before independence Lagos was a teaming lively city drawing inhabitants from the tribes and villages throughout the country. Following Isoko customs, young Ben's lodgings were in a neighborhood inhabited by fellow Isokoians.

Like many parts of the non-western world, the trade union movement was divided by international power politics. The West, headed by the Americans were supporting and promoting their brand of unionism, which was based upon capitalism. The East, headed by Russia, was backing unionists who favored communism. Ben was drawn to the segment of the union movement which was ideologically associated with Marxism.

Africa has been riveted with tribalism and still is. The trade union movement in all African countries was not. Workers were drawn from villages to employment and the exciting life of the big cities where newly established industries were located. Like their worker counterparts in Western Europe and North America, Nigerian workers were drawn into the trade union movement as their only means to obtain decent wages and conditions of work.

One of Ben's strong points was he wasn't easily intimidated even though his physical statue was not big. He made up for his lack of stature with a will of iron. Attributes made for a future trade union leader.

Ben was introduced to the union that represented food workers. Shortly after his introduction, a major strike occurred which shut down the food processing sector for a few days. Ben's unwillingness to be intimidated by management during the strike won him great respect with the work force. Ben was introduced to representatives of the future Nigerian Labor Congress (NLC) after the settlement of the strike. Most of the representatives were young firebrands like him. They also had been drawn to the "big city" from villages in the south, west and north of the country.

Individual trade unions were made up of various ethnic grouping: likewise union officials and organizers represented various tribes. One unique African trade union aspect absent from North American unionism was the establishment of trade union youth wings. In years to come youth wing leaders were often men in their late 30's or early 40's-not really youths. More mature persons had greater influence and status with young trade unionists, especially with those newly arrived from villages in rural areas.

The birth of the trade union "youth league" was brought to fruition. Previously major political parties each had youth wings but were only representing their respective regions in the country. The trade union youth league was one of the first with members and leaders drawn from the numerous tribes and regions in the country.

From the early days of recorded civilizations, mankind has had a few "haves" and many more "have-nots". Originally, due to limited communications, the majority who were not well off accepted their position in their respective societies. Whether or not their acceptance was one of resignation is not described in early history. The divide between the "have's" and "have-not" moved with them as humans began their movement from one place to another.

The Europeans who came to colonize the continent of North America were of the belief that their respective society was far superior to the indigenous societies which they were to discover but not understand. As the colonial process proceeded, the lack of semi-skilled and skilled manpower played a role in the mass migrations of western Europeans to the new world. The expeditions were originally financed by the wealthy acting either on behalf of European royalty or on behalf of their own vested interest. This pattern was followed when Africa was colonized by Europeans

The wealthy from Europe were drawn into the search for what was later to be referred as "black gold" once the search for oil went international. The "informal oil cabal" was gradually opened to European and North American entrepreneurs that were helping to finance oil exploration in the Middle East, Africa and South America. Areas in communist controlled countries were not targeted since the state controlled all matters dealing with oil exploration initially.

The power of the cabal grew by leaps and bounds in North America especially after World War II. The future was very rosy in spite of the cold war between capitalism and communism. Both needed oil to develop their respective natural resources and economies. The only potential fly in the ointment for the cabal would be the discovery of an alternative source of power not related to oil. The control of the production and distribution of petroleum was and is a key element in US government's foreign policy.

Prior to World War II, village folklore credited the Edherue extended family with secret remedies'; one was a system to generate unlimited amounts of alcohol from sea water. Unfortunately in this case, folklore was never substantiated with proof. Regardless, at the time the family didn't have the financial resources to undertake any commercial economic steps never mind alcohol generation from sea water.

Was it possible that political assassinations in the 1960's were petroleum related? Unlikely but whether the tragic events that took place could have been avoided is unknown even as this is being written. The government led investigation into the killing of John F. Kennedy laid the blame on one person Lee Harvey Oswald. Oswald was portrayed as a mentally unstable former military person fixated on Communism. After investigation findings were made public, to this day, there are pages and pages of material associated with the assassination that remain highly classified and closed to the public: maybe forever? Why? Unfortunately for the world, Jack Ruby killed Oswald before he could be legally prosecuted. Ruby was portrayed as a mentally unstable individual prior to his conviction for the Oswald killing. Ruby died in jail from cancer so it is reported.

While Cannon was living as a Peace Corps volunteer in the Philippines, Ben was gradually becoming more and more enamored with Marxism. Much to the chagrin of his family, he was spending less time on his high school studies than on trade union matters.

Many young people throughout Nigeria were drawn to Lagos. It was a large city full of attractions that were completely absent from village living. One could always find a place to reside with a family member or an extended family member from one's tribe. Lagos attracted the best and the brightest because it offered excellent education and employment opportunities compared to the countryside.

Ben's life in Lagos brought him into contact with other young Nigerians who were also attracted to Marxism. The trade union movement provided the medium for these young persons to test out their Marxist ideological beliefs. Nigeria was also just starting to industrialize in a meaningful manner at the same time.

Most of the industrialization took place in the Lagos region. This made it easy for Ben to become a player at a young age in union youth groups. Young males from the north, east, southeast and western parts of the country joined him. While there were cultural, religion and educational differences between the peers, the overriding commonality in their Marxist beliefs overrode these differences.

Testing out one's beliefs brought the budding radicals into conflict with older trade unionists that were more main stream. They were adherents of western type unions that favored capitalism and consumerism. However both groupings established youth wings. Both groups obtained financial assistance from their overseas ideological mentors.

Russia channeled its assistance thru the World Federation of Trade Unions (WFTU), which was headquartered in Eastern Europe. The United States channeled its assistance thru the American Federation of Labor-Congress of Industrial Organizations (AFL CIO) overseas arm for Africa called the African American Labor Center (AALC). Additional assistance from western countries was channeled thru the International Confederation of Free Trade Unions (ICFTU), which was based in Western Europe.

It wasn't too long after the end of the 2nd World War that the international differences between the East and the West became more of a military issue than an ideological one. China came under the control of the Communist party in 1949 after a civil war. The West backed the losing side. A few years later, the forces of West and East battled each other in Korea. While the Korean conflict was taking place, France was gradually losing control of its colony of Vietnam. Once the French withdrew in 1956, the United States gradually became embroiled in the conflict until it became known as the Vietnam War of the 1960's. Fortunately in Nigeria, the battle between East and West wasn't of a military nature until the civil war started on May 30, 1967.

While Nigeria was gaining Independence the West and East were in competition as to whether Marxism or Capitalism would become the major influence. Both Eastern and Western countries praised the newly independent government. It was touted as a government of national unity. The internal domestic situation was starting to unravel even before independence. Major tribes, of vastly different cultural mores and religions, inhabited all the regions of Nigeria. The former colonial power didn't make the elimination of tribalism as one of its priorities. In fact, they used tribal differences as a divide and rule governing mechanism.

All the good will in the world does not substitute for daily interaction. After decades of divide and rule, which enhanced mistrust, superstition, and envy, it was not realistic to expect independence to be the panacea to even the playing field. With the removal of the oppressor, it was not long before politicians, who put their families' or tribes' before their neighbors and country, replaced the former oppressors.

The West had very big expectations for independent Africa even if many people viewed Africa as one unit not as several countries. Maybe guilt was a prime factor in the wish for Africa's success. Was it realistic to expect the new leaders of Africa to ride around on bicycles after independence instead of Mercedes Benz's cars? Was it realistic to think there wouldn't be any corruption after independence? The West had its full of corruption. The only difference was in the West it is below the surface, not out in the open like Africa. Was it realistic to think Africans wouldn't help their fellow family members or their tribe after they assumed political control as opposed to helping the general populace? These questions are as appropriate in 2014 as back at the time of Independence in Nigeria.

The 1963 national census in Nigeria which was to update the nation's population helped usher the military into the body politic after it failed. Allocation of revenues, parliamentary seats, provincial governments, and many more factors were effected by a census. The planned census in the Northern Nigeria area ran into problems when Islamic leaders opposed the census. They didn't want non-Moslems entering into their compounds. They viewed this as a violation of their cultural and religious mores. How can you undertake a meaningful census if you cannot count the population?

Once the military undertook its first coup on 15 January 1966, some people felt it would only be a matter of time before there would be regional/tribal issues within the military itself. Religious riots broke out in the Northern and Eastern sections of the country. The majority Muslim ethnic groups forced minorities to flee back to their original tribal places of origin after many people were killed. The military leadership began to discombobulate, as did the country.

Eastern Nigeria ceded from Nigeria on May 30, 1967 and formed a breakaway country called Biafra. This action resulted in Africa's first modern civil war in Africa's most populated nation. This was the situation facing Ben and his fellow radicals as they were coming of age in the Nigerian trade union movement.

4

Confluent Conflicts
South Vietnam, Congo, Nigeria

SOUTH VIETNAM

In 1965, most Americans were supportive of their government's role in South Vietnam. The military draft had yet to turn into a massive protest movement. Cannon's prior military service in the 1957-1959 period meant he was not eligible to be drafted. Should he accept the CRS employment offer he could be going to South Vietnam as a civilian not as a soldier. Once Cannon accepted the employment offer from CRS as 1965 drew to a close, he learned his first assignment was to take him to South Vietnam in early 1966.

Cannon was about to meet a person in South Vietnam who would have a profound effect on his future, Lawson Mooney. Mooney wasn't a big man physically, but he projected himself with greater confidence that made him bigger than he actually was. He had a slight mustache and a full head of hair. When he smoked, he held his cigarette in his left hand. He also used his left hand when making a vocal point of importance. To some, he might be called a con man due to his gift of gab. To others, he was a person who felt equally at ease with senior military officers and diplomats. Either way Mooney was never lost for words.

Mooney was a product of Somerville, Massachusetts. He stayed in France after World War II. He would become a part-time actor and sculptor before marrying the daughter of a French plantation owner. While managing a plantation in Madagascar, he was recruited by the same major non-government organization that hired Cannon-CRS. After a few years work in Africa, Mooney and his family were transferred to South Vietnam where he would be the CRS program director.

When Cannon arrived at Ton Son Nhut-Saigon's airport, it was still smoldering from the mortar attack by the Viet Cong. After Cannon cleared Customs and Immigration, he saw a sign with his name. Next to the Vietnamese sign holder, there stood Mooney smoking a cigarette looking very cool not bothered in the least by the smoldering airport. Next to him stood Stan Garnett who was also a former Peace Corps volunteer from the Philippines. Cannon did not meet Stan before when they were both were volunteers.

Cannon arrived into a completely different atmosphere than his arrival in the Philippines back in 1963. There was no special orientation. No local family who would host Cannon.

After the airport, Cannon and his two suit cases holding his possessions were taken to a Vietnamese catholic orphanage Santa Maria on the outskirts of Saigon. This was to be Cannon's residence while he was worked in CRS/South Vietnam's main office. The Vung family who operated the orphanage came to Saigon as refugees from North Vietnam. Orphaned children occupied the first two floors of the complex. Cannon was allocated a bed on the third floor in a dorm like room. There was a big closet against one wall to store one's personal effects. Stan lived in a self-contained flat at the opposite end of dorm. A Vietnamese couple served as cook and custodian for the CRS staff living in the orphanage. Mooney and his wife and two teenage daughters lived in an old colonial style house downtown.

The day after arrival, Cannon drove into the city in the passenger's seat of a Chevrolet sedan. Cannon was taken aback at the amount of motorbikes on the road-they seemed like they were everywhere. It was hard to understand how Stan didn't hit anyone on the drive to the office. It took a while to get used to the Saigon traffic before Cannon started to drive.

Cannon's first introduction in the CRS office was to Mooney's wife Lisa who served as the office manager. Then Cannon was introduced to the Vietnamese members of the staff-the majority of whom spoke English. This was fortunate since Cannon didn't even possess elementary French which was spoken by many Vietnamese. After the introductions, Mooney and Stan briefed Cannon on the CRS program and the role they envisioned for him: a field liaison with implementers of the various programs.

Cannon registered himself with the US Embassy. Later he was introduced to staff at the USAID office who dealt with CRS especially those who worked in the Food for Peace section.

A few days after his arrival, he was traveling to Danang with a suitcase full of money for Catholic Archbishop Chi. Cannon was told a reservation was made in a local hotel in Danang for him. He could get a local taxi to the Archbishop's office and residence to deliver the suitcase. Cannon slept with the suitcase under his hotel bed. What good that did in retrospect is questionable. The money would facilitate the usage of some Catholic owned properties by the US Marines as they expanded their main base in Danang. Cannon never knew exactly how much money he carried. Rumor had it that it was close to at least half a million dollars.

Once the Danang assignment was completed, Mooney had found himself a man willing to go anywhere in the country on assignment for him. While in the field Cannon would sleep wherever he was offered a bed. After completing an assignment, it was back to Saigon for a few days of rest before his next assignment.

The eighteen months of Cannon's assignment in South Vietnam took place in 1966-1967. Cannon traveled throughout the entire country infrequently by bus but most often by planes operated by Air Vietnam, Air America and the US military.

Cannon's field assignments were to arrange the supply of US donated PL-480 food commodities or check to see whether they were received as by Catholic nuns and priests operating programs and/or to check whether they had received shipments from Saigon programmed for their distribution. Secondarily the same process applied to medicines that were to be distributed. The surplus US grown foods were supplied and shipped to South Vietnam by the US government as part of its aid program to South Vietnam. The US government also shipped medicines donated to the Catholic Medical Mission Board for CRS. His other main assignment was to act as liaison to the US military's program of Civic Action. Pl-480 food commodities were shipped to recipient units who distributed the commodities in the hearts and minds battle between the West (US) and the communistic East (Viet Cong) to win support from the local population.

Cannon actually thought his work would make a difference in the hearts and minds battle. This proved to be untrue from a historical view and it remains as untrue in the 21st century. You cannot bomb areas and people constantly then give them some food or build a classroom or some other building and expect the recipients to love "you" and fully believe in your cause.

There were all kinds of people drawn to South Vietnam. There were young career types with the US State Department who viewed an assignment in Vietnam as a pre-requisite for their career ambitions. There were businessmen who were there to cash in on the bountiful economic scene. There were crooks that were able to make fortunes if they didn't get caught. Then there were insurance people who really made money insuring every major construction endeavor undertaken by the US government. For them it was if they had their own printing press kicking out US dollars twenty-four hours a day seven days a week

Life in the major South Vietnamese cities was unique. The beer was decent, the women were beautiful, and food was great. Cannon liked starting the day with a bowl of Pho (noodle soup) and coffee with sweetened tinned milk. One could save a few dollars at the same time. Living in an orphanage was a humbling experience. While in Saigon, Cannon would daily see the inhumane effect on children who became orphaned as a result of the war. Cannon's life gradually became discombobulated. Good things were being done for civilians at the same time others were being killed and injured.

US military personnel were always coming through the Saigon office. Mooney and his staff were terrific hosts. Frequently there were after work gatherings that usually ran well into the evening with lots of good food and drink. Cannon met Vietnamese who he socialized with. He was fortunate in meeting Madame Nge who ran an orphanage in Saigon, not in the one Cannon stayed. She was forced to flee North Vietnam back in the 1950's. It was always a pleasure to visit Madame Nge. On occasion she would host a dinner party at one Chinese restaurant or another in the Cholon (Chinese) section of Saigon. The food was always terrific. She eventually had to flee Vietnam too after it fell to the North Vietnamese. She eventually died in the USA.

One night over a few beers, Mooney informed Cannon that he was considering the sale of certain selected commodities to Chinese businessmen in order to obtain local currency to expand the office's operations. He said bulgur wheat, which didn't appeal to the Vietnamese diet, was an excellent source of pig feed. Powder milk, which frequently caused diarrhea because local water was polluted, was used by the Chinese to make ice cream, which they sold to the US military. Even decades later while in France visiting with Mooney, Cannon never was able to confirm whether or not US donated commodities were sold to the Chinese in Saigon by his buddy Mooney.

There were other instances in which US donated goods were sold instead of being distributed to the needy for which they were originally destined. There was one instance when, a young guy like himself employed by another American non-government organization, sold an entire ship load of donated goods. These goods would then re-appear for sale on the black market. Unfortunately he was caught and spent some time in a Vietnamese jail before being thrown out of the country. If my memory is still working I think the commodities were sold to a group of South Korean "businessmen".

Lawson Mooney and his team were only judged by CRS headquarters on the amount of donated US supplies they could get out into the provinces. Movement of supplies was easy if you were able to plug into the US military distribution channel since there were planes and truck convoys crossing the country daily. In retrospect, it is questionable whether a non-government organization, such as CRS, should become such a close partner in an overseas war with the US military? This question is still being debated among some segments of US society decades later.

Before Cannon knew it, eighteen months had flown bye and it was time to depart South Vietnam. Not that much attention was paid to the political status of the war by Cannon. He still believed it was the good guys (US) against the bad guys (Communist Viet Cong/ North Vietnam)

CRS had transferred Lawson Mooney back to Africa before Cannon's assignment was over. Cannon had listened too many of Mooney's tales about Africa. So when he was offered an assignment to the Congo he accepted same even though it was experiencing mercenary problems. Little did Cannon know in 1967, after accepting the CRS Congo post, that he would work in Africa for close on thirty years until his last assignment in Nigeria ended in 2004?

CONGO

Cannon returned to the US for a short vacation before heading off to the Congo. While at CRS headquarters in New York city Cannon had an opportunity to meet Madubuko Diakite. A Peace Corps friend of Cannon, Elaine Bosak was dating a person with a deep connection with Nigeria- Madubuko's stepfather MCK Ajuluchuku was a senior official in the Biafra regime. The friendship that developed was instrumental in Cannon's marriage a few years later. We all stayed in touch throughout the years regardless of our whereabouts and do so to this day.

Cannon's first direct experience with Africa took place in Liberia. His journey to the Congo was interrupted when the plane was forced to land at Roberts Field due to a massive sand storm coming off the Sahara. The airline put the passengers up in the best hotel in Monrovia at the time-the Ducor.

The first major cultural shock that took place was when Cannon found out that the Liberian currency was exactly the same as the US currency back in the United States. How could this be, since Liberia became independent on 26 July 1847? Cannon always thought independent countries had their own currency not that of the former colonial power. Could Liberia's use of US currency be considered a form of colonialism? Up until that time, the term colonialism was only a meaningless word used by Communists.

Once the storm passed, Cannon proceeded to the Congo later named Zaire before it became the Congo again many years later. Upon arrival, Cannon had his second cultural shock. His passport was confiscated at N'djili Airport after he refused to cough up a few dollars. Cannon only received his passport back after coughing up a few dollars as recommended by his boss.

In the late 1967, the Congo was still suffering from its mercenary problems in the eastern part of the country. The staff, which Cannon joined, included a former colleague from South Vietnam, Bill Donaldson, with whom a house was shared in a suburb of Kinshasa. Cannon learned that his new boss had never been out of the US before assuming responsibility for the Congo multi- million dollar aid programs.

It was obvious the Congo program was going to be run according to Mr. Mullen's experiences in America even if there was little or no relationship to the Congo. As soon as Cannon got settle, he began to lobby for a transfer to Nigeria were the civil war had just started. Cannon knew he had to get away from Mr. Mullen who behaved as if he was still working in the US.

There were two experiences in the Congo that stand out and are worth a few sentences. Donaldson and Cannon were given an assignment to visit the port of Matadi and to review projects funded by CRS. Driving out of Kinshasa, the VW bug vehicle was stopped at a check point by Congolese soldiers. The soldiers used their weapons to motion Cannon and Donaldson out of the vehicle. The soldiers, in French, asked why we were carrying weapons as they were pointing to the VW's twin exhaust pipes. Fortunately Donaldson's spoke better French than Cannon and after a humorous conservation was able to convince them to allow him back in the vehicle. He started the engine and got out of the vehicle and suggested one of the soldiers place the palm of one hand against the exhaust pipes. Soldiers smiled and allowed us to proceed.

During Cannon's time in the Congo, there was a liberation war being waged in the next store country Angola. There were two major groups fighting against the Portuguese. One was the MPLA- The Popular Movement to Liberate Angola led by Agostinho Neto. The other group was organized by Angolan exiles living in the Congo: UPA- Union Popular Angola led by Holden Roberto.

Roberto had lived most of his life in Kinshasa and spoke some English. Prior to Cannon's arrival in the Congo, Holden had established contact with CRS. Cannon was told by Mr. Mullen to accompany an Angolan to a site that was to become a school not far from the Angola border. The Angolan introduced himself as Holden Roberto. Whether he was or was not who he claimed to be was never found out. To Cannon's knowledge, CRS never funded Roberto's planned school. In all likelihood, any monetary assistance which Roberto might have received would have been used for military purposes. One meets a strange set of characters when working in the development field.

Work might have been a problem, but the nightlife in Kinshasa was great. There were a few night clubs with excellent live music that opened late at night and closed early in the mornings. There were a couple of restaurants which specialized in European type food. They were decent but expensive unlike the night clubs. The first sojourn to the Congo was so short that Cannon's limited French hardly improved from the basics he acquired in South Vietnam. Early in 1968, Cannon was informed by CRS headquarters he was being reassigned to Nigeria.

NIGERIA

The Nigerian military undertook its first coup on 15 January 1966 a by-product of the failed national census according to the view of some Nigerians. Eastern Nigeria ceded from Nigeria in May, 1967 to form a breakaway country called Biafra. This action resulted in Africa's first modern civil war in Africa's most populated nation.

Initially Cannon was given assignments which required travel throughout northern Nigeria which wasn't directly affected by the civil war. The infrastructure was in good shape during those days. The roads were good. The rail system functioned. The indigenous airline sector was just starting to develop. During one trip, Cannon was completely surprised to run into a Catholic priest who attended the same grammar school Cannon had in Providence. The Dominican priest was elevated to a bishop for Sokoto. Guess the Catholic Church figured he had plenty of experience living and working among members of the Muslim religion in Nigeria, and this should serve him well later as a Bishop in Pakistan.

While traveling throughout northern Nigeria, Cannon started to get a feel for the differences among the major tribes in the country. The majority

Hausa and Fulani of the North were almost entirely Moslem. Religion formed a major part of their daily lives. Many of the service providers in the non-agrarian sector were either transplanted Nigerians of the Yoruba tribe from the West or Ibo from the East. They viewed life through a different prism as opposed to the tribes of the North besides being mainly Christian.

Cannon was able to find a small self-contained apartment in the port area of Apapa where his office was located. There were a couple of western style grocery stores in the area, but most of the buying and selling occurred with roadside vendors. Cannons diet focused on Nigerian food. It was heavy on starches and meat. Gradually some friends were acquired with whom Cannon would go night clubbing on weekends. Nightlife in Lagos was terrific for a bachelor.

After some six months, Cannon's employer decided it should get directly involved in the Biafra war relief effort via the International Committee of the Red Cross (ICRC) operating in areas controlled by Nigeria's Federal Government. A former colleague from South Vietnam, Stan Garnett was brought to Lagos with his newly acquired wife. Another single guy was transferred. Additional staff later joined this small team. The team worked through the office of the Nigerian Red Cross in Nigeria but under the auspices of ICRC.

Cannon was given a Nigerian Red Cross jeep and told to head off to the East. The first place he operated out of was Nsukka which was formerly a university town. He was housed in a vacant university lectures house on the campus where the Red Cross ran its operations. Later he moved further east to Abakaliki outside of Enugu where he resided with an Irish Catholic priest and group of Catholic sisters who stayed at their parish church and school throughout the war. It was good that Cannon did not have a problem eating Nigerian food since that was all his hosts were able to purchase during his stay with them. Other temporary assignments were undertaken throughout the area. Cannon completed his 6 month assignment prior to Christmas 1968.

Another one of Cannon's temporary assignments was to locate a source of local food outside of the East which could be purchased for distribution to the people in the East. He ended up in a small town called Lokoja which was located on the River Niger. Lokoja was a transport hub for food stuffs grown in the north, such as rice, peanuts (called groundnuts in Nigeria) and legumes. These items could be transported by small boats down the Nigeria into river front towns under the control of the Federal government.

Cannon first off needed a place to operate from. As an employee of a Catholic NGO, it was logical that he would seek and find the location of the local Catholic Church. The Bishop of Lokoja, a French Canadian, offered Cannon a bed in his rectory. Additionally he provided invaluable information relative to the traders who Cannon could contract as potential suppliers of locally grown food stuffs. Cannon's stay wasn't entirely devoted to work.

While in Lokoja, Cannon had his first water-skiing experience. A Catholic priest provided the skis and boat. Cannon drank quite a bit of the River Niger before learning to let go of the tow rope. After a couple of tries, Cannon was proficient enough to stay upright to enjoy the pleasure of water skiing.

Cannon's slow process of his political ideological transformation continued which had commenced in South Vietnam. It was enhanced in the Congo where the country was experiencing mercenary trouble often on behalf of foreign governments. Cannon's experience in the east of Nigeria (liberated Biafra/occupied Biafra) was another step in the slow process of his political and ideological transformation.

While Nigeria was at war internally, the trade union movement was breaking up into tribal factions, which were exacerbated by East/West politics. Many of the early trade union leaders originated in the East or West. They ended up taking Sides during the war as did the entire populations in both regions. During Cannon's time in Nigeria during the civil war, he didn't cross paths with Ben Edherue.

5

Apartheid-First Experience

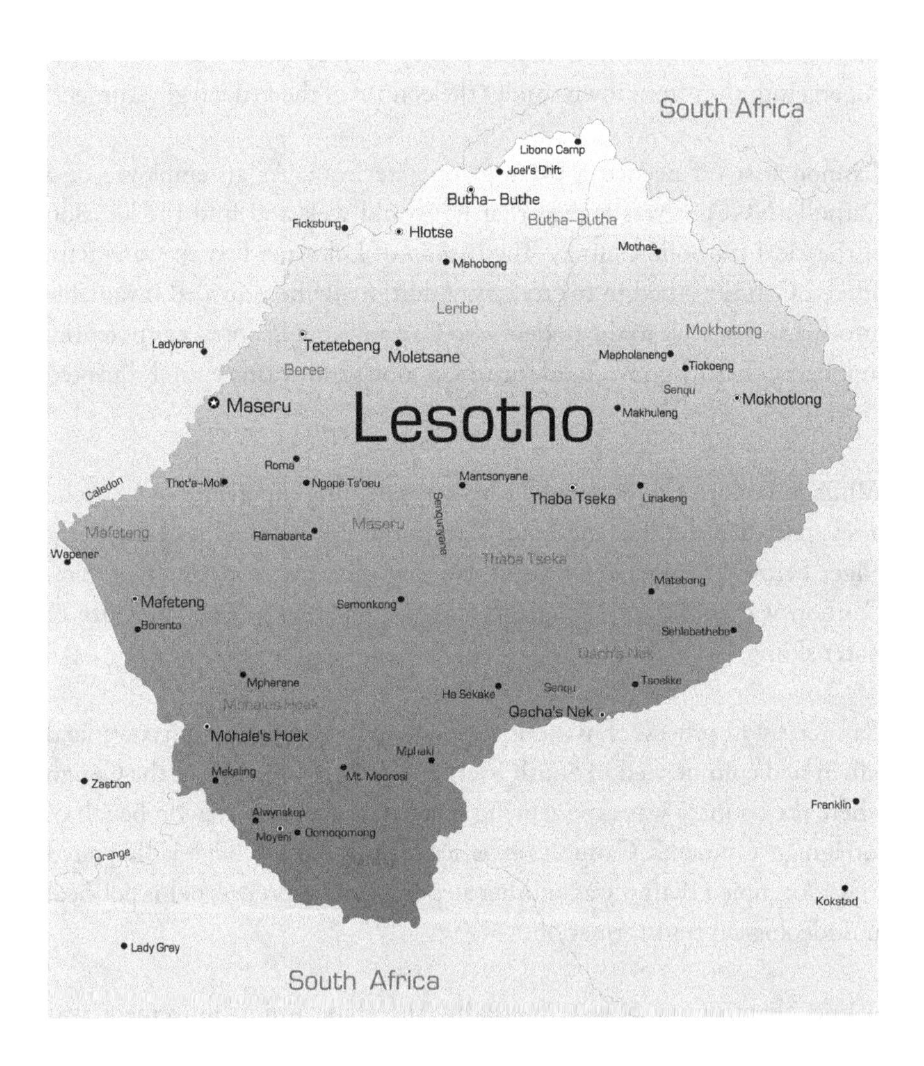

INTERLUDE

What started out as a desire to effect positive humanitarian development after the Peace Corps was starting to wane! The West seemed to believe it knew what was needed for the development of third world people with little, if any, local input. Henry Mullen in Congo exemplified this know-all belief. He believed he could come directly from the USA and implement a program for Congolese people without their input. It wasn't until decades later that what was taking place could possibly be seen by Cannon as a form of neo-colonialism

The holiday season in 1968 was a turning point in the personal life of Cannon. He traveled to Sweden to spend the season with his former Peace Corps friend Elaine (Bo) and her boyfriend Madubuko (Buko). They had moved to Lund, Sweden in 1967 to escape the racism which existed in the US, such as the pursuit by the FBI of the Black Panthers. The US wasn't a great place to be for a mixed black and white couple at the time.

Sweden was a drastic change from Africa. Not only were the people 99.9% white (just like the Ivory Snow soap commercial), but also the weather was completely opposite Africa's warm. It was cold. While in Lund, Cannon was to meet a circle of expatriates drawn to Sweden for various reasons. One in particular, a male of Asian background, was driven there as a victim of South Africa's apartheid regime as a teenager. Others were deserters from the US military who didn't want to serve in South Vietnam. Still others were exchange students on study programs.

While in Sweden, Buko and Bo introduced Cannon to a teenage Norwegian that was staying in Lund with her relatives, Kari Moe. Kari was a tall blond beauty attractive enough to appear in local movies produced by expatriate University of Lund students. Kari spoke English-mostly acquired when she was a member of an Outward Bound troop performing in the USA.

After a whirlwind courtship of some ten days, the pair thought it would be a great idea to get married. Due to Kari's age, she needed to secure the approval of her father who was a resident in Trondheim, Norway. After receiving Kari's fathers' approval, a civil marriage took place in Norway in January 1969. It was doubtful whether Mrs. Cannon really comprehended what was in store moving to Africa. Cannon had no idea what marriage was about nor did his new wife. Two days after the civil marriage, the couple flew out to Africa.

Much to the chagrin of his employer, Cannon arrived in Nairobi, Kenya with a wife. To compound matters, she wasn't a Catholic. Cannon was reunited with Lawson Mooney and another friend and his wife the Garnett's in Nairobi. The Garnett's were previously in Nigeria with CRS.

Nairobi wasn't at all like Monrovia, Kinshasa nor Lagos. While it was on the continent of Africa, it felt more like a westernized city in Europe (Kenya had a moderate climate) like Europe. Nairobi had wide boulevards with the lane dividing middle islands planted with a wide variety of flowers.

There was a very big British presence in the city even after independence of 12 December 1963. Some of the small service providers were still British and many more of Indian origin. What took a while to sink in was the British settled and colonialized Kenya while they only did tours of duty in West Africa. Later some of Cannon's friends in Nigeria used to say: "Thank God for West Africa's bad climate".

Before Cannon could proceed to his new assignment with CRS as the Program Director in Lesotho, he needed to get married in the Catholic Church. Kari was a Lutheran but she was non-practicing. The Diocese of Nairobi wanted her to undergo six weeks' of Catholic education before they would agree to perform a Catholic wedding for the Cannon's. Kari could not understand the reasoning behind this position since the Lutheran faith is not completely different than Catholicism.

A Catholic wedding was necessary since Lesotho had a very large Catholic population and Cannon would be working closely with the church there. After a few days in Nairobi, Mooney was visited by a priest friend who expressed a willingness to perform a Catholic marriage in Machakos, a small town some 65 kilometers south of Nairobi, even though Cannon's wife wasn't a Catholic. At that point in time, Machakos was not a part of the Diocese of Nairobi but was in the process of becoming its own diocese.

A small private wedding mass took place witnessed, by the Mooney's and Garnett's. There was a small group of Kenyan children who performed as the choir. While the Church was basically empty, it was still a moving ceremony. Afterwards, a lunch was served in the priest's rectory. Under very unusual circumstances a great day was had by all.

Once the honeymoon was over, the Cannons flew out of Jomo Kenyatta Airport for Lesotho. There were no direct flights to Lesotho since it was a tiny country completely surrounded by South Africa. Upon arriving in Johannesburg at the Jan Smuts Airport, Cannon had his first taste of apartheid.

LESOTHO

Cannon's Italian heritage blessed him with a swarthy complexion and black hair. He was close to six feet tall and weighed close to 155 pounds. Many people often thought he was from one of the Middle East countries. After honeymooning on the beaches of Mombasa, he was quite tanned, whereas his Norwegian wife was very blond. The immigration officials didn't allow the Cannons to enter the country. The customs and immigration people thought the couple was mix raced which was illegal in apartheid South Africa. Instead, they were forced to spend the night in a room that was located above the arrival hall in the international terminal before catching their small commuter plane to Lesotho the following day.

The Cannon's flight to Lesotho was smooth. Upon arriving at the Maseru airport, the plane was forced to circle the airport a few times due to cattle grazing on the grass runway. The runway was very small since the airport was located right in downtown Maseru. After the cattle were dispersed, the plane was able to land without difficulty.

The Cannons were put up in the only hotel in Lesotho's small capital Maseru. It still had hitching rings and posts along its main street for those who rode their horses into the capital. It was a tiny place to begin a new marriage. It offered the Cannon's plenty of time to get to know each other after such a short courtship.

It's told that just prior to Independence (4 October 1966) the only tarred road in the country was from the King's Palace in Maseru to the South

Africa border, courtesy of a royal visit by Princess Elizabeth who later became the Queen of England. The rest of the roads were dirt.

Lancers Inn was owned and operated by a white family who lived just across the Orange River in South Africa. After the Cannon's unpacked, they proceeded to the Inn's lounge outdoors for drinks. Here Cannon's predecessor introduced him and his wife to some of his friends. While introductions were taking place over drink a black face peered through the outdoor hedges separating the hotel from the road. The next thing the predecessor was running out of the hotel trying to catch the intruder. When asked later what that was all about, Cannon was informed the intruder (Desmond Sixishe) was working as an informer on behalf of the South African government.

Many years later Desmond turned against the apartheid regime and became deeply involved in Lesotho politics. As a son-in-law of Prime Minister Leabua Jonathan, he was instrumental in moving the once right wing Government towards the Eastern bloc community much to the chagrin of the apartheid regime in South Africa.

The Cannons were eventually housed in a renovated teachers' cottage that belong to the Catholic Diocese of Maseru just on the outskirts of the capital. At that time, Lesotho's capital hadn't yet installed its first set of streetlights. A small circle of friends were soon cultivated. A weekend didn't go bye where there wasn't a party in one house or another.

Eventually, the Cannons got involved with some Peace Corps people as well as some volunteers from England. Little did they realize that their involvement with the Peace Corps would place them into a black-white confrontation among the staff? The Cannons' befriended the Warrington's, a black couple. Sam was the Peace Corps Deputy Director. The director was a white guy. What provoked the dispute between Sam and the Director wasn't out in the open. Matters came to a head. Senior staffers from Peace Corps headquarters in Washington came to Maseru to investigate the dispute.

During the investigation, the Warrington's left their Peace Corps provided housing and moved into the small Cannons' cottage to wait out the investigation. One day, the 3rd secretary from the US Embassy, which in those days was located on the third floor of a dry cleaning establishment owned by a colored refugee from South Africa, visited the Cannons to ask if they were housing the Warrington's. He was told he had no rights to come into the Cannon house unless invited. The Cannon's stood by their friends.

Peace Corps ruled in favor of the white Director and eventually removed his black deputy Sam Warrington. It wasn't bad enough that one had to live with racists South Africa on one's door step: racism within the Peace Corps was another issue. Cannon's eyes were starting to open.

The development work Cannon was directing focused around the utilization of US Public Law 480 Title Two commodities. The commodities included bulgur wheat, non-fat powdered dry milk, cooking oil, flour and a few others. These commodities formed a significant portion of the United States Agency for International Developments (USAID) program overseas. Title Two commodities were shipped from the USA to the port of Durban, South Africa. Once they cleared customs (Lesotho was a member of a customs' union with South Africa), they were transported by rail to rail heads in South Africa near the Lesotho boarder, then trucked into Lesotho. The Pl-480 Title Two commodities were either distributed as a supplement to a child's nutrition program or used a partial payment for work done on self-help projects such as the building of mountain roads and small earthen dams.

These agriculture products and by-products, over produced by US farmers, were purchased by the US government and made available to US non-government organizations for overseas distribution as part of USAID. Whether these foods were normally consumed by the recipients or not, was never questioned. Once during a serious food shortage, USAID supplied yellow corn (maize) meal to Lesotho. People in Lesotho and Southern Africa did not eat yellow maize. Yellow maize was used for animal feed. It was very difficult to convince the recipients that yellow maize meal was good to eat.

Some years later this seemingly erstwhile availability of surplus commodities for overseas distribution, produced changes in eating patterns of recipients. They also built up future markets for the commercial sale of US agriculture commodities. Bread, unknown to Africans before the arrival of the white man, eventually became a staple of urban residents in many African countries. Was this a long range policy goal of PL-480 US donated commodities or merely a coincidence?

Within the Cannon's first year in Lesotho, they were informed a baby was to join them. A big decision had to be made as to where the future child would be born: in apartheid South Africa which had excellent medical facilities for whites or little Lesotho where medical facilities were limited to say the least. It was decided that the baby should be born in Lesotho: not to carry the stigma, at the time, of having South Africa appear on one's birth certificate. Fortunately Cannon's work helped him come into contact with a small Catholic mission hospital in the village of Roma located not far from Maseru.

The hospital was an offshoot of the University, which originated as a Catholic institution, which later became the University of Botswana, Lesotho and Swaziland. The only potential complication to the forthcoming birth was a drive of some thirty-five kilometers to the hospital over not too good roads. When the time arrived however, the Cannons drive to Roma went off without a hitch.

The doctor in charge of the hospital was a European lady volunteer from Switzerland who perfected her profession on the World War II battle fields of Europe according to rumors. Whether this was true or not, it still made for interesting conservation. The doctor informed Cannon that his wife would be attended by a Basotho mid-wife until it came time for the actual delivery. When Cannon questioned the doctor about her availability, he was told millions of children are born throughout the world without doctors being present. He should have more faith in humanity.

While Mrs. Cannon was in the delivery room which was big enough to hold two beds, Cannon was joined by friends from Maseru who decided it was time to hold a party. The party was only interrupted by the delivery of a healthy baby girl. The delivery was conducted by the Doctor and a Basotho midwife.

After the delivery, the decision to have Chandra in Lesotho was re-enforced by the mother and child being together in a small cozy room throughout their hospital stay able to host visitors at any time during day light hours. Mother and child thrived in this cozy environment. The entire cost for the birth was less than $100 US dollars.

Before Independence on 4 October 1966, the majority political party was the Basutoland Congress Party (BCP) led by Ntsu Mokhehle a sure shoe-in to be elected Prime Minister. The politics of Mokhehle were an anathema to South Africans. He actually believed in a form of socialism, which the white apartheid regime directly correlated with Communism. To combat the possible election of an independent socialist country in their mists, the South Africans brokered a new party the Basutoland National Party (BNP) and convinced a former associate of Mokhehle to become its leader. Leabua Jonathan was a strong Roman Catholic ex-gold miner in South Africa. With great South Africa support in the form of money and food and the backing of the Catholic Church, Leabua won/stole the election.

It wasn't too long before Parliament turned into a political battle between supporters of Mokhehle and supporters of Jonathan putting developmental issues to the background. At that time, the constitutional monarch, King Moshoeshoe II, who was a relative of the Prime Minister, began to meddle in party politics against the wishes of the Prime Minister. Eventually the Prime Minister forced the King into temporary exile in the UK. The first post- independence election in January 1970 resulted in the defeat of Jonathan's ruling BNP.

Shortly after the election, a coup attempt was mounted against Jonathan's government. It could have possibly succeeded if the Special Branch and the small Armed Unit of the Police didn't jump into the fray under the leadership of British expatriates fully supported by South Africa. Some of the more vocal BCP supporters who opposed Jonathan were arrested. Some were housed in a nearby jail, this was located across the highway from the Cannon's cottage.

One of the more interesting friends the Cannon's first made in Lesotho was Joe Molefe. Joe was a South African political refugee forced into exile as a result of his participation in the Pan African Congress (PAC). Every African over 16 years old was required to carry a pass. The pass, issued by the apartheid government, allowed the bearer to be in a white area. The PAC promoted a mass action campaign against the pass law. The police opened fire on PAC supporters in the black township of Sharpeville on March 21, 1963. Over 60 were killed and more than 180 injured. Those killed and injured were shot in the back. Joe was a participant in the Sharpeville mini-revolt before fleeing to Lesotho.

In retrospect, it was probably easier for South Africans to monitor the comings and goings of Molefe in Lesotho than it would have been if he were off in the UK. Lesotho was much smaller than the UK and was completely surrounded by South Africa. It was easy for the South Africa spy apparatus to function in a country it completely surrounded. Additionally they were able to coerce and recruit a few Basotho mine workers while they worked in South Africa. The South Africans were further assisted in their efforts to monitor Molefe by a few white expatriate British policemen who were either seconded to the Lesotho police force or hired as contractors usually by the British government.

Molefe had to check-in with the Lesotho Special Branch weekly as a refugee. Joe supported his family as a stringer for the British Broadcasting Company (BBC) and by operating a transport business, which consisted of one vehicle. Any friends of Joe Molefe became suspect in the eyes of the South African regime. They were viewed as radicals. The Cannons befriended an expatriate member of the Lesotho police force and his wife. Ted Irving later informed the Cannons they were coming under the attention of the South Africa security services because of their friendship with Molefe.

Fortunately, Joe Molefe lived long enough to witness the demise of apartheid and the election of Nelson Mandela as President of South Africa.

How ironic was it that Cannon was also to return to Lesotho years later and also witnessed the beginnings of a new South Africa ruled by the majority of its citizens.

When the Cannon's traveled into Bloemfontein, (the nearest South African city some 100 miles away), the apartheid plain clothes personnel-male and female followed them openly. It was worst for Mrs. Cannon who was a striking blond Scandinavian woman who didn't understand why she was being followed. All she was doing was shopping for clothes. The absurdity of the political and racial paranoia of South Africa can be illustrated by the next sequence of events.

Cannon was diagnosed with a nasal problem in Maseru. The medical people recommend he go to Bloemfontein to have an operation since they had better facilities. Cannon drove himself over the border and to the hospital where he was told he would be hospitalized overnight after the operation. After the operation, Cannon woke up in a ward that was full of white South Africans. Upon waking, Cannon proceeded to the nurses' desk asking for his clothes. After getting dressed, with gauze still in his nostrils, he was discharged. Despite being groggy, Cannon then drove back to Maseru.

Upon returning to Maseru, Cannon was visited in his office by two white South African security personnel who said he was being investigated for fraud in South Africa. Cannon was told he bounced some checks purchasing goods. Cannon asked what authority these people had in Lesotho. He was told they basically had the run of the country and could do as they pleased.

Cannon contacted his friend Ted Irving in the Lesotho police who used his clout to pull off the South Africans. Cannon learned that someone in the hospital's reception staff (they were all white in those days) stole some blank checks out of his belongings and forged his signature on checks to make three purchases of goods in Bloemfontein.

The Cannons were asked to report to the South African border post after the aforementioned instance. After checking with friends at the newly built and opened US Embassy in Maseru, they proceeded to the border in a vehicle driven by a friend who could keep abreast of events from nearby. Once inside the border post, they were escorted to the office of the Commander who then tried his best to convince the Cannons of the benefits and rational of apartheid. The analogy used was two straight lines. After Mrs. Cannon asked what would happen when the two lines joined, the public relations promotion stopped and the Cannons were able to leave. The Cannons were later informed that the PR spokesperson was a colonel in the South Africa's Bureau of State Security. From that day onwards until the Cannon's left Lesotho in 1971, they had company whenever they were in South Africa.

As it happens in every country outside of one's own, the people you have become acquainted and friends with gradually begin to disperse. They either return to their country of origin or are transferred to another overseas assignment while local friends stay put. One of the first to go was the United Nations Development Program (UNDP) representative who had the audacity to suggest to the United Nations that UN aid to Lesotho be curtailed since non-elected personnel were running it. Needless to say, if the UN recognized Papa Doc Duvalier in Haiti, they would have no problems in dealing with the Jonathan regime. Throughout the many, many years after the UNDP Resident Representative Bob Lederman's departure, the friendship developed in Lesotho grew in spite of personal whereabouts with him and his family. Bob was an honest civil servant who spoke the truth which got him a demotion to UNDP Deputy in Nigeria on his next assignment.

When the Cannons arrived in Lesotho, the United States Embassy for Lesotho and the US Ambassador to Lesotho were located in Lusaka, Zambia. The regional United States Agency for International Developments (USAID) office responsible for Lesotho was also located in Zambia. The US Consulate in Maseru was located on the 3nd floor of a building, which housed a dry-cleaners shop on the ground floor.

The US finally built an Embassy in Lesotho in 1971. At the same time, USAID established an office. Lesotho being such a small African country (about the same size as the smallest state in the USA- Rhode Island) drew some very talented young State Department junior officers. Cannon befriended a junior State Department officer in the newly established Embassy who would later rise to the rank of Ambassador. When the Cannon's returned to Lesotho in 1986, they met two other junior officers who would rise to the rank of an Ambassador of the United States. Truly amazing!

There were other Basotho who would become well known. One Basotho who the Cannon's first met when he was released from jail after the 1970 coup attempt later became a well-known international artist: Mohau/ Meshu who exhibited in Europe, South and North America. Another Basotho rose from the Lesotho Planning Department to become the Secretary Treasurer of the World Bank and would later have a law passed in apartheid- free South Africa that would allow him as a foreigner to become the Deputy Director of the Bank of South Africa. Bishop Desmond Tutu headed the Anglican Church in Lesotho before becoming the Archbishop in Cape Town, South Africa. The late Chris Hani, a hero in the fight for South Africa's freedom, who was killed in the prime of his life, also had once resided in Maseru with his family as well.

With the Cannon's starting on their 2nd group of expatriate friends and their Basotho friends starting families and moving elsewhere, they started to wonder what was next. CRS informed them a move was afoot to assign them to South Korea. The program in South Korea was run by a member of the Catholic clergy. Cannon would go from being country program director in a small place to deputy country program director in a much bigger place. With a small baby and the prospect of another few years remuneration based upon one's Christian belief, the thought of continuing employment with a wonderful organization such as CRS wasn't as appealing as after departing Peace Corps as a bachelor.

The Bishop of Maseru was not at all pleased to hear Cannon would be departing Lesotho. Cannon always tried to keep Bishop Morapheli informed regarding CRS program developments even though the program was non-sectarian due to the reception of US government funds. Cannon did his best to keep his personal religious beliefs and practices away from his work.

Cannon's informed the office of Prime Minister Jonathan that CRS planned to transfer the Cannon family to South Korea and his replacement would be Eugene Rosera. Much to the delight of the Cannon's, the Prime Minister held a farewell party, at his official residence, in their honor. The Cannon's received beautiful hand-woven mohair rugs as farewell gifts. Cannon also received a personal letter from Prime Minister Jonathan, which appears in the appendages.

6

Academic Renaissance

Canada 1971-1972

Once the Cannons decided they were not going to South Korea, it was necessary to find an alternative since it was certain they would no longer have employment with CRS. The Cannons were in for a drastic change: a possible move to North America. One of the projects that Cannon supported in Lesotho was operated out of the University of Botswana, Lesotho and Swaziland's Extension Department. The project was to provide education to Basotho farmers who formed cooperatives to maximize potential crop production by combining individual small plots of land. Tractors were provided to the cooperatives. Direct technical assistance to the cooperatives was provided by Peace Corps volunteers who lived amongst the cooperative communities. The UBLS Extension Department Director was a Canadian, Dr. Hugh Gillis. He was previously associated with St. Francis Xavier University in Canada.

Cannon was informed of a new start-up graduate program in Adult Education at the University of St. Francis Xavier in Antigonish, Nova Scotia by Hugh Gillis. He recommended a phone call be made to the Director of the Adult Education program to see whether a place could be secured. Cannon made the call and was informed he would be accepted into the course starting in September 1971 based upon the recommendation she received from Hugh Gillis. Additionally, the tuition fee would be waivered.

Prior to returning to Providence, Rhode Island the Cannons passed through New York City for a de-briefing. Cannon departure from CRS went smoothly and there was an option to return after graduate school. The next step was a visit with parents in Providence before going onwards to Nova Scotia

While in Providence, Cannon ran into an old grammar school friend who informed him he might be eligible to access the G.I. Bill. This Bill, established after World War II, provided financial assistance to military veterans' for education purposes and was based upon the active duty time one spent in uniform. To Cannon's welcomed surprise, he was eligible to receive $ 125 per month as a full-time student.

How to get to Nova Scotia from Providence? The best option was to hire a car which could carry a few of the belongings of the Cannons. Upon arrival there, Cannons found they were too late to secure a place in the married students' complex. The Adult Education staff directed them to a house in the center of Antigonish: a small town in which the university was located. The house was completely furnished. The rent cost was $ 75 per month plus utilities and it was only a 15-minute walk to the campus. The owner of the house was affiliated with the University hence the minimal rent.

Much to Cannon's surprise there were other students in the program who were not Canadians. One was from Bolivia and two others from Hong Kong. They originally went to Antigonish to study at the Coady International Institute. The Institute was named for a pioneer in Eastern Canada who was instrumental in the establishment of credit unions during the depression years. The Canadian government made available grants to foreigners wanting to acquire credit union skills, which could help their communities in their respective countries.

The second surprise, which awaited Cannon, was the entire focus of the program was changed from its first year of operation. The students would no longer attend lectures and classes. The new focus was on contractual learning. Each student was to be responsible for designing his or her own program of learning, which would be task orientated. Each student was required to write up a program of learning, setting learning goals, objectives, and tasks to be undertaken. The Adult Education staff would review same and either accept the student's submission or return it for further revision and elaboration. Not only was Cannon surprised, the other eleven students were equally surprised. Three eventually dropped out of the program.

After the Christmas holidays in 1971, the Cannons moved into a beautiful home across the street from the campus. A spinster heard of their predicament (unable to get into student married quarters) and offered them access to a small flat within her house. There would be tasks to be undertaken to assist the landlord such as providing wood for the stove, snow shoveling, periodic shopping, etc. The monthly rent would be $ 75, which included all utilities. Fortunately the landlord was a bit deaf, hence Cannon's daughter Chandra could properly exercise her lungs without any reproach usually associated with landlords.

Cannon was finally starting to get into an academic groove at the start of 1972. This was the first time he didn't have to work while studying. In the past it was difficult to read background reference materials due to insufficient time. During the graduate year in residence, Cannon was able to develop new reading skills by consuming numerous books and periodicals. These reading skills would turn into a passion for the remainder of his life.

The implementation of tasks needed to be undertaken to acquire the objectives in the learning contract signed with the Adult Ed department proved difficult. The staff despite being always available for feedback on one's progress didn't seek out the graduate students. Their philosophy was the students were mature adults who should know when they needed external guidance or help and ask for same.

Trying to identify potential learning tasks in an unfamiliar environment provided a big challenge. The tasks were to be completed in the year's campus residency. For the first time in Cannon's life, he was challenged intellectually: previously it was only a matter of studying enough to pass an exam.

Cannon was fortunate to team up with two Canadians. They both had vehicles. Cannon and the two Canadians form an investigation team to determine the feasibility of implementing a community-identified project in the town of Westville which was about 50 miles south of Antigonish.

A survey was designed and pre-tested based upon the data collected during previous visits to the town of some 4,000 residents. A sample population of one percent was identified who would be interviewed to determine possible community projects. The data collected identified recreation and entertainment as the two priority needs of the community. Projects in these areas however were beyond the ability of graduate students. The survey findings of the investigating team were made available to the town fathers.

Cannon's second learning task was a social awareness project undertaken with some of the more radical students at the Coady International Institute. This was Cannon's first exposure to persons who didn't view communism in the same light as Americans yet they were also Catholics. Cannon was able to find a kindred soul at Coady who was also an expatriate American, Emilio Garza.

The project with the Coady students was even more of a learning experience for Cannon because it was his first exposure to people from South America. These students often referred to the US as a neo-colonial power not as a development partner. They were big supporters of "liberation theology" which was a new phrase to Cannon.

Cannon later learned a Dominican priest from Peru, Fr. Gustavo Gutierrez was the prime proponent people must be liberated from unjust economic and social conditions prevailing in much of South America. In the mid 1980's future Pope Benedict the 16th, then Cardinal Joseph Ratzinger officially critiqued liberation theology. Ratzinger believed some Catholic theologians had mixed up the Marxist critique of capitalism with Catholic theology.

It was at Coady that the philosophy of the late Brazilian radical Paulo Freire was first encountered. Freire was the pioneer in promoting an educational belief that the poor and impoverished learned better if they took responsibility for their own education by becoming subjects, not objects, in the learning process.

An additional task was to design an evaluation of a two-week residential labor education course sponsored by the Atlantic Region Labor Education

Centre, which was conducted by the St. Francis Xavier University's Extension Department. This task provided Cannon with face-to-face trade union practitioners for the first time.

Various evaluation techniques were designed to acquire feedback as to whether the course objectives were met as well as to measure the participants satisfaction with the curriculum, the education techniques employed, the resource personnel used and the facilities made available by the university.

Throughout the process of implementing various tasks to acquire skills that were part of Cannon learning contract to obtain a Masters' Degree in Adult Education, Cannon was fortunate to have been able to read some ninety-five books and publications, which greatly broadened his intellectual horizons.

Two other events took place in Antigonish which enhanced the learning experience at the University. Mrs. Cannon brought forth a lovely baby boy in June 1972 named Marc. At the time of this birth, Canada's health care system was financed by a sales tax, which meant the Cannon's did not have to get a loan for hospital costs. Cannon was able to be inside the delivery room when his son was born. It was another fantastic experience similar to that of his daughter Chandra in Lesotho except it was more formal- sans party.

Fortunately for Cannon, his being married with two children was not a hindrance in the self-directed graduate program. Cannon could cook, shop for food supplies and undertake other home tasks during the daytime, because daily university classes were not part of the graduate program. This gave Kari a break from the kids and allowed her to take an extension class at the University.

Based upon Cannon's experiences overseas in the Philippines, South Vietnam, the Congo, Nigeria, and Lesotho, he was drawn to Coady International Institute's foreign students. The how and why a fellow American Emilio Garza was at Coady remains a mystery. It was rumored that that the CIA used Canada as a refugee for some of its personnel who needed a temporary place and seclusion for a short break from their career.

Emilio Garza was a Chicano from Texas. He was average in his height and physical built. His hair was thinning and he wore black horn rim glasses. Emilio was very self-confident and was a riveting instructor in the classroom. His family, a wife and two teenage sons had accompanied him to Antigonish. They lived in a colonial rented house on the outskirts of the town.

Cannon learned that Emilio had been previously employed by the American Federation of Labor/Congress of Industrial Organizations (AFL-CIO) overseas arm in Latin America. In the book **INSIDE THE COMPANY: CIA Diary** by Philip Agee, Emilio was referred to as a recruited and controlled agent of the CIA. This accusation was never proved nor disavowed.

What role the late Garza had in Cannon getting a position later with the AFL-CIO's overseas arm in Asia was never made known. What can be said is Garza was instrumental in directing Cannon on a new path in international development. If Cannon had not met Emilio Garza, it is unlikely he would have found a career in the international trade union movement. Whether Cannon would have spent the remainder of his working career overseas is also questionable.

Living across the street from the University and Coady Institute afforded Cannon an opportunity to socialize with students from developing countries in the Cannon's residence. Institutional food in North America wasn't what most of the foreign students were accustomed to, especially the Africans. Rice was served in the form of a desert-rice pudding. The Africans were shocked to be served rice as a desert not as a main staple. Foreign students had access to the Cannons' kitchen with the following two conditions: they had to bring the food that was to be prepared and secondly the Cannons were to be included in its consumption.

Breaking bread resulted in very interesting conversations which was often driven by Marxist beliefs and attitudes. For the first time in Cannon's intellectual development, a new world view was starting to open.

International development was being seen through new eyes. Needless to say, many a fine meal was consumed.

The African foreign students were quick at mastering the substitution of North American foods for those from their respective countries. Yams couldn't be obtained to make pounded yam- a favorite with the West Africans. The replacement was instant mashed potatoes, which could be made to take on the texture of pounded yam- a sticky rounded ball. Another substitution basic was cooking oil, combined with tinned tomato paste, replaced palm oil for cooking. Unfortunately there was no Canadian substitute found for palm wine. We just had to get by with Canadian beer, expensive but decent.

In addition to the strange foods, the foreign students at Coady Institute had to become accustomed to winter. The cold and snow were shocking even with the heavy winter clothing donated by the community annually. There was one exception, the two students that came from Lesotho in Southern Africa. Their country experienced snow in the mountains. The freezing temperatures created conditions in Lesotho's mountains for skiing much to the disbelief of Canadians.

Just when winter seemed over, the town was hit by a freak snowstorm on the day of the seniors graduating ball. It was hilarious to see these Canadians in their rented gowns and tuxedos trying to navigate in knee-deep snow. As can be imagined the snow didn't last. Prior to the onset of summer, Cannon was only finishing his self-selected learning tasks and activities.

The next hurdle to climb was putting one year's activities into a thesis. Without access to a typewriter, putting together a draft was time consuming. This was difficult with a small child running about and meeting the needs of a new baby Marc who was born in June 1972. Eventually a hand written draft was compiled and a typist found who was willing to type it for a very decent wage.

By the end of July, Cannon's draft thesis was in a state for presentation to his advisor. The first objective of the draft thesis was: a) to determine whether a graduate student in Adult Education acquired or improved the adult education skills of- communications, group processes, interpersonal competency, planning and data collection/interpretation. The second objective was to provide enhanced experiences in communications and planning skills. The acquisition of these skills were to be acquired or improved via a series of action tasks juxtaposed to specific measurable objectives for each skill. He lucked out. It was accepted, with only minor revisions.

The final thesis entitled: An Adult Educator's Description and Evaluation of Skill Development was submitted and accepted by the Department of Adult Education on September 1, 1972. The following words were penned onto the blank page by the Chairperson of the Department "With very best wishes & hope that you continue your determination to learn. It has been a pleasure to work with you."

Norway 1972-1974

The Cannon's departed Antigonish, Nova Scotia with no definite employment prospects in store. The family traveled to Providence, Rhode Island to stay in the unfinished basement of Cannon's parents. Trying to secure a job in the Adult Education field was a throw-back to getting a high school teaching job in 1963. Again it was who you knew not what you knew that served as the door opener. Cannon wasn't able to kiss arse this time either. Hence employment in Rhode Island didn't occur.

Fortunately, while still in Antigonish, the Cannon's started to communicate with the University of Bergen in Bergen, Norway. Cannon still had additional education eligibility remaining under the GI Bill. It was learned that one could use the GI Bill in Norway if Cannon could enroll in a post graduate program.

In September 1972, the Cannons were on the move again. This time they were moving to the homeland of Mrs. Cannon: Norway. Bergen, Norway was located on the North Sea. It was in the process of becoming a very important player in the international petroleum industry.

Offshore oil had recently been discovered. The discoveries of oil lead to a resurgence in Norwegian nationalism which was reflected in referendum defeat as to whether Norway should join the European Union. Norway was on a roll.

Initially the Cannons were placed in student flat built for two individual students. It consisted of two bedrooms with a connecting kitchen and shower. One bedroom housed the two children and the other bedroom served as a dining/living room as well as the bedroom for the parents. It was a tight squeeze for a family of four but had to make do until married quarters became free in January 1973. This initial placement proved a blessing because the Cannons were able to meet a family of three from the Sudan who lived in the next apartment complex who were also enrolled in the Anthropology department at the university.

The University of Bergen was starting to welcome foreign students. It was recommended that foreigners enroll in Norwegian classes first prior to starting study in their respective discipline. Classes were conducted at the university in downtown Bergen. The university was approximately eight kilometers away from student housing.

The Cannons found Norwegian living expensive, in comparison to Canadian living. They had to secure a student loan to supplement the monthly allotment of $ 125 received under the GI Bill. Even with the added monies from a loan, Cannon's lived on a very tight budget. Towards the end of each month, before the next monthly loan was deposited in Cannon's bank, he would walk to the university to save bus fare and sometimes back as well.

Professors who had previous field experience in Asia as well as Africa staffed the Anthropology Department. It was this department that accepted Cannon. It was also the same department that the man from Sudan, Mohammed was enrolled in. The University stipulated that lectures and classes were offered in English prior to the Cannon's arrival. Unfortunately this proved to be only partially true. The majority of the lectures and classes were in Norwegian.

Another complicating issue was the requirement that each enrollee had to have a University of Bergen recognized matriculation. This was easy for Norwegian students and other from European countries but not for North Americans. Some of the foreign student advisers were not familiar with education standards and programs especially in the US and Canada, thus they found it difficult to correlate foreign degrees with matriculation.

Cannon received his Masters' of Art Degree in Adult Education from St. Francis Xavier University in Canada in October 1972. Even with a Bachelor of Arts degree and a Master of Arts degree, Cannon was told he still needed to be matriculated according to Norwegian procedures. Eventually the bureaucracy came around to accepting Cannon's two North American degrees allowing him to commence studying in the Anthropology faculty. Unfortunately, Cannon's command of Norwegian wasn't sufficient to fully comprehend academic lectures. A compromise was reached whereby it was agreed that Cannon could write two papers in lieu of attending most lectures and then deal with the next step-the thesis.

The married student's quarters, which the Cannon's moved into, were patrician compared to the single quarters. They were located on the top of a mini mountain just in back of the single student's complex. There were no foreign families living in this complex.

Mohammed and his family departed Norway for England in early 1973. He felt the University wasn't following thru on its promises and commitments. Fortunately, his government concurred and paid for the family's transfer to England so he could continue his studies. It is impossible for a white person to comprehend what a black person goes through living in a white society.

The Cannon's in Africa were not personally subject to racist behavior per se, only political monitoring by white South Africans. Cannon's Mediterranean complexion, combined with his Afro hairstyle and black full beard stood out in the Norwegian culture. Norway was populated by people with blond hair, blue eyes and very white skin.

Cannon began to feel what racism is like when he started to get short-changed at a few grocery stores in Bergen. Mrs. Cannon wouldn't believe her husband's complaining about his getting stiffed when he did their grocery shopping in Bergen. It wasn't until she actually witnessed the occurrence that she finally believed him.

Another incident took place in public one afternoon in the city. Cannon and his wife were having a brief argument while he was pushing the baby carriage. An older Norwegian man approached Mrs. Cannon and asked her if the foreigner next to her was bothering her. Much to the chagrin of the older man, he was told to mind his own business and that the foreigner was her husband.

The Cannons had daily routines. He would get the kids breakfast ready, prepare a food shopping list, and get dressed. He would take the bus or walk to the University. Mrs. Cannon would go off to work at her part-time job at the married students' day care center. Cannon would return in the late afternoon in time to help prepare the evening meal. After eating, the kids were put to bed and Cannon read before heading to bed. Unlike most other students living in the married students' quarters, the Cannon's had neither television nor an automobile. The routine was broken at the weekend when Cannon went to the only Catholic Church in Bergen on Sunday.

Cannon gradually stopped going to his Norwegian lessons at the University. Ninety-nine percent of the academic lecturers were in Norwegian. Cannon's Norwegian comprehension wasn't sufficient for him to follow the complete lecture. Instead he spent his time in the library. While all the Norwegian professors and assistant professors spoke English, cross-cultural communication was still fraught with frequent misunderstandings. It became obvious that Cannon's chances of getting a post graduate degree at the University of Bergen were slim to say the least.

When the university closed in May 1973 for the summer, the Cannon's departed Bergen to stay with Mrs. Cannon's mother and step-father on a tiny farm in southern Norway not far from the city of Stavanger. They were able to make use of a tiny rustic furnished apartment in the loft of the farm barn within walking distance to the main farm cottage.

Summers were a pleasure. Due to the proximity with the equator, the sun didn't set until well into the late evening hours. Lots of time was spent outdoors. It was a great place to jog due to the lack of much vehicular traffic. The farm was within one hours walking distance of the nearest small town Bryne, which served as a diversion from life on the rural farm. The children were thrilled to be away from the small-married students' quarters. They were even more thrilled to be with their grandmother and step-grandfather.

Bo and Buko, the same couple who introduced Cannon to his wife, visited the Cannon's from Sweden. After a few days on the farm, the foursome was able to depart by road for the trip back to Sweden. The trip came at the same time Mrs. Cannon was starting to reduce breast-feeding Marc, their son born in Canada. Grandma had her hands full for the first few days the Cannons were away from the farm to say the least. By the time the Cannon's returned from Sweden, Marc completely adjusted to bottle feeding, thanks to the yeoman efforts of Kari's mother, Liv.

In the early 1970's Sweden was a haven for deserters from the Vietnam Conflict, who were welcomed and taken care of by the welfare system. It was also still a popular destination for people who were fleeing racial persecution in many parts of the world. The Cannons were able to touch base with many of the people who they knew back in 1969 before they went to Lesotho. It was great to get away from the conservativeness of Norway but a bit concerning wondering about the kids.

After returning to Norway, Cannon devoted the majority of his time to writing free hand, the agreed upon papers for his academic adviser. Life in the married students' quarters moved along well. By April 1974, it became apparent that Cannon wasn't making progress with his pursuit of a post graduate degree. The folks at the University of Bergen were not able to envision what "international education" meant to an international student. Following much recrimination between both parties, the University relented and gave Cannon the equivalent of a post graduate diploma in Social Anthropology: whatever that was meant to stand for.

7

The Good and the Bad

CALAIS, MAINE

The four Cannons returned to the USA in the summer of 1974. They moved once again into the unfurnished cellar of his parent's small house in Providence and Cannon set about trying to find a job. One instant during that summer stands out. A visit from a childhood friend who also attended St. Pius grammar school and was making a career for himself in the US Marines.

Cannon's path had crossed with Jimmy Keeley in Danang in 1967. At the time Cannon had taken over the CRS regional office for the northern most provinces of South Vietnam. One day in an Officers Club, in came Jimmy Keeley. Jimmy had moved up from being an enlisted Marine to a Captain. After a few beers of catching up on where we both had been since 1960, we agreed to meet the following day. We stayed close until Cannon moved to Nha Trang to set-up another regional office there for CRS. Jimmy went back to the field.

Jimmy pitches up with a girl-friend. All six of us are now hanging out in the basement of the Cannon's parent's small house much to the chagrin of Cannon's Italian mother Lena. She wasn't supportive of the life style in progress at the time. Her conservative social mores and staunch Catholic beliefs were offended by couples sleeping together who were not married. Cannon's Irish father, John, didn't voice any opinion on the living arrangements. Later Cannon learned his views coincided with his wife.

Publically Cannon's parents were civil to Jimmy and his girlfriend. In those days, older folks might not have approved of the social happenings of the times, but they were polite enough to welcome house guests regardless of their private feelings. We had a great time together before Jimmy and his girlfriend departed. Unfortunately years later, after only a few years into retirement, Jimmy died from all the Agent Orange he inhaled while doing battle in South Vietnam.

Cannon was told he could get a job in Providence through family connections; but fate intervened. Cannon answered an employment advertisement in the Boston Globe for a position in Calais, Maine. After a telephone interview, he was given the job as curriculum developer with Maine Indian Education (MIE) for one year with a possible extension depending upon funding.

Calais, Maine was located in Washington County and it was about as different as anything Cannon had seen or experienced before. Located on the St. Croix River, which served as a boundary with New Brunswick Canada, it was originally inhabited in June 1604 by French expeditionary forces under the leadership of Pierre du Gua Sieur de Mons and Samuel de Champlain. It was the first settlement by Europeans north of Florida on the North American continent according to many.

Calais grew into a small city of some 3,600 people located about 20 miles northeast of Eastport, Maine in Washington County. Washington County was about the size of the state of Rhode Island but had only some 35,000 people. There was a small library about an (20) minute walk from Cannons place. It was a built on the banks of the St. Croix River. The library was stocked with a wide variety of books and was a member of the Maine Library Association. If a book was requested which wasn't on the shelves, the library could usually obtain a copy within a few days from another one of Maine's libraries. The Cannons were able to rent a small house in Calais that was within the financial range of the salary paid by MIE.

MIE was the creation of the Passamaquoddy and Penobscot tribes. The First Nation Passamaquoddy People were housed on two reservations in Washington County: one northeast of Calais in nearby Princeton, and the other just outside the city of Eastport. The Penobscot reservation was located near the University of Maine in Old Town-approximately 90 miles south of Calais. Maine Indian Education (MIE) Superintendent's office was located in Calais

MIE was created to oversee the primary school systems on two Passamaquoddy reservations and one Penobscot reservation in eastern Maine. These primary schools were established by Catholic missionary societies back in the early 19th century. After these mission schools became public, it was only a matter of time before the First Nation people took control of their own education facilities.

It didn't take long for Cannon to realize that significant change wasn't in the cards for MIE. The two tribes had a law suit pending against the State of Maine in which they rightly claimed millions of acres of land throughout the state. These acres had been appropriated without their consent in the years gone by. Until the land claim issue was resolved, the state of Maine and the federal government were not in a position to fully fund MIE. The curriculum developer position was federally funded. Only a few positions in the Superintendents' office were funded by the State of Maine.

To perform his duties, Cannon applied for his first ever bank loan ever to purchase a 2nd hand car. The bank declined Cannon's loan application on the grounds he had no credit rating. This was Cannon's first dealing as a married man with a commercial bank. He tried without success; to explain to the bank manager cash was the only medium of exchange he used while working in Africa and as a graduate student. This was one of Cannon's first culture shock in the USA: credit as opposed to cash.

One of Cannon's colleagues at MIE was kind enough to give him a $ 900 personal loan needed to purchase a second hand VW Beetle. Chandra and Marc painted the rust spots with red primer paint over the exterior of the vehicle. It was named FRECKLES. It was a great little car that served the family for a good many years.

The Cannons were fortunate that their rented house was just up the street from a family that was native to Calais. A deep and cherished friendship would develop between the families. The Bernardini family had children in the same age bracket as the Cannons. It wasn't long before it became know that their Italian name was graced with Irish ancestry, just like Cannon.

At the time of the first meeting between the Cannon family and the Bernardini family, neither were aware that a friendship would blossom and last for decades to come. Without the new friendship, life in the unfamiliar milieu would have been difficult. Cannon would never had experienced snowmobiling; ice- fishing, trapping, lobster trapping, flounder fishing, clam digging and one or two other outdoor activities.

Was it ever possible that someone would try to dig clams with a toilet plunger? To illustrate Cannon's city background naivety, some people he met told him that one could get clams out of the riverbed faster if you used a toilet plunger. The suction would bring the clam to the surface. One can imagine the look on the faces of Bernardini and his high school buddy Jerry Olsen when Cannon showed up with his six-pack of beer and a toilet plunger instead of a clam rake. They just about pissed themselves laughing at Cannon's feeble attempts to get clams using the plunger. From that day onwards, Cannon friends would never let him forget about the toilet plunger and clam digging.

When June 1973 rolled around, Cannon's job with MIE ceased after US government funding stopped. He was able to secure an administrative job with a health non-profit managing their offices in Calais and Machias about 45 miles south of Calais. Cannon wasn't happy working in the health field in the US. Cannon's main task was to ensure the numerous state and federal government reports were submitted on schedule. Nor was Cannon thrilled with the constant driving back and forth between Calais and Machias in an old 2nd hand VW.

One day out of the blue, there was a knock at the front door of the Cannon house. This signaled strangers to the area since people in Calais knew the side door was the main house entrance. Upon opening the door, Cannon came face to face with two white adult males dressed in suits. One asked if he was Peter J. Cannon. When Cannon answered in the affirmative, the 2nd showed his Federal Bureau of Investigation (FBI) badge. He said they were checking references for Emilio Garza. This seemed strange since Cannon assumed Garza had closer friends from his passed, that would act as better references than Cannon.

In spite of the strangeness of the purported visit, they were invited into the house. Before Cannon answered any questions he asked them to show driving licenses and credit cards to confirm their identities. The agents had a bemused look on their faces but produced the two forms of additional identification requested by Cannon.

They then proceeded to ask a series of questions about Emilio Garza. They said FBI clearance was needed before Emilio could become a member of the US delegation to the annual meeting of the International Labor Organization (ILO) in Geneva, Switzerland. Garza was nominated as a delegate for the American Federation of Labor-Congress of Industrial Organizations (AFL-CIO) as part of the overall US delegation to the tripartite ILO: government, labor and business.

When they finished, off they drove never to be seen again at the Cannon's residence in Calais, Maine. Prior to Cannon's departure from Antigonish, he obtained a telephone contact number for Emilio Garza. Cannon contacted Emilio to inform him of what took place. He was pleased with what Cannon told him. Shortly thereafter, Emilio contacted Cannon about a position with the AFL-CIOs overseas arm working in Asia, the Asian American Free Labor Institute (AAFLI). Cannon interviewed for the job in Washington and was hired thus ending the stay in Calais, Maine. Did the FBI visit have any relationship to the AFL-CIO job offer which followed the visit? Cannon was required to get a security clearance while employed by AAFLI.

One day another surprising occurrence took place in Calais. Kari Cannon told Cannon she was taking instructions in the Catholic faith. Cannon was no big fan of Fr. Andy the local priest. He was constantly preaching about hell during his Sunday homilies. Kari found Fr. Andy a different person than Cannon and was successful in her instruction and was later confirmed by Fr. Andy.

Once the family moved, no one was aware that in the future years, Calais would become the 2nd home for the Cannons while overseas and the Bernardini family would become Cannons family away from Rhode

Island. It would also become the retirement city for Cannon when his overseas working career ceased in the first decade of the new 21st century.

Cannons experienced many of the wonderful attributes and joy of life in rural USA. The scenery was awesome throughout the year even in harsh winter conditions. The issue of class and status were not important. What were important was honesty, hard work and a sense of humor.

Rural living also provided the Cannon's with their first exposure to the injustices suffered by Native American Indians. Their original way of life was long ago fragmented. Their tribal values often conflicted with modern society as a whole. Employment on their reservations was absent. Self-esteem very low. Living conditions were bad. Prospects for the future dim.

WASHINGTON, DC

The Washington, DC area was a complete change from Calais, Maine. Initially, a friend from Cannon's days in South Vietnam, Stan Garnett offered his basement as a temporary respite until an apartment was secured. The apartment complex chosen in Bailey Crossroads, Virginia-a few miles south of DC and was the same complex that the Garnett's stayed in when they relocated to DC. It was relatively cheap, integrated, on the bus line, close to a shopping center, schools and a Roman Catholic Church.

It wasn't long before the Cannon family settle into a routine. However, Cannon's job at AAFLI wasn't what it originally seemed. It mirrored the State Department in its hierarchy. Cannon became the desk officer for the Philippines and South Korea. Two other new hirers were made desk officers for Bangladesh-Sir Lanka, and Fiji- Malaysia.

It soon became apparent that one did nothing besides move paper from one's desk upwards to the next desk in line. This desk then moved it higher until it reached the Executive Director. These tasks were a far cry from what Cannon had done previously in Lesotho. As the Country Director for CRS, he was responsible for a program valued at over a million dollars per year- responsibilities far above those of a desk officer. Cannon began to wonder whether Emilio Garza did him a favor or what?

The Executive Director of AAFLI was an old hand from New York City who came out of the International Ladies Garment Workers Union. Some of the names of higher ups in AAFLI and the other overseas organizations of the AFL-CIO also appeared in the 1975 book **INSIDE THE COMPANY-CIA Diary** written by Philip Agee. If any of the allegations raised in Agee's book were true, Cannon's career had taken a complete 180 turn from being a Peace Corps volunteer. To Cannon's knowledge, none of the individuals noted bothered to sue Agee for slander. Did this mean the allegations were true or did it mean they had no bearing upon AAFLI's work?

Cannon was eventually sent overseas on temporary assignments. The first assignment was to work with in Bangladesh with Garza. It wasn't clear why Cannon was given the temporary assignment to Bangladesh. Garza had opened the office initially yet he was soon to assume a regional role working out of Sir Lanka. Was Cannon being "groomed" to replace Garza in Dacca?

The AAFLI office was in a second-class hotel. It resembled a hotel room more than an office. To get around the city, Garza had rented an old 2nd hand vehicle, with a driver. While Cannon was trying to figure out what he was supposed to do in Dacca and the rest of Bangladesh, Garza was living in the Intercontinental Hotel getting himself ready to move to Sir Lanka.

After Cannon was introduced to some folks at the US Embassy and a few trade union leaders, Garza left. Cannon was left on his own. Garza left Cannon with the impression that his main task was to increase the number of trade union projects, especially in the port of Chittagong.

One of individuals Garza introduced Cannon was to accompany him on a trip south of Dacca. Stops were made in Saleet first and then Chittagong. Was Cannon in for a surprise when his traveling companion took him into offices displaying the hammer & sickle flag saying they were offices of unions affiliated with his federation! AAFLI/Washington was surprised with Cannon's reports since Garza had been dealing with said individual before Cannon's arrival in Dacca. Was it possible that an old trade union pro like Garza could be conned? Or was Cannon instructed by Garza to work with this federation to obtain information that could be useful to other US bodies? Since Garza died, Cannon will never know.

Nothing was ever mentioned about him becoming the AAFLI Representative in Bangladesh thereafter. This should have been a clear sign that the leadership of the AAFLI wasn't too happy with information provided by Cannon, which contradicted its perception of the trade union persons being supported by the AAFLI program in Bangladesh.

Free trade union development internationally was meant to oppose communist sponsored trade unions and what Cannon reported was just the opposite. This should have made Cannon fully aware that his work had little to do with development as defined by the Non-Government Organization (NGO) community. Unfortunately it took Cannon longer to come to this conclusion.

Between overseas assignments, Cannon was fortunate to re-establish contact with his former Peace Corps boss, Mr. Leonel Castillo. Leonel was the first ever Hispanic appointed to the senior position of Commissioner for the US Immigration and Naturalization Service by President Jimmy Carter.

Leonel kept his family in Texas when he moved to DC so he was happy to partake in some home cooked meals at the Cannons. The task of the Director of Immigration and Naturalization was extremely daunting before computers were introduced. Until that time, all applications and files were kept in manila folders in overcrowded offices. Another problem was the lack of technology available to police the border with Mexico. I can remember an article appearing in the Washington Post indicating that the Service had doubled the number of aircraft policing the border. Later Leonel said yes this was true- the number went from one to two.

The 2nd temporary assignment was to South Korea. It took place a few months after the one to Bangladesh. The AAFLI office in Seoul was completely the opposite of Dacca. It had all the trimmings of a state side office: plenty of local staff, modern office equipment; a few project vehicles, a big South Korean project counterpart, and a close relationship with the US Embassy. Cannon's major task was to investigate a number of income generating projects. They had been proposed by unions affiliated with the national center which were seeking money from AAFLI.

The Director of the AAFLI office was a friend of Garza. Both had served in South America with the American Institute for Free Labor Development (AIFLD) another overseas' arm of the AFL-CIO. Ryan had his large family well established and he thrived in his role. It was common that business often took place in social circumstances frequently in restaurants with numerous "toasting" to international trade union friendship and solidarity between the Federation of Korea Trade Unions (FKTU) and the AAFLI/AFL-CIO. Since a curfew was in place from 8PM to 6AM, these socials often didn't break up until after curfew was over. Initially Cannon thought these gatherings were great fun, but after a few in just one week's time, his liver began rebelling.

At one of the socials, Ryan regaled Cannon with stories from his days with in AIFLD. One of these stood out in particular. He and another AIFLD representative were the bag men to funnel funds into Guyana for the trade unions that were instrumental in organizing the overthrow of the elected president Cheddi Jagan. Years later, the Head of AIFLD was proposed by newly elected President Clinton as his Ambassador nominee for Guyana. Unfortunately for the nominee, Cheddi Jagan was elected a 2nd time as President. Suffice to say, Jagan refused to accept Clinton's nominee.

While Cannon was in Seoul, he was introduced to the Peace Corps staff. This proved a blessing in that he was able to move into the Deputy Director's house from his hotel. Hotel living for Cannon was tedious after an extended period of time; hence the offer to move into a house was deeply appreciated.

Greg had a fantastic Korean style home near the Blue Palace, the resident of the Korean President in downtown Seoul. At the time old styled Korean homes were heated using coal via a system of channels cut into the floor. It had all the amenities of a western home but with a Korean soul. It was within walking distance to the AAFLI office. This allowed Cannon to get a better feel for the Korean people. One always sees things differently on foot rather than riding in an enclosed car.

When Cannon returned to Washington after the three-month assignment, it became clear that AAFLI was planning to send him back to Seoul as Ryan's assistant. If Cannon had been a bachelor, the assignment would have been great: but with a wife and two small children, he wasn't ready to sacrifice neither his marriage nor his liver for the Korean "socials" needed to build international trade union solidarity.

When Cannon was officially told he was going to be sent back to South Korea as a program officer, he was not going to accept the assignment. Cannon's father John passed away on August 13, 1977 after a long battle with cancer, leaving his mother alone. Cannon used his father's death and his being an only child as a reason to decline the posting and left his employment with AAFLI.

The family moved back to Maine. This time to Southern Maine, in the ritzy Kennebunk area, where they were able to rent a nice home along a stream just outside of town in a place called Days Mills. The year was 1977. Mrs. Cannon in a space of eight years of marriage had moved houses seven times - a real trooper. The Cannon kids made friends with a nearby family who were able to help them in adjusting to their new primary school. The parents gradually made friends with another couple in Kennebunk that had lived overseas and with a Catholic priest from Lithuania.

Life wasn't too easy in the winter, but it was fantastic in the summer. The family could splash around in the stream next to the house. A mini pool was carved out of the rocks by the small dam that had been built years previously. Kennebunk was only about a three to four hour drive from Rhode Island. Cannon was able to reconnect with his Rhode Island relatives, some of whom even visited. Visitors included the Garnett's' from Virginia, Louis Bernardini and Gerry Olsen from Calais. The Calais visitors asked Cannon if he was still seeking clams with a toilet plunger. Other visitors included the Lederman's from Toronto (old friends from Lesotho), and Dr. Hilmi Desai from Sweden who was instrumental in introducing the Cannons back in Christmas 1968.

One of the free- lance consultant assignments Cannon accepted, while living in Kennebunk, was with a small one man firm from the DC area who was awarded a Government contract to evaluate the activities of the AFL-CIO's overseas arm for Africa, the African American Labor Center AALC).

Cannon was part of a three person team which included the director of the consultant firm Dr. Fliks and a former USAID Director in Thailand, Mr. Rey Hill. The countries visited were Ghana, Togo, and Kenya. There wasn't sufficient time to visit Zaire.

The activities of the AALC were very similar to those of AAFLI with one exception. The AALC had staff that was trained in the establishment and promotion of credit unions as adjunct services for host country trade union movements. Its main task was the same as that of AAFLI and the other overseas organizations of the AFL-CIO: to combat left wing and communist influence within African trade union movements while promoting democracy and American style democratic trade unions.

When it became time to write the evaluation report, Cannon was a dissenter. He couldn't concur with his consultant partners that the promotion of credit unions wasn't relative to the goals and objectives being funded by USAID. The AFL-CIO's role in combating the spread of left wing communistic ideology was too important a part of the US Government's overseas policies to be derailed by a consultant's report Especially in its policy against the USSR seeking votes from non-aligned countries at the ILO annual meeting in Geneva of which trade union movements participated. In the end, the report probably was read by a few people in Washington and then put aside to gather dust or be used as a book rest.

The AFL-CIO's role in combating the spread of left wing communistic ideology was too important a part of the US Government's overseas policies to be derailed by a consultant's report. Cannon's dissent in the evaluation of AALC most likely played a part in a consultant job offer from AALC.

It helped that Bayard Rustin, a key organizer of the 1963 March on Washington, led by the late Dr. Martin Luther King, wrote a recommendation letter (see appendages) to the AALC Executive Director. At the time of writing, Bayard was the President of the A Philip Randolph Institute- a prime mover of the March on Washington. The consultant task was to develop a plan of operation for the Central Organization of Trade Unions (COTU) Kenya's trade union movement, regarding the operation of its planned trade union college.

The AALC had for years been a backer and supporter of COTU's Workers Education Institute (WEI). WEI conducted trade union education seminars throughout the country holding them either in local education premises or in small hotels. AALC was the financier of the WEI staff and provided it with materials, supplies and transportation.

COTU was able to secure an educational levy under one of the Trade Union laws in Kenya. The levy could be used for a specific task for a specific time as approved by the Minister of Labor. It was applicable to every worker in the country who was a trade union member. Their employer was required to deduct the levy sum from the members' salary each month, cut a check and send it to COTU. These funds were used to build COTU's residential Labor College. No external funds were used throughout the construction phase. This was a first in Africa, and maybe throughout the developing world.

It was an assignment that Cannon relished since it was interesting one and had great potential for a residential trade union educational premise for Africans. The final product of the assignment was a report submitted to the Central Organization of Trade Unions (Kenya) entitled "Tom Mboya Labour College- Plan of Operations" which was accepted by the Executive Board of COTU.

Tom Mboya was a young Luo trade union leader who was instrumental in Kenya's fight against the British for independence. Mboya was a cabinet minister in the post-independence Kenya Africa National Union's (KANU) government. He was the Minister of Economic Planning and Development at the time of his assassination on 5 July 1969. Mboya came from the Kisumu region in which the college was located. Mboya was killed before he could reach his true potential as a leader in Kenya. It was fitting that COTU would name its labor college after their deceased colleague.

The Secretary General of COTU, Juma Boy, asked AALC to hire Cannon to help COTU get the proposed college operational. One of Cannon's letters of support for employment with AALC was from the late Bayard Rustin who was instrumental in the 1963 March on Washington. In 1979, Cannon was offered a position with AALC in Kenya, which he accepted. The plan was for Cannon to live in Kisumu, Kenya where the college was being built.

8

Cold War Warrior

KENYA

The Cannon family was on the move again. While Cannon was under taking the consultant assignment, he was befriended by some expatriates in Nairobi who were well established in Kenya. One of them, originally from Denmark, who married one of the first Brits to take up Kenyan citizenship, had a magnificent house in semi-rural suburb of Nairobi. She offered to share it with the Cannons until they moved to Kisumu. While residing in said house, the Cannons had visits from Mrs. Cannon's mother and later by her younger sister. It was decided to home school the two children until the Cannons moved to Kisumu. Later when it became apparent that the Labor College wouldn't be opening immediately, the Cannon children were enrolled in Roslyn Academy- a religious operated primary school. Much to the surprise of the Cannon children, their days of being schooled leisurely were over.

AALC underwent some staffing changes in 1980. The Country representative responsible for dealing with COTU was reassigned to headquarters in Washington. His logical replacement, who worked with trade union credit unions regionally refused to play the role of COTU's bag man. Cannon instead of moving to Kisumu, became the AALC Kenya representative based in Nairobi and thus assumed the bag-man's role.

What did a bag-man's role entail? It entailed making cash available to the COTU Secretary General. The cash was earmarked for education workshops and seminars. Frequently the Secretary General used the cash to further his position as the COTU leader. He did this by awarding his supporters seminars or workshops. They in turn solidified their positions by selecting their supporters to participate in the programs. They received travel expenses and daily per diem. There were instances when it wasn't 100% sure if a seminar or workshop had been held but receipts for same were always received.

Trade union education, in some instances, took second fiddle to the needs of COTU's leadership efforts to keep the lid on left winger elements within the federation. Having COTU on the AFL-CIO and the US side at the ILO and African trade union ventures was a key unwritten element of the AALC program in Kenya.

The Cannons moved from the Archer residence to a house near the University of Nairobi off of Riverside Drive once he became the representative for the Kenya program.

Much to the surprise of the Cannons, one Sunday while attending Mass at Consulata Church in the Westland's section of Nairobi, they were able to renew acquaintance with the late Fr. Carlo Capone. They met Capone just prior to their marriage in 1969 in Nairobi. Besides being a Catholic priest, Capone was a medical surgeon and an internationally renowned expert on child health and nutrition. Carlo was a terrific human being close to the entire Cannon family.

Cannon had his own private tribal and trade union tutor working within the AALC Nairobi office: the late Pius Odhiambo. Pius was a Luo who had fought with the British during World War II. After being demobilized, he eventually landed a position with the Kenyan civil service ending up in its Cooperative department. After retirement he was lured to work for COTU and later enticed to join AALC with COTU's blessing.

Cannon spent hours getting his daily tutorial on the politics of the Kenyan tribes and how this impacted upon COTU. The tutorial was like having one's own professor one-to-one daily. It was a tremendous learning experience which laid the foundation for future trade union assignments.

The majority of trade unions have their bases of support in urban areas. Urban areas are populated by various tribes from the entire country. Individuals are drawn to urban cities from rural areas with the hope of a better life. Frequently, they see that the road to success isn't what it seemed, but by becoming members of a trade union, they can get ahead better than by staying on their own or with their own tribe.

Another impediment of trade unions development in Africa was the lack of democracy in Cannon's view. After independence came to Africa in the late 1950's and early 1960's, democracy frequently was side lined either by one- party states or by military coups. Often the only indigenous body to hold democratic elections was trade unions, even if the elections sometime are a bit disingenuous to say the least.

Progress towards the opening of the Tom Mboya Labour College was hindered by the internal and tribal politics within COTU. Besides organized religion, there were, and still are, few organizations in African countries that have memberships which cross tribal lines.

Before the labor college could open, COTU had a schism within its officer bearers. Trade union leaders frequently moved from the left to the right and back. The motivating factor was whether they could more advance their national trade union career. Hence they often re-aligned themselves for national elections. Yes COTU was a democratic body but it had an African hitch to its democracy.

COTU's constitution reads that the President of Kenya has the power to confirm the three top positions within COTU after a national trade union election is held. The Luo tribe, who were from the Kisumu region bordering on Lake Victoria, dominated COTU. According to Odhiambo, this dominance went back to pre-independent when the Kenyan trade union movement was led by Tom Mboya. Even after Kenya's independence on 12 December 1963, the Luo continued in their leadership of COTU, much to the chagrin of the Kikuyu tribe. The Kikuyu tribe was the largest in Kenya and Kenya's first President Jomo Kenyatta was from this tribe.

When COTU held one of its first national elections after Kenya Independence a slate of officers were elected with minor representation from the dominant Kikuyu tribe. President Kenyatta approved the three top office bearers after inserting a fellow tribesman, James Karebe, into the post of Deputy General Secretary.

COTU devoted its energies towards national trade union elections in 1980, 1981, and 1982. Trade Union elected officials led decent lives especially if their unions representative members in the thousands. They also had access to other goodies such as trips overseas or study tours overseas providing they were supporters of the leadership of COTU.

Prior to COTU elections, elections were held by the affiliated unions who made up COTU. These elections entailed lots of interesting maneuvers. One of which still seems unique: the voting delegates were often put on buses and taken to hiding places where they were kept in isolation until being bused to the location where the vote was to be held. Delegates were held in isolation to prevent them from shifting sides. The competing slates were both hidden, but the slate with the most money had the advantage since they could provide more amenities (food, booze and ladies) for their delegates while they were being hidden.

The Secretary General of COTU, Juma Boy, was also a Member of Parliament from the South Coast. His power base though, was derived from his being the General Secretary of the Dockworkers Union in Mombasa. It was natural, in retrospect that trade union politics were often caught up in national political politics. Juma Boy's main political foe politically in Mombasa was Sharif Nassir.

In 1980, Nassir put forth a candidate to challenge Juma for the leadership position in the Dockworkers Union. To the surprise of many, Nassir's candidate Yunis defeated Juma in May 1980.

AALC was faced with the loss of their major supporter in Kenya. From that point onwards, all energy was focused on seeing that Juma acquire another union so he could maintain his post as Secretary General of COTU. With AALC's support, Juma was elected General Secretary of the Petroleum Workers Union in August 1980.

COTU had as one of its members the Journalist Union. Through this contact, one could get anything printed in the major dailies in Nairobi, if you were willing to fork out some cash to a reporter. It didn't matter whether what appeared in the press was correct or incorrect, the desired report/topic would appears in one of the daily papers since libel suits weren't a staple of Kenyan democracy.

Shortly after the Petroleum election, Juma's victory was questioned by one of his opponents within COTU. Fred Omido was the head of the Metal Workers Union and was an ally of James Karebe, Juma's long standing Kikuyu nemesis. Fred was jovial and personable in his dealings in person with Cannon but didn't earn the nickname Fred the Red for nothing.

One of the papers ran a front-page story accusing Cannon of interfering in COTU politics. The accuser quoted in the article was Fred Omido who had aspirations of becoming the Secretary General of COTU. The article misspelled Cannon's name but it was obvious to anyone with knowledge about trade unions in Kenya at the time who the article was accusing.

Upon reading the accusation, Cannon thought this could develop into a major problem for both himself and the AALC. Would the Kenyan Ministry of Labor start an investigation into the program of the AALC? Would AALC be accused of meddling into the internal political affairs of the Kenyan trade union movement? Would Cannon and his family be declared persona non grata? Would the Cannons be deported from the country? Would Cannon be thrown under the bus by AALC headquarters as a quid pro quo for them to retain their Kenyan program?

Cannon knew if he could keep his cool and remain out of the press, this accusation would blow- over. What Cannon didn't know was what the reaction of the US Embassy would be? Cannon didn't have to wait long.

On Monday morning following the Sunday's publication, Cannon received a phone call saying the US Ambassador would like to see him immediately. The Ambassador gave Cannon a major dressing down saying the publicity placed the Embassy in a very bad light. Cannon was able to look the Ambassador in the eye and deny the entire allegation in the article since the article misreported facts. Cannon didn't lie, but Cannon didn't state what he was actually doing that provoked the article. Previous to the article, Cannon was told he could refer to the Ambassador by his first name-Bill. After the article, it was Mr. Ambassador.

Cannon's major task was to work with the Secretary General of COTU and not with individual unions affiliated with COTU. The AALC was totally committed to the COTU re-election of the Juma Boy slate. Initially back in the early 1960's, Juma Boy went to East Germany where he attended trade union educational courses. Cannon was never informed when Juma switched from the East to the West nor why. Regardless it was before he became the General Secretary of the Dockworkers Union and the

Secretary General of COTU because AALC wouldn't have been his main backer since their prime unwritten task was to only support Pro-Western non-leftists trade union leaders in Africa

Cannon learned that one of his "unspoken/unwritten" job responsibilities was to create ways to get funds to Juma Boy using means outside of the regular program budget. This was the main reason why a staffer named Daniel who had seniority over Cannon took a transfer out of Kenya as was noted previously. Cannon was able to find ways to access cash to support Juma Boy since his opponents were getting cash from Eastern bloc countries that had Embassies in Nairobi.

Cannon was introduced to a few Asian traders who were happy to get dollar checks and pay street market exchange rates for Kenyan schillings. The sums received were made available to Juma Boy in cash for his campaign to retain the position of Secretary General for COTU. All Juma Boy had to do was provide Cannon with hotel receipts and signatures indicating money was received for transportation and local per diems to attend education seminars throughout the country. This proved easy since one COTU union was the Hotel Workers –who's General Secretary just so happened to be a big supporter of Juma Boy. It is very questionable whether making cash available for use by Juma Boy promoted the development of the Kenyan trade union movement and enhanced the well -being of its members as was being claimed by the AALC.

While this was going on, Cannon gradually became a witness to what was taking place in Uganda. The owner of the house, which Cannon moved into after Daniel's departure, was originally from Uganda. He told a very interesting story about life under Idi Amin.

After his personal vehicle was stolen outside of Kampala, Philip purchased a new Peugeot in Nairobi. Before taking it back to Uganda, he broke the side windows, placed big dents over the entire vehicle and messed up the paint. He said he did this because most of Amin's soldiers, especially those at checkpoints, had no interest in stealing cars that were battered. Battered cars did not look like new cars to Amin's soldiers even if their motor was brand new.

In the 1960's, Kampala was home to a trade union residential college built by the International Confederation of Trade Unions (ICFTU) where many African trade union leaders received their education. Uganda's trade union movement was well educated and well respected until Amin's time. Many trade union leaders who opposed Amin were forced to seek political refuge in Nairobi during the bad days. Cannon's predecessor provided assistance professionally and personally to some of these individuals, hence there was always a steady stream of Ugandan visitors' to the AALC office in Nairobi.

A few of the exiled trade union leaders after the overthrow of Amin started to return to Kampala, especially those from President Obote's tribe- the Acholi. AALC called on one of its senior staffers Charlie Taylor to go into Uganda to help resurrect the morbid National Organization of Trade Unions (NOTU).

Cannon's office provided back up services for Taylor in Kampala and became a focal point whenever a Ugandan trade unionist was visiting Nairobi. It wasn't long before Cannon became well versed in the political intrigues taking place within NOTU. Tribalism had raised its ugly head.

Nairobi was also a stopover for trade union leaders who had international flights to catch to attend numerous international meetings, seminars, workshops, conferences, etc. which they were invited to by East or West trade union organizations. They often did a little shopping for their families and friends before heading home. Trade union leaders from the OATUU (Organization of Africa Trade Union Unity), ICFTU, Zambia, Tanzania, Malawi, Mauritius and Somalia were often in Nairobi.

Cannon was often called on and frequently hosted these visitors for a lunch or dinner. Many times, he was called upon to advance loans or even pay for their hotel accommodations as well as providing rides to the Jomo Kenyatta Airport. These tasks were part of winning hearts and minds necessary for support of the AFL-CIO and US government's position at the annual ILO meeting and other international trade union forums.

The AALC office had one visitor who was a key trade union activist during the late 1950's and early 1960's in the time of the late Tom Mboya. Aggrey Minya originally came from Western Kenya. He became estranged from Mboya and was defeated by Mboya for the post of general secretary of the Kenya Federation of Registered Trade Unions in the late 1950's. In subsequent years he was more marginalized by each of Mboya's successors. When Cannon met Aggrey he was basically living on handouts.

Cannon liked Aggrey, who when sober, had great stories to tell. Aggrey often referred to some trade unionists as "trade union eaters" not leaders. Eating was a term frequently used in Kenya and other African countries to denote corruption.

Throughout 1981, unions affiliated with COTU held national elections. One election was very important to the reign of Juma Boy as COTU's Secretary General. Ochola Mak'Anyengo, a former trade union heavy weight, was trying to make a trade union comeback. He was previously in jail for supposedly trying to overthrow the late President Kenyatta.

Mak'Anyengo made a successful comeback and was elected General Secretary of the Railways and Harbors Union. He was also a Luo and his support for Juma Boy was a key in the battle for the leadership of COTU. The Luo's continued to be the predominant tribe in the politics of COTU during this period.

Juma Boy's predecessor at the helm of COTU was Denis Akumu, a Luo, who became the first General Secretary of the Organization of Trade Union Unity (OATUU). After assuming his new post with headquarters in Accra, Ghana, Akumu drifted away from the AALC and the West. OATUU started to take assistance from the East as less and less from the West. In October 1981, Akumu presented Gaddafi with an OATUU award in Libya much to the chagrin of the AALC. It wasn't clear whether Akumu would use his influence with his fellow Luo's to support Juma's reelection or not?

Some of the International Trade Union Secretariats had offices in Nairobi. These were organizations that represented trade unions in one particular industry only. A Nigerian, Roxy Udugowa headed one of these, the International Transport Federation. Roxy was a friend of the AALC from his days as a trade union leader in Nigeria. He kept Cannon abreast of the East/West struggles over the leadership of the huge Nigerian Labor Congress (NLC) and its role within OATUU.

Besides the ITS's, a few other international organizations had offices in Nairobi. Like the AALC, they represented either a particular political party or another trade union federation seeking political influence in line with their political ideology. The Frederick Ebert Stiftung (West Germany), the Swedish LO working with OATUU, and the International Labor Organization (ILO) were some of those with offices in Nairobi.

With so many organizations seeking political influence, it was a dream to think some Kenyan trade union leaders wouldn't take from whoever offered assistance regardless of ideology. Other trade union organizations, while not having offices in Nairobi, were very active whenever they came to town. These include Histadrut from Israel, the Canadian Labor Congress (CLC), and the World Federation of Trade Unions (WFTU) which represented Eastern bloc countries.

The WFTU split from the ICFTU after WW II. It drew its main support from various trade union movements behind the Iron Curtain. It also created industry counterparts to the international trade secretariats associated with the ICFTU. The WFTU became the prime supporter of state controlled trade unionism opposed to democratic trade unionism. The WFTU battled to influence developing country trade union movements. AALC was one of the WFTU western opponents in Africa. Trade union movements in Africa were in the forefront of the battle to win hearts and minds between the East and West. The welfare of the workers took back seat to this political tussle.

Cannon and Odhiambo traveled to Sudan where discussions were held with Ginawi and other leaders of the Sudanese trade union movement about potential education program. Nothing of any significance developed though Ginawi eventually made a visit to Kenya to check on various credit union activities being undertaken by COTU.

One thing about the trip to the Sudan was unique. The air plane had to stop in Juba, Southern Sudan (now an independent country). Upon disembarking, Cannon and Odhiambo visited the duty-free shop. The items for sale consisted of Omo (a washing powder) very popular and an Orange drink (name forgotten). That was it.

It wasn't only international trade unions that had internal political problems. The AALC did as well. The AALC staff conference in April 1981was held in Cairo, Egypt. The AALC staff split in two over the overbearing know-it-all conduct of the former representative in Nairobi, the late Nate Gould. Many staffers felt the late Doug MacQuillian, who also once worked in Nairobi, was being under- cut as the deputy director of AALC by Gould. Gould was white: MacQuillian was black which may have been an issue between the two. Cannon backed the MacQuillian side which ended up losing. Gould survived and Murphy the AALC Director never forgot those who opposed his man Gould. Taylor, who also supported MacQuillian expected to become the AALC Representative in the newly independent Zimbabwe, was passed over in favor of a newcomer Jim Harris. Taylor went on to Swaziland and left AALC as a bitter person after decades of honorable service. This should have served as an early warning to Cannon as to the type of individual who was running AALC.

While these comings and goings were taking place, the Cannons were living what they thought was a normal family life. Chandra and Marc were both students in an intergraded private religious school in Nairobi. They developed many friends from varied backgrounds. Kari developed a group of friends of her own none of whom were involved with trade unions.

Cannon tried to keep his work with the Kenyan trade union movement separate from family life. At times this was impossible, especially when the AALC and Cannon were hosting dinners for Juma Boy and his supporters. It was a given Kari would attend since she would be seated next to Juma Boys city wife who spoke excellent English: his first wife who didn't speak good English resided in his rural home. Kari also was called upon to perform similar functions when the dinners were for trade union visitors from the US.

The Cannons socialized with a small group of friends who were associated with the business sector. Most of these associates were not Americans nor from Norway the homeland of Kari. Life was enjoyable in Nairobi which was a terrific small city. The city possessed most amenities associated with life in the West which also made overseas living not a problem.

Throughout 1982, COTU union leaders were offered numerous overseas trips by Eastern as well as Western suitors. This also held true for union leaders from Uganda and other nearby countries. These trips offered people an opportunity to access hard foreign currency, which is always welcomed in any developing country. Cannon very frequently was directed to give these leaders traveling money, usually US dollars, to assist them should their trip be interrupted by some unforeseen reason.

The bookkeeping for these allocations was the responsibility of the office in Washington. Some unionist going to Eastern bloc programs also sought AALC travel assistance without success. The late Justice Mulei, who eventually became COTU's Secretary General, was turned down in his requested for foreign exchange to attended the WFTU World Congress in Cuba.

Trade unionists from all over Africa passed through Nairobi in 1982 as well as trade union visitors from the United States. Cannon spent long hours at the Jomo Kenyatta Airport waiting for these visitors or driving them to the airport on their way out of Kenya. They came from Zimbabwe, Mauritius, Israel, Malawi, Sudan and a few other countries.

In 1982, Cannon continued outfitting the Tom Mboya Labour College (TMLC) with equipment and furnishings. AALC was asked to recruit an economist for the College, which they did in the person of Dr. Charles Cambridge. Cambridge was originally from Guyana and his late father was the head of the Guyana trade union movement in the 1960's. Charles never did reside in Kisumu before leaving Kenya after one year. COTU would set a date for the opening of the labor college only to rescind it later.

Cambridge joined the Cannons in traveling to Kwale –south of Mombasa, for the opening of Juma Boy's new house. The house was enormous in comparison to those in the area. One could see out to the Indian Ocean even thought it was some (15) kilometers away. The chief guest was a very powerful Kenyan politician at the time, Member of Parliament (MP) Charles Njonjo who later fell out of President Moi's good books. Njonjo was famous in Nairobi for saying he gave his domestic help an English-type breakfast each morning. This showed how rich he had become as well as his superiority to the average Kenyan. AALC was the only foreign group invited to this "official" house opening.

KENYA COUP ATTEMPT

Cannon thought his days of being around wars and coups were over when he moved to Kenya. Was he surprised one night when deafening shooting awoke him! Cannon walked to a bedroom window to look out. He couldn't see flashes of bullets flying in the night. Kari and the kids were awoken by the loud noise. The shooting was far enough away from the house that Cannon wasn't too concerned about the immediate safety of his family. Kari and the kids were scared until Cannon reassured them what took place was strictly a Kenyan matter that would have little or no bearing on expatriates. Everyone return to bed until the next morning.

Early the following morning on August 12, 1982 he received a phone call from Fr. Capone informing him that elements of the Kenyan military had attempted an unsuccessful coup the past night. Fr. Capone resided in the Consulata Church rectory. It was located just off the main Westland's roundabout circle on the highway leading out from Nairobi to Nakuru and further onwards to Kisumu. Capone had a front seat to the fighting at the Westland's roundabout.

Cannon also received a call from a Welsh friend, Phil Jenkins who was on a mini safari just outside Nairobi in the Nakuru area. Jenkins two teenage step daughters were in their home alone near Consulata Church in the Westland's section not that far from the Cannon house. Cannon was asked whether he could check on their status.

The Cannon house was off Riverside Drive. To reach the Jenkins house, he had to drive east past sections of the University of Nairobi before he could reach the dual highway. The dual highway went into downtown Nairobi one-way and out of Nairobi to Westland's the other way. The highway had a few military road blocks. There were some abandoned cars along the highway which were shot up. Fortunately by driving calmly and slowly Cannon was able to reach the Jenkins house to find both girls OK. To Cannons surprise there were also two young male friends who were visiting. The drive back was just as excruciating but uneventful because it was shorter and didn't have as many military road blocks.

Cannon drove later that same day into his office in downtown Nairobi which was located opposite a few government office buildings. After checking the office and finding nothing amiss, Cannon took a walk to the nearby Post Office. There were dead bodies still laying on many of the streets. They had yet to be removed.

Cannon had pre-booked a short safari at a Mountain Lodge near Mount Kenya for himself and his son. They were to leave the next day. The trip was postponed until Cannon held further consultations with Fr. Capone. Capone was in contact with his fellow missionaries in the countryside who said it was safe to travel, especially if you were white. Father and Son drove out of Nairobi on August 20th to see some elephants. The drive to Mountain Lodge the game park was without incident. The lodge was full, with many Americans, including Sandra Day O'Connor who was appointed as the first female Supreme Court Justice in the US by President Reagan. The coup attempt was the major topic of conversation in the lodges' dining room. Normally dining room conversation at a safari lodge would be totally focused on the types of wild life seen.

After returning from Mountain Lodge, it was back to work for Cannon. He had to make arrangements for visitors from Sudan led by the Secretary General of the Sudan Trade Union movement Brother Ginawi. Cannon put them in the Hotel 680 which was in very close proximity to the main Nairobi mosque since the entire delegation was Muslim. Cannon assumed the guests wanted to be close to a mosque. After fetching the delegation of (3) and driving them to their hotel, Cannon briefed them on their surroundings.

Throughout their (4) day stay it was questionable whether they went to the mosque much. They were very active participants in the Hotel's bar scene and quite popular with the ladies of the night according to some of Cannon's friends who frequented the same watering hole. Gould told a story that when he was traveling to Sudan he was always asked to bring a few bottles of "salad dressing". The salad dressing favored by Ginawi and his colleagues was Johnny Walker Red.

In October 1982, Cambridge's replacement arrived in Kenya. The Davis family was making their first trip to Africa. Cannon had no idea what they were told by AALC/Washington. Arriving not too long after the aborted coup, Cannon booked them into the best and most famous hotel in Nairobi- the Norfolk Hotel. He figured they needed to see Nairobi at its best for first impressions sake before moving onwards to Kisumu. Kisumu was to Nairobi as Bangor, Maine is to New York City. Later Cannon learned the Davis's resided in Providence, Rhode Island (his hometown) before coming to Kenya.

It wasn't too long after the Davis's were getting settled in Kisumu that another expatriate arrived who was to be stationed at the TMLC. Jorgen Petersen was recruited by the ILO from Denmark. Jorgen was also making his first trip to Africa, but without a small child unlike the Davis's. Jorgen had a teenage daughter. It didn't take Jorgen and Joe too long to realize they were colleagues not opponents at the TMLC. They quickly learned to form a united front to avoid being taken advantage of especially by the new TMLC Principal Jackton Akumu who was more interested in furthering his own financial pockets than in running the TMLC.

As noted previously, COTU was able to build the college with the monies contributed from Kenya trade union workers. The Government gave COTU legal authority and permission to place a levy of a few cents per worker per month to get construction funds. The builder was kicking back funds by cutting corners from the original building materials specifications. The

Quantity Surveyor, who was responsible to oversee the contractor's work, was from Mombasa and was Juma Boys' friend. Everyone was happy-just like in Rhode Island: what mattered was who you knew-one's connections.

AALC helped outfit the college from pots and pans to curtains in the dormitories along with furniture and commercial kitchen equipment. It was Cannon's task to get quotes from local businesses and evaluate the quotes. Many businesses in Nairobi were not big enough to complete and deliver to Kisumu the items they quoted for. Before final contracts were entered into, Cannon would provide samples of quoted items to Juma Boy for his approval. Once approval was secured, Cannon would write a check to the winning bidder and establish a time for the delivery of items to Kisumu. The college was built to house some 100 residents.

Juma Boy successfully won the COTU national election in 1982 after it was postponed from 1981. Juma was also a Member of Parliament (MP) and a member of the ruling Kenya Africa National Union party (KANU) led by President Moi. He had no difficulty in getting Moi's blessing for his slate of candidates prior to the election.

The 14th of January 1983 was set to officially open the Tom Mboya Labour College. Guess who the guest speaker was? If you say President Moi you'd be correct. Juma Boy had no other option available but to ask the President of Kenya and KANU to officially open and dedicate the college. Cannon had the task of writing Juma Boy's welcoming speech which praised Moi much more than was necessary. Juma was thrilled especially after Moi showered him with praises in his dedication speech and official opening speech.

It was originally envisioned the COTU Executive Board would vote and approve an annual budget for the college. The College Principal would be the chief Operating Officer who would be responsible for reporting expenditures back to COTU. This would mean the COTU Treasurer would need to relinquish a portion of his financial power within COTU. It proved to be a daydreaming idea.

Once the college opened the tribalism within the COTU hierarchy gradually became a major stumbling block towards the college's operation. The COTU Treasurer was a Luo who had his differences with Juma Boy and who had support from half of the Executive Board, especially his fellow Luo's.

Instead of allocating an annual budget to the TMLC, the Treasurer periodically would send funds to Kisumu on an ad hoc basis. One of the reasons, besides differences within the Executive Board, for this stop gap approach was many COTU Executive Board members did not trust the honesty of the Principal of the Labour College Jackton Akumu (not a relative of Denis Akumu). Needless to say this approach led to the gradual demise of the College. It couldn't even program events properly or provide necessary maintenance for the buildings and for purchases needed for food, teaching supplies and equipment.

Since the TMLC was not being fully utilized, some of its staff started to get more involved in internal COTU politics. Accusations and counter accusations flew far and wide including charges of misappropriation of funds. One could visibly see that the maintenance and upkeep of the complex started to diminish. Repairs that were needed were not undertaken. If a piece of equipment broke, it wasn't replaced. Instead of cooking with electricity as happened when the college was opened, the TMLC kitchen cooks returned to using charcoal. Materials needed for education programs were not available on a regular basis. Books and equipment for the library only existed if they were purchased either by the Yanks or Danes.

Trade Union members were not being educated as envisioned when the TMLC was built and opened. Their education took a back seat to the internal political divisions with COTU and to the competition of different ideologies of donor organizations. Each thought their way of doing things was the best for COTU to follow. It gradually became oblivious to Cannon that the political aspect of international trade union solidarity far outweighed the developmental aspect.

Some western trade union programs refused to hold their education programs at the TMLC. They held them in hotels in Nairobi and at times in Mombasa instead. They said the selection of venue wasn't influenced by COTU internal politics. But in reality, those for whom they worked directed them not to use the TMLC since it was too closely associated with the Americans.

The AALC's political agenda frequently juxtaposed with the US government. This was mostly the case when a Democratic President led the US government. Democrats usually were allies of the AFL-CIO hence it wasn't too hard to be on the same page at the annual series of ILO meetings in Geneva.

It became a different story when the Republican Ronald Reagan was elected President of the US. One of his first major actions was the busting of the Air Traffic Controllers Union in the US. He used his authority and power of the presidency to fire the entire membership since they were government employees. Cannon's personal thoughts were gradually become more attuned to the incongruities of his job.

Cannon was facing middle age. He had a wife and two small children. He had a decent paycheck. He lived a good life in Kenya. The incongruent nature of the job seemed like a part of normal life living in Africa, which was difficult to fathom for a non-African in spite of Cannon's daily education by Odhiambo.

Was it more important to support US policies in Kenya or was it more important to implement programs that benefited Kenyan trade union members? When one's eyes start opening to reality, at first, it is very difficult to accept if it contradicts what one is seeking to accomplish. If a major aspect of ones work is questionable, it is sometime easier to put it aside and continue what one had been doing work wise.

The Cannons neighbors and best friends from their days in Calais, Maine visited the Cannon family. The Bernardini's arrived shortly after the official opening of the TMLC. They had won a raffle, which included free airline tickets to Europe. Cannon while in Egypt to attend the AALC staff meeting had the good fortune to be able to fly out to the Valley of the Kings to visit a few opened tombs. It was a truly remarkable experience, to see artifacts from some 4,000 years back, when his European white ancestors were still living in caves.

Cannons suggested the Bernardini's visit the Valley of the Kings which they did. Their visit to Kenya was fantastic: game park viewing plus lounging on Indian Ocean beaches south of Mombasa. Both families enjoyed lots of great seafood and lots of drink. Cannons were able to get friends to baby-sit their kids during the visit.

Cannon's Italian Mother and her sister came to visit in 1983. It was the first time for either out of the USA. Cannon was able to meet them in the airport's receiving area after clearing customs. His Mother was walking very slowly. Once Cannon picked up the hand bags of his Mother and Aunt Mary he realized why.

Their hand carry bags were full of food. They weren't aware that one could buy tinned tomatoes, pasta, etc. in Nairobi. Their thoughtfulness was much appreciated. Both were shocked to see that the house they stayed in had running water, flush toilets, electricity, etc. They said they were expecting something out of a Tarzan movie.

The highlight of their visit was a game park safari, which took them to a few parks in northeastern Kenya as well as to Mount Kenya. Cannon hired a car and driver. Chandra Cannon, age 11, was placed in charge of the trip and served as tour guide. From all reports and pictures, they had a great time. Probably a better time, than if Cannon or his wife went along. There was only one main glitch.

The rented car suffered a flat tire in one of the parks. This happened in front of a pride of lions. A few tour buses, parked between the lions and the car so the tire could be changed. The bus drivers helped, but when the lions moved they jumped back in their buses, rightly so. This caused anxiety until the driver of the rented car was able to change tires since there were lots of other wild animals in the vicinity. At a later date, Cannon was informed by his Mother and Aunt that his daughter was the perfect guide and host for their safari. It was the highlight of their later years.

A highlight of a different nature from 1983 also comes to mind: a seminar put on by another international trade union organization at the residential Two Fishes Hotel south of Mombasa. Cannon was invited to participate by the sponsors. It turned into a circus. Most residential seminars include room and board for the participants who also receive a daily per diem for incidental expenses. Trade Unionists are always saying their daily per diem is inadequate.

In this seminar, the participants took the sponsors recording secretary hostage and refused releasing said person, who was in possession of all the seminar documents, until they received additional per diem payments. Eventually the sponsors caved in to the participant's demands and gave them more per diem. Only then was the recording secretary allowed out of his room along with the seminar papers.

Another highlight was a visit from a representative of the Polish labor movement: SOLIDARNOSC. J. Milewski was the Solidarity representative outside of Poland in Brussels, Belgium. Milewski was visiting African trade union movements to solicit their support for his detained colleagues inside Poland. He told a very interesting story about the 1st massive Solidarity meeting. At said meeting the leaders had very little understanding about conducting democratic meetings. They let anyone speak who wanted which resulted in the meeting taking numerous days.

Cannon never paid too much heed to the United States as being perceived as the land of milk and honey. That is until a TMLC staffer from Juma Boy's tribe was chosen to attend a one months' study tour in the USA in September. He pitched up in the AALC Nairobi office with a brief case on his day of departure. Cannon asked where his travel luggage was. Ali Masi told him he was seeing it. It contained a pair of socks and change of underwear. Ali Masi said he'd get all the clothes he would need while in Washington. It goes to show, that one doesn't need to over pack when traveling abroad: in Africa anything is possible.

Out of the blue in July 1983, Juma Boy became ill while Cannon was on leave in the USA. Juma Boy was flown to the UK where he died either on the operating table or immediately following surgery. Being a Muslim, his body was immediately returned to be buried in his birth village south of Mombasa. Joe Davis, the resident economist at the Labour College, represented AALC at the funeral along with the AALC Executive Director who flew in from Washington.

COTU's Deputy Secretary General, Justin Mulei who was from the Kamba tribe, succeeded Juma Boy. Mulei had different ideas as to who COTU should be associated with. He was a believer of non-alignment. COTU could get access to more funds and fewer restrictions if it broadened its base away from the AALC. His behavior resulted in a new split among COTU Executive Board members, especially those who were part of the late Juma Boy's inner circle.

While all these machinations were taking place, the Cannon kids were growing up. After a brief period of home-education, Chandra and Marc were enrolled in a religious school called Roslyn Academy which stopped a grade six. They eventually transferred to the International School of Kenya (ISK) to continue their schooling after grade six. Both kids learned to read and to enjoy it since there wasn't a television in the household. They only got to watch television and VCR movies when they were at their friends' houses.

The Cannons' social circle was fairly small. One particular friend was named Karl Marx. His wife's maiden name was Joan Castro. Kari met Joan at one of the services at Consulata Church. Karl was a strong and firm believer in the capitalist system despite his name. He was a career employee with Colgate Palmolive. While in Nairobi, Karl managed the Colgate factory in Kenya and served as its regional director for East Africa.

The Marx's were born in Guyana in South America. They eventually relocated to Canada after the Marxist Cheddi Jagan was elected Prime Minister after Independence. They had neither desire nor plan to return to Guyana. They were transferred out of Kenya to Costa Rica where they eventually settled.

Karl and Joan were terrific hosts. They always had tons of food for guests as well as loads of drink. Frequently on weekends the Cannon's would drive to the very large Marx house to enjoy their company. The Cannon kids always had a great time at the Marx's playing with their kids and getting to watch television or DVDs.

Shopping in Nairobi was easy in comparison to some other countries in Africa. One could purchase most western type food stuffs as well as a terrific assortment of locally grown fruits and vegetables. The one exception was apples. Kenya produced beer which was far superior to American beer. Access to wine was a bit limited after Kenya stopped the importation of wine from apartheid South Africa. On selected Sundays throughout the year, there was horse racing at a lovely track called Ngong. Life was good.

Prior to Christmas 1983, Cannon was paid a surprise visit from a cousin from Rhode Island on his father's side of the family. Cannon had no idea that Joey was coming to visit. One morning he received a phone call from the US Embassy saying there was an American there saying he was a relative of Cannon and wanted to know his office location? It was Embassy policy not to provide information to persons coming off the street.

Cannon took the short five minute walk to the Embassy. After being cleared at the main desk, Cannon was met by the Labor Attaché. George proceeded to inform Cannon the visitor had left. On the way back to his office, Cannon decided to pass the Post Office to check his mailbox. There he found his cousin Joey who had arrived the previous night and had checked into a hotel across from the Post Office. Cannon asked his cousin what you are doing here. The reply was "visiting you".

Seems like the cousin was having some problems in the USA and decided he needed a break. Fortunately being a lawyer, he wasn't stuck for funds to come up with to get to Nairobi, Kenya from Providence, Rhode Island. When Cannon went to check him out of the hotel, he learned his cousin's credit card wasn't valid. It had expired.

You might imagine the surprise looks on Cannon's wife's face when he walked into their home with Cousin Joseph. The kids were moved. One gave up his room, to move in with the other, so Cousin Joseph had a place to stay. Cannon asked whether his family in Rhode Island was aware he was traveling to Kenya. The response was no. After a while, it was suggested he call the US so his family at least knew where he was. It wasn't too long thereafter when Cannon had a call from Joey's father demanding answers as to why his son was in Nairobi.

All Cannon could say was his son was safe. He had a place as long as was needed to get his head back in order. Uncle Joseph implied that if Cannon were not so adventurous his oldest son would not have ventured so far away from home. Didn't make any sense or did it?

Cousin Joseph had a terrific time in Kenya. He had a once in a life time experience to meet Cannon's jogging buddy from New Jersey-Bob Welch. Both had attended Georgetown University in Washington, DC, but in different decades. He also met the Welshman Phil Jenkins who came to East Africa as a youngster just prior to independence. Phil spoke excellent Swahili and always had a fridge full of excellent cold Kenyan beer plus a zillion interesting stories.

There were also numerous trips to Ngong Race track to watch thoroughbred racing the "Sport of King's". Joey was introduced to some jockeys from the UK by his Georgetown buddy Bob. He had a chance to meet Frank Mobley a great jockey from England who in his fifties was still skillful enough to regularly boot home winners.

There was also a visit to Lake Victoria and Kisumu to see the Tom Mboya Labour College. We stopped on the way to visit with one of the first Brits to become a Kenyan citizen, Chris Archer whom we met at Lake Naivasha. Later, afternoon tea was taken in an old tea plantation hotel in Kericho. It was a setting right out of a novel or movie. In the evening we stayed at the Sunset Hotel, Kisumu which had the most fantastic sunset nightly that Cannon ever saw in his life. The evening sun set by disappearing into beautiful Lake Victoria.

The Cannon's treated Cousin Joey to a safari in Maasai Mara over the New Year's weekend. He was flown out to Governor's Camp where he had his own tented room, which included an internal toilet and shower. When Joey returned to Nairobi, he said he had a terrific time. Only one night was his sleep disturbed by a coughing type sound on the outside of the tent. African old hands say the sound was most likely caused by a leopard. If Joey knew that he might have suffered a heart attack since he also was a city kid from Providence

While Cousin Joey was away for New Years' Eve, the Cannons were guests of the Marx's at the private Bacchus Club in Nairobi. It was their first visit to the "Members Only" club, which catered to wealthy Nairobi residents. At the club, the Cannons bumped into his jogging buddy Bob Welsh who was entertaining visitors from Nigeria. The fun night was only marred with the news that there was a successful coup in Nigeria. What a way to begin 1984!

Shortly after the start of 1984, Cousin Joseph decided it was time to leave. The Cannon kids were happy to get back to their separate rooms and Cannon's liver was happy to get a rest

In 1984, work with in Kenya followed much the same patterns of the previous years since the goals and objectives of the AALC remained the same. The promotion of democracy and human rights via the development of the trade union movement was politically valid especially as a counter to the communists.

What was starting to be questionable in Cannon's mind was the word "development". Was it possible that the political evolution equates to development? Do human rights equate to a full stomach for a worker? How do you measure development? Could one say a tea picker in Kericho working as a laborer, on a tea plantation owned by a multinational corporation receiving subsistence wages is a participant in development?

AALC/Washington continued to send out American trade union people to Kenya and elsewhere to conduct programs or to undertake studies. One comes to mind, Walter Lypka, of the Graphic Communications Union. Part of Walter's brief was to visit Uganda to see what might be done with National Organization of Trade Unions (NOTU) in the printing and communications area. Like most Americans, Walter hadn't been to Africa previously. Nairobi wasn't that much of a shock since it was a fairly western city. Kampala was another matter.

We booked into the Speke Hotel in Kampala in the late afternoon. We had a few beers with the NOTU folks who came by the hotel to greet Walter and to give him some idea of a schedule. That evening, we went to the hotel dining room to eat. The menu listed various foods available- a typical hotel menu from the days when Kampala was functioning city. Walter studied the menu then asked Cannon what he was going to have. Cannon said he didn't know until the waiter came. When the waiter came Walter ordered fish. Cannon asked him what food the hotel had. He was told eggs and bread and that's what Cannon ordered. Walter was a fast learner. He said he changed his mind and would have the same as Cannon.

Prior to leaving, Walter asked if we could drive out to a shrine for the Ugandan Catholic martyrs just outside of the city since he was also a Catholic. The martyrs later were elevated to Saints by Rome. Arrangements were made with NOTU to hire a car and driver. On the way to the site, the car was stopped at a military checkpoint. A soldier stuck his AK 47 in the window and asked Walter "Do I know you?" Cannon told Walter to slowly draw out his passport and show it to the soldier while Cannon started talking to him. First off, Cannon asked him whether his family were all in good health; what village was he from; etc. before getting to the fact that we were visitors from the United States on our way to the shrine. The soldier waved us through the roadblock without even looking at Walter's passport. Walter was really happy to leave Uganda the following day. Back in Nairobi, he said he probably would not return to follow up any potential programs because of his busy schedule in the US.

When walking the streets in Nairobi, one never was sure whom one would encounter since it was such a transit point for so many people. One day Cannon came across an old friend from his days in Lesotho in the late

1960's-Joe Molefi. Joe was a South African refugee who went into exile after the Sharpeville trials in South Africa. Another person was Jonathan Jenness who worked in Lesotho with the United Nations.

The biggest surprise was bumping into an old friend from Cannon's days in the Peace Corps. Elaine Bosak and her man Roland Hartland were visiting with another ex-Peace Corps volunteer Pam Benson. The Benson family was part of the USAID/Kenya program and the International School of Kenya's staff. The get together which followed was terrific.

The AALC staff conference in 1984 was held in Lesotho. It was sort of a home coming for Cannon since his first child was born there in 1969. The visit was marred by the death of an old friend Mike Everett. Cannon was able to get away from the conference long enough to attend Mike's funeral at the small Anglican chapel in downtown Maseru and to renew acquaintances with many Basotho who attended the funeral.

Desmond Sixishe also attended the funeral. He was the person who peered through the bushes on behalf of the apartheid South African government when the Cannon's first arrived in Lesotho in 1969. Since that time, both he and the Prime Minister's politics had drastically changed. They were now aligned with the USSR and strongly against the white South African government.

Nairobi continued to be an attraction for US political delegations. Cannon had the opportunity to meet the Speaker of the US House of Representatives Tip O'Neil among others. Hudson Kabanga, a Zambian friend with the Zambia Trade Union Congress (ZTCU), was always in and out of town until he passed away late in the year. Hudson was the first trade unionist Cannon knew who died of AIDS which he contacted with the help of too many lady friends.

President Moi confirmed Justus Mulei as the COTU Secretary General in April 1984. AALC and Cannon weren't the main focuses in Mulei's vision for COTU but were viewed mainly as a reliable source of funding. It wasn't too long after the confirmation of Mulei that Cannon identified a potential replacement and started the grooming process.

Joe Mugalla was a long time unionist from Western Kenya. He had spent years being the number two in his union and was the recipient of a US scholarship for trade union members at Harvard University. He was normally very gregarious but became less so when he was under the weather (too much drink).

Cannon convinced Joe to join him at the Nautilus Club. He could lose a few pounds and also meet a wide range of people including the US Ambassador who worked out daily in the as early morning hours. Sometimes, after a workout, Mugulla and Cannon would have breakfast and talk strategy. All the strategy focused on establishing broad based/multi tribal trade union alliances. Many of the smaller unions within COTU were run by individuals who always needed money. Many of these could be convinced to support Mugulla especially those compensated for delivering delegation votes. Mugalla eventually was elected COTU Secretary General defeating Mulei after Cannon left Kenya in April 1986.

Marc transferred from Roslyn Academy to the International School of Kenya (ISK) in Nairobi when he reached grade six. He joined his sister who made the same move a couple of years before. It was easier having both children in the same school than different ones.

The Cannon's thought it would be best for their eldest child Chandra to attend high school in the US. It would afford Chandra the opportunity to better prepare for her future education. She was accepted into St. George's private boarding school in Newport, Rhode Island. The school was close enough for Cannon's mother Lena to visit as well as some of his cousins. Kari accompanied Chandra to Rhode Island and enrolled her in September 1984. Cannon stayed in Nairobi working and taking care of Marc while Kari was away.

Chandra attended St. George's for one year. She said she was too homesick for her family and Africa. She also noted that the school was more for the wealthy than for a daughter of a man working with trade unions. She enrolled in ISK upon her return to Kenya

Marc was the beneficiary of a visit from an AALC staffer from Washington. Byron Charlton was in Kenya to view progress at the TMLC before moving on to Kinshasa, Zaire to meet with Glenn Lesak who was formerly in Kenya. Glenn invited Marc to visit him. The Cannons agreed in spite of Marc being eleven years old. Marc accompanied Byron, but not without a few hiccups at the airport. Byron was questioned about Marc. You see Byron was black and Marc was white. This caused some confusion initially with Kenyan officials at the airport. Marc had a great time in Kinshasa before flying alone back to Nairobi on Air Zaire where they put him in 1st class. Could it have been this experience that initiated his champagne tastes?

A tragedy befell the Cannons and the entire AALC organization on the 26th of September 1984, when Pius Odhiambo had a heart attack in Maseru, Lesotho and died. Not only did AALC lose a stalwart staffer, but Cannon also lost his African father figure. The previous year, Pius went to the US to undergo heart surgery. The operation was so successful that he even stopped drinking his favorite beverage of vodka and hot water. The AALC/Nairobi office was never the same without him nor was Cannon for that matter.

Before Cannon knew it, the Davis family had completed their assignment at the TMLC. Joe was a terrific teacher and well loved by participants and TMLC staff. It was hard on Mrs. Davis with a young son. Kisumu wasn't the greatest place for services and facilities for a young child. Both Davis's had made commitments back in the US before coming to Kenya and were eager to return home. They returned to the USA where Joe was planning on completing his Ph.D. in Economics.

The AALC hired Robert Hardy to be his replacement at the TMLC. The Davis's house in Kisumu wasn't larger enough for the Hardy family. They stayed in The Kisumu Hotel until Bob was able to find and rent their new home. Cannon did not get on as well with Bob Hardy, as he had with Joe Davis. Maybe it was a clash of personalities? In Cannon's view Bob wasn't as effective a teacher as Joe Davis was: this was also the view of some of the Kenyan staff at the TMLC.

Cannon periodically traveled to Kampala to undertake assignments with NOTU and to serve as their paymaster. He frequently traveled with thousands of US dollars in traveler's checks for NOTU's activities. Cannon would obtain receipts from NOTU before signing off on the checks. Cannon later learned NOTU had arrangements with some business people in Kampala who gave local Uganda shillings for the checks. At times it was impossible to discern Cannon's own signature, which changed drastically from signing so many checks.

Cannon's friend Phil Jenkins told him about a British buddy who was living and running a small construction business in Kampala. Cannon eventually found the house of Roger Woods high up on a hill overlooking the city and Lake Victoria. Roger recommended a Greek guesthouse in town near the old golf course which he said was a thousand times better than the Speke Hotel. There were trips to Kampala when Cannon's luggage consisted of traveler's checks for NOTU and butter and bacon for the Guest House- a very interesting combination.

NOTU was constantly changing its leaders. Cannon often held long discussions with NOTU people such as David Wogute, Robinson Kasogi, Humphrey Luande, and others about the pitfalls of unions depending upon governments in Africa. Cannon's view was whatever an African government gave an African trade union movement, they could just as easily remove it as they deemed fit.

Unfortunately Cannon's advice fell on deaf ears. David Wogute, one of the first NOTU Secretary Generals after the fall of Admin, wanted NOTU to establish a Labor Party in the hopes of his becoming a Parliamentarian. He was eventually removed from NOTU via an internal coup. The revolving Secretary General's chair continued when the Uganda Liberation Army (ULA) under General Yoweri Museveni toppled Obote. Kasogi and others followed in Wogute's footsteps becoming too closely aligned with the next new government. They too were replaced by another NOTU internal coup.

AALC continued its support for COTU focusing in on activities at the TMLC. Cannon often taught a class or two whenever AALC sponsored seminars were held. This task was one of the more enjoyable ones associated with his Kenyan work. The trade unionists were very receptive to learning especially on the topic of grievances handling at the work place.

Teaching at the TMLC afforded Cannon the chance to drive from Nairobi to Kisumu-a beautiful drive. Probably the best two views were those going into Kericho thru the tea plantations and over the mountain leading to Lake Victoria. Cannon usually stayed at the Sunset Hotel, which was so aptly named. At sunset you could watch the sun drop into Lake Victoria a magnificent site no matter how many times one witnessed it. Another pleasure was having access to restaurants which served great lake fish.

The only unpleasant side of these trips to Kisumu was the problem with the TMLC Principal. It grew so bad, that Cannon and Akumu were hardly speaking beyond exchanging greetings before COTU eventually fired Akumu. It was assumed that Akumu was fired because of financial issues.

One never knew whether the AALC sponsored education programs were producing results or not. It was next to impossible to evaluate whether seminar participants were able to put into practice trade union tasks such as grievance handling, collective bargaining, occupational safety and health, etc. However there were a few instances where the AALC program was providing on-the-job skills to trade union people in Kenya. One such example was a Job Evaluation conducted by Frank Lunney of the US Steelworkers for union members at the Firestone factory in Nairobi. Here union staffers were actually getting taught US proven negotiating skills not just theory. Unfortunately programs of this nature were too infrequent even though one could say they were truly developmental since they actually changed people's work life.

The annual AALC staff conference took place in Washington, DC in 1985. For Cannon, the highlight of said conference was the participation of the AFL-CIO international legend Irving Brown. At this time, Brown was the AFL-CIO's representative in Europe. He gave a tutorial on Poland that was excellent. He was positive that should the Polish Solidarity Free

Trade Movement succeed, it would be the start of the collapse of the USSR. Brown was a prophet in his own life time.

A by-product of the staff conference was the visit to Kenya of James McCargar who was recently hired to help with the AFL-CIO's international publications. Jim was an old friend of Irving Brown's from their days together in Europe after WW II. In 1963 James wrote "**A Short Course in the Secret War**" which was published under the pseudonym of Christopher Felix. In the third edition published in 1992, James was revealed as the true author of the book called "The Thinking Man's Spy Book" by the New York Times Book Review.

Cannon met Jim at the Kenyatta International Airport just on the outskirts of Nairobi. Cannon had never met Jim hence he was holding a sign with his name printed on it. A tall very distinguished looking man in his 60's identified himself as Jim McCargar. On the drive to the city, Cannon briefed Jim on the program which had been set-up for him. A booking had been made at the InterContinental Hotel which was within walking distance to the AALC office.

While in Kenya, Jim spent lots of time with the Cannons. In spite of Jim's baldness, it was self-evident he was very comfortable in the company of the opposite sex. When first introduced to Mrs. Cannon, Jim kissed her hand European style, thus cementing his charm.

It was only years later that the Cannons learned that Jim was one of three foreign persons honored by the King of Norway for his exploits there during WW II. Another was Bill Colby who later became the Director of the CIA. Jim was a gifted and an amazing friend. His friendship lasted much longer than the Cannons years with AALC. Unfortunately his publication ideas were not used by COTU. The AALC consultancy became a one-off affair.

Cannon pushed COTU to establish a Women's Department. They had a women's section but it really didn't have any organizational stature within COTU. As a first step, Mulei agreed to hire Katherine Maloba who had been active in women's issues within COTU. AALC then arranged a trip for her to the USA so she could be exposed to what the US women were doing within the AFL-CIO structure. While Maloba was in the US, she invited the AFL-CIO to send a women's delegation to Kenya.

On the 28th of June 1985, an AFL-CIO Women's Delegation of nine arrived in Kenya. It was co-headed by two women who were members of the AFL-CIO Executive Board Ms. Barbara Hutchison and Ms. Joyce Miller. Pat Topping an AALC/Washington staff member accompanied them. From day one, there was competition between Hutchison and Miller as to who was the true leader of the visitors' team. They both received fruit baskets upon arrival at the Hotel Intercontinental. If (1) banana was missing from one, Cannon heard about it. Despite this small issue, the trip was a complete success. Later Maloba left COTU to become an African representative for an International Trade Secretariat (ITS) affiliated to the International Confederation of Trade Unions (ICFTU).

On the 20th of January 1986, the AALC opened its annual staff conference on the Isle of Mauritius, in the Indian Ocean. Mauritius is one of the most beautiful tropical islands in the world. It was natural for AALC spouses to want to accompany their husbands for this conference. In addition to Mrs. Cannon, the AALC/Nairobi Secretary of long standing Mrs. Linda Konditi also attended.

The conference was held in a top notch beach hotel. Rooms led out into the Indian Ocean. The food was terrific, especially morning egg omelets which were enhanced with locally grown very hot red chili peppers. Kari got to meet some of the other AALC spouses for the first time. While the menfolk were participating in morning and afternoon meetings, Kari enjoyed the pristine beach. Nights were it was free for dining and dancing. Socially the conference was great.

Professionally for Cannon it was a disaster. The AALC Director informed him at the conference that he was to be transferred back to the Washington office in April. His predecessor Nate Gould, noted previously, would replace him. This decision surprised and shocked the Cannons. Cannon thought he was doing good work in Kenya. The testimonial letters in the appendages seem to support Cannon's view. Cannon had no choice but to accept the decision. Was Murphy getting back at Cannon for his role in opposing Gould at the Cairo staff conference?

The Cannons thought they would be spending many years working overseas for the AALC. Murphy mentioned Egypt and Nigeria as other potential job possibilities initially, but as the conference proceeded no more was spoken about either. What job would Cannon be doing in DC? Would he be replacing Gould as the Deputy Director? Murphy was non-committal throughout the conference.

With heavy hearts, the Cannons returned to Nairobi. Cannon spent February visiting trade unions in Nairobi informing them of his transfer to Washington and that he'd be replaced by Nate Gould in April.

In March, Cannon accompanied the Regional US Labor Attaché Mr. George Dragnich to Uganda to introduce him to Uganda trade union officials. A highlight of said trip was the visit of US Ambassador Robert Houdek, an old friend from his days as Deputy Chief of Mission in Nairobi, to NOTU offices in Kampala. This was a first for NOTU. The TMLC held a farewell party for the Cannons and Jorgen Pedersen, whose assignment was finished, in March: a festive but sad time.

Cannon was given a strange assignment prior to his departure from Kenya. He was instructed to meet a colleague, George Martens in Kinshasa, Zaire. They were to investigate the potential of resurrecting the partly finished Labor College outside of the city. The AALC Representative, Glenn Lesak (an old friend from his days in Kenya) was in charge of Cannons and Martens program. He put Martens and Cannon up in a house in the former Organization of African Unity (OAU) village. In those days it was the practice of any African country hosting the OAU Heads of State conference, to build an entire complex to house there guests even if they only stayed in them for a few days.

The College's proposed site was like a mini city including the skeleton of a massive sports stadium. The initial construction was done a decade before when things were much better in the country. It was apparent it would be highly unlikely that the Labor College site would be resurrected due to the lack of funds. A report, with a positive spin for good will was written for UNTZA President Kombo. This was yet another AALC task whose purpose was questionable except, if one took it as a political gesture which Kombo could use in his dealing with Zairian President Mobutu.

While in Kinshasa, Cannon broke his ankle while out jogging. Fortunately he and Martens had completed the field work on the proposed Labor College. If this wasn't enough, Cannon was shocked to hear his old Vietnam boss Lawson Mooney was living in Kinshasa working for President Mobotu.

Prior to departing Zaire, Cannon was able to break bread with Lawson and Lisa Mooney. Cannon's colleague Glenn Lesak was familiar with Mooney. Mooney and a former AALC representative Peter Lobarth were well known as competitors purchasing Zaire art. Glenn was kind enough to drive Cannon to their house. They lived a nice house in one of the more expensive expat sections of Kinshasa.

It was wonderful to set eyes on Lawson and Lisa. The years since Vietnam had not been too good to Mooney. He didn't look well nor was he the gregarious person he had been. Lisa said Lawson had health issues besides not aging well. Yet it was great to see them after so many years. The last previous time together was 1969 in Nairobi at Cannon's wedding.

Living in Kenya was a terrific culinary experience for the Cannon family. There were numerous local restaurants in Nairobi and surrounding areas. There were Indian restaurants which offered a wide selection variety. One of the favorites was a placed called Mohinder's Corner located in the Eastleigh area. The food was terrific and cheap in spite of a few bullet holes in the walls-courtesy of a patron who had too much to drink one night. Another was a Chinese restaurant operated by a friend of Karl Marx. Joseph's place offered a wide selection of dishes and had cold beer to wash the food down.

The Carnivore, based upon a concept from Brazil, was famous for its meat. A wide variety of meat was served from large hand- held swords. The waiters carved off portions according to one's choice. It was a meat lover's paradise. Cannon never could get over how much meat his colleague Glenn Lesak could consume.

Mombasa was famous for its fish dishes as were the tourist hotels on the coast south of Mombasa. There was a unique restaurant on the coast whose name Cannon cannot recall. It was underground in a cave right off the Indian Ocean.

Before departing Kenya, Cannon had his 2nd exposure to HIV/AIDS. One of the leading trade union figures, which headed up a major COTU affiliate as well as being a senior officer bearer in COTU was hospitalized with Kaposi's sarcoma. At the time nobody was mentioning HIV/AIDS but later it would turn out to be a major problem throughout Kenya.

Cannon received numerous testimonial letters regarding his work in Kenya: the US Ambassador; the Minister of Labor; the President of COTU; the Chief Executive Officer of the Kenya Federation of Employer's were some of those received. See Appendages.

On the 6th of April 1986, Cannon departed Kenya with heavy heart for the unknown of the AALC Washington office. Mrs. Cannon stayed behind to allow the children to finish their school year at ISK and to pack their household effects to ship onward to Washington, DC.

9

Militant Unionism in Nigeria

After the fall of Vietnam in 1974 if you're an American, or the liberation of South Vietnam if you're a North Vietnamese, the cold war took on added intensity. This was especially true in Africa, where the USA and the USSR were competing ideologically for the hearts and minds of Africans. This competition also involved the international trade union movement as previously noted. Another competition existed as well, between western trade unions for influence within the African trade union movement.

The US trade union movement at this time, in addition to members' dues, also received US tax payers' monies via the US government for its programs in South America, Asia, Africa and later Central Europe. The Europeans accused the AFL-CIO of being just an extension of the US government because they received government funds. Some of the younger Europeans forgot the role the AFL and CIO, before their merger in 1954, played in the rebuilding of Europe after WW II. These younger Europeans developed their views during the Vietnam years and most were opposed to the US involvement in Vietnam. They were even more opposed to the AFL-CIO's support for the South Vietnam's trade union movement. The Eastern bloc nations associated with the USSR went further saying that the AFL-CIO overseas was an arm of the US Central Intelligence Agency (CIA).

Cannon became very aware of these accusations while trying to help COTU operationalize the Tom Mboya Labour College. One would think the major problem would arise from the East's accusations but this wasn't completely true. Some of the Europeans were very active in the International Confederation of Free Trade Unions (ICFTU) which also had a few Africans on its staff. The AFL-CIO was a founding member of the ICFTU but later withdrew for a few years because of issues, some of which arose from Vietnam. Other Europeans were very active in bi-lateral programs supported by their respective trade union movements. Their ideology was left of that of the AFL-CIO, especially those coming from Scandinavia.

The Europeans kept in the closet the fact they also received monies from their respective governments for many years. If they did acknowledge it, that was okay since their governments were "good" being social democrats, etc. as opposed to the US government being capitalist which was "bad".

Late comers to the bilateral trade union assistance programs in Africa included the Canadians. Many of their overseas representatives felt a closer bond with their European counterparts than with the Yanks representing the AFL-CIO. Each bilateral organization felt it had a program to offer COTU which was far superior to that offered by the AALC. One of their selling points was they were not as stringent when it came to the expenditures of funds by the local recipients. Another was that some of them were willing to work with some individual Kenyan unions opposed to COTU's closeness to the Americans. Too much time and energy were expended trying to mitigate petty problems arising from the aforementioned than against the USSR and its Eastern European allies. Not enough time and energy was put towards developing trade union skills such as collective bargaining, occupational safety, and organizing non-union workers. This was true in Nigeria as in other countries in Africa.

Ben Edherue was a very active player in the Nigeria trade union movement starting in the early 1980's. Like many other countries in Africa, the trade union movement in Nigeria was a key player in the fight for independence from the British. The British even went so far as to send out trade union personnel prior to independence in order to re-direct the trade union movement away from the pro-independence forces. One British goal was to bring the young Nigerian unions closer to their form of economic trade unionism.

The independence tide in Africa wasn't to be denied regardless of what the colonial masters did or didn't do to sway the outcomes. Nigeria was no different than other African countries. Once Nigeria became free on October 1, 1960, it wasn't too long thereafter that internal strife broke out within the trade union movement. Tribal influences competed with political ideological views. Further strife was exacerbated once the civil war broke out after the first military coup in 1965.

The USSR became a very strong backer of the Nigerian Federal Government as part of its effort to put down the secession attempt of 30 May 1967 by the Eastern province Igbos. Soviet aid provided military aircraft and pilots as well as training for Federal Government military officers. It was only natural that the USSR also became very active in providing assistance to Nigerian trade unions. Among its major projects it supported was the building of a large three-story trade union complex in downtown Lagos At one point there were at least three groups of unions all claiming to be the major national trade union center representing Nigerian workers.

Not only was the USSR providing assistance, western countries were also trying to influence the Nigerian trade union movement. Some European countries had bilateral programs, as did the AFL-CIO's African American Labor Center. In the late 1960's, the Nigerian Military Government mandated the creation of one national trade union center- the Nigerian Labour Congress. The competition between the East and West didn't pass with the establishment of the NLC, instead it intensified. It was also compounded by the playing-off of one assistance movement against another. For many years, it wasn't possible American trade unionists to obtain a residence permit to reside in Nigeria. Without a permanent presence only ad-hoc projects could be conducted. Some trade union organizations would just send monies for projects.

Ben, along with a cadre of other young men, was part of the youth wing of the NLC. Ideologically they were drawn to socialism since their view of capitalism was darken by the role some Western businesses played in supporting the rebels who were seeking to break their country apart during the civil war period. Their idealism was also drawn to one of the basic tenants of socialism: **from each according to his ability, to each according to one's needs!**

Unlike capitalism, which in Ben's eyes meant much wants more. Another very positive attraction towards the USSR and its affiliates was their support for liberation movements in Africa trying to obtain independence, especially those in southern Africa. Western countries in particular especially the USA were viewed as supporters of the status quo or worst as supporters of anti-communist governments who were racists like South Africa.

Unfortunately for Ben, the Nigerian military were not the best of friends with the NLC especially during the periods of the 1st military junta (1966-1978) and the 2nd junta (1983-1998). It was not uncommon for people to get arrested, when carrying out their trade union duties in the early days following a coup. Even if trade union organizers were not arrested, their movements and work were closely monitored by the military's intelligence service.

During these periods of military rule, all western trade union movements acted together in trying to pressure the Nigerian military to release any trade unionist arrested. This was the only area in which trade union "solidarity" was actually practiced not just verbalized.

In the days, prior to independence, union leaders had to visit each work site at least once a month in order to collect subscriptions (another term for dues), which were used to fund the union activities and pay overhead costs. It might be said union leadership were in closer contact to its rank and file (membership) when hand collecting subscriptions. The drawback was the number of people needed to collect monies monthly. It was also an invitation for dishonest unionist to further their monetary nests by pocketing the monies collected.

Ben and his fellow comrades were products of the "modern" trade union movement. Once the collective bargaining process became institutionalized, the means of subscription collection changed. Unions stipulated in the collective bargaining agreements which workers were covered. Unionized workers could agree to having their monthly subscription deducted from their wages; the employer then agreed to deduct said sum and write a monthly check to the union for the workforce covered under the collective bargaining agreement (CBA). Under this process, the respective union was able to obtain subscriptions for the entire workforce covered by the CBA. Unions did not need to spend long hours trying to meet individual workers at month's end to collect dues in person.

While many viewed the new process as a boon, especially after governments codified laws which institutionalized the subscription process, some felt otherwise. Whereas it was difficult to secure monies to operate trade unions when subscriptions were collected by hand, the leadership didn't have the problem of becoming estranged from the rank and file because they were in monthly face-to-face contact.

It is natural that people of the same views intermingle with each other. This is doubly so for trade unionists for in unity there is strength. The draw -back to mingling with one's brothers is that you only get one point of view. If this happens enough, sometimes unions cannot see the trees for the forest. Trade union leaders and those employed by trade unions gradually become estranged from their membership as well. If one only ends up speaking with people of the same beliefs, gradually you end up preaching to the same choir. For trade union movements' to grow and prosper, they need to constantly acquire new members. This can only be done through organizing. One organizes the unorganized that are not within one's circle of communicants.

While western trade unions were in a period of declining membership, the trade union movement in Nigeria was growing more rapidly. Nigeria was well off in the early 1970's. The oil boom had basically made the country debt free but at a cost. It was no longer self- sufficient in food production. The NLC devoted resources to organize the farm workers as well as those working in the manufacturing formal sector in mostly cities. More success was achieved in the cities than in the rural areas.

Ben traveled extensively. He was acquiring an on-the-job education in the tribal realities of Nigeria, especially as to how they impacted upon trade union politics and politics in general. Many of Ben's comrades wanted to establish their own Labor Party.

They had models from Europe to draw upon and tacit support from selected bi-lateral trade union programs. This view flew in the face of the Americans who were firm believers that trade union movements should support political parties not run them.

This was another example of the Nigerian trade union movement getting caught between ideological opposites from the West. Gradually it dawned on the comrades that aid offered almost always comes with strings attached. This was true in Nigeria and elsewhere in Africa. In spite of these drawbacks, Ben and his buddies stayed committed to the NLC, although a few of them drifted away into the private sector if they acquired additional skills through higher education.

The trade union movement was split ideologically. Some of the leadership had been educated in the USSR or affiliated countries, while others were educated in western countries. It wasn't surprising that after completing studies abroad, the returning union leaders' ideology reflected that of the country in which they were trained. Naturally the returnees became ideological enemies within the trade union movement.

Whenever a major national election arose inside of the Nigerian Labour Congress (NLC), internal ideology and the prevailing government in power affected it, The prevailing power was the military for long periods of time from the late 1960's to the mid 1980's, regardless what General was in charge. To be a NLC officer bearer required great survival and navigational skills.

Throughout this time, the NLC and whatever government was in power both were internationally very pro-active in the anti-apartheid movement. Most of the NLC's international supporters from the West were also involved in the anti-apartheid movement but to varying degrees reflecting their ideological basis. It was many years before the US government initiated sanctions to show its displeasure with the government of South Africa.

Very few NLC leaders and even fewer of its youth league leaders, such as Ben were aware that the AFL-CIO frequently was in conflict with the US Government on policy matters effecting workers. Thus the AALC was often perceived, rightly or wrongly, as being an arm of the US government. This perception was fueled by representatives of European and even Canadian trade union representatives who were competing for political influence within the NLC.

Money doesn't buy ownership, influence or loyalty in Africa. It only rents it. The youth league members became very adept at playing-off one donor versus another. Tell them whatever they want to hear, but get their funds.

It was natural that AALC program assistance was geared to those unionists who were pro-democracy and pro-American. The AALC had no control over was who attended its in-country education programs since participants were selected by the NLC. During this period Ben wasn't a supporter of the AALC.

Across the continent, Cannon was gradually becoming aware of the foolishness of the competition among western trade union programs. It became all the more apparent as Cannon and some COTU colleagues were trying to promote the TMLC with visiting trade unionists coming through Nairobi. The COTU dreams of the TMLC becoming a Pan African education center utilized by all international donors gradually fading away

The NLC had an even tighter role to walk. It had to function regardless which General was in charge of the government. While months and even a few years might pass, the military government would periodically come down on the NLC and even detain some of their members. Unfortunately for Ben and his comrades, the NLC youth league members often found themselves in jail. Additionally, the military frequently provoked splits within the NLC for their own political ends. United We Stand- Divided We Fall.

10

Return to the Mountain Kingdom- Southern Africa

During the spring of 1986, Cannon started looking for housing in the Washington, DC area for his soon to be arriving family. Living overseas, the Cannons were able to save some money but would it be enough to make a down payment on a townhouse in one of the most expensive cities in the USA?

A misfortune had befallen a trade union colleague which resulted in a change in plans for the Cannons. The AALC representative who was responsible for the recently established program in South Africa fell ill. Michael Lescault lived in Lesotho. Since the leader of the Lesotho trade union movement was a great friend of AALC, it was easy for Michael to acquire a residence permit and to travel in and out of South Africa after he obtained a South Africa visa.

Michael almost died while being treated for a major illness in South Africa. While he made it out of surgery, he had lost the use of the lower part of his body. Eventually the AALC decided Michael needed access to US medical care. He was to be transferred back to the USA. The AALC needed an immediate replacement for Michael since its program for South Africa was a key component in the AFL-CIO's opposition to apartheid.

Cannon's was not happy with his return to Washington professionally. After a few weeks back in Washington it was apparent Murphy had no plans to move Cannon into the deputy's post once occupied by Nate Gould. Cannon sat in a sparsely furnished office with little to do awaiting word what was to be his new role with AALC. Before a new headquarters role was assigned, Cannon was named as Michael's replacement in early May 1986.

Cannon was thrilled with this new blessing: his prayers were answered-another overseas assignment. Fortunately the Cannon family had not yet moved out of Kenya, nor had a townhouse been purchased in the Washington, DC area. The family effects would be shipped to Lesotho where the Cannon's started their married life and where their eldest child Chandra was born.

Cannon returned to Lesotho in the June 1986, some 17 years after his first arrival. Naturally the capital, Maseru, had changed. There was even a Hilton Hotel in the capital: the same capital which had horse hitching posts on Main street back in 1969. In the middle of June, Michael went back into a hospital in Bloemfontein, South Africa after having a medical setback which prevented him and his family from leaving Lesotho. He spent close to a month being treated before he would be strong enough to fly back to the United States in August.

Lesotho is a small mountainous country completely surrounded by South Africa. It had a population of about 1.9 million people. It was between 29 and 31 degrees south and 27 and 30 degrees east. Its size if approximately 30, 355 km squared. It was about the size of the State of Rhode Island where Cannon was born. Imagine being completely surrounded by another country whose political system was completely opposite your countries?

The first task Cannon undertook was to go to South Africa's embassy in Maseru to apply for a visa to go into South Africa. No problems were anticipated since his predecessor Michael had one. Was Cannon in for a surprise! The initial application was refused. No reason given. Cannon was told to come back in a few months if he wanted to apply again. Cannon would wait three to four months before re-applying. Throughout Cannon's stay in Lesotho, after each time the entry visa was refused, Cannon would wait a few months and re-apply. The end result was always the same. It did not change until the South African Government unbanned the African National Congress (ANC), the Pan African Congress (PAC) and the South Africa Communist Party (SAPC).

Cannon was perplexed when the South African embassy refused to grant him an entry visa, into their country. He had no idea why this visa application was denied yet his predecessor Michael was granted a visa. How could Cannon implement the AALC program in South Africa if he could not enter the country? What would be the reaction of AALC/ Washington to this? How would this decision impact on Mrs. Cannon and the children who were to arrive in Maseru soon?

A house was located to rent, oddly enough, the Cannon's had been inside it previously in 1970 when it was rented by the CARE representative and his family. It was located within walking distance of Machabeng International High School where Chandra and Marc were enrolled. The house had a small one bedroom annex which could serve as an office.

Lesotho is completely different from Kenya even if both are located in Africa. The first difference occurs upon arrival at the airport. Kenya's main airport in Nairobi is large and modern. Lesotho's main airport on the outskirts of Maseru is tiny. Chandra voiced her teenage dismay upon entering the arrival hall-life for her was going to be different than in Nairobi.

During Cannon's introductory visit to the US Embassy in Lesotho, he was ushered into an office that looked and felt as if it wasn't used too often. In walked a person who introduced himself as a staff member. The first thing he did was to turn on a tape player. The music was country & western not one of Cannon's favorites. Cannon was asked how he planned on implementing the AFL-CIO's program with the black trade union movement in South Africa when he couldn't even get into South Africa.

It was obvious with the music scene, that the person Cannon was with had other duties in the US government besides the State Department. If additional confirmation was necessary, it was his knowledge of Cannon being refused a visa into South Africa. Said individual and Cannon soon became jogging partners and social friends.

The Cannon's personal effects from Kenya arrived prior to the Cannon family. Once they were cleared through customs they were delivered to the Cannons home in the Maseru West area of the capital. The house had adequate facilities so each child had their own bedroom. The bedrooms were separated from the other rooms in the house by a steel door: a precaution against robbers. It didn't take long before the Cannons were able to re-establish friendships with people they knew in the late 1960's and make new friends.

On the 12th of June 1986, the apartheid government of South Africa declared a State of Emergency. Over 5,000 people were arrested and detained. Many of them were trade union activists. If Cannon couldn't enter South Africa before, it became even more difficult for him to contact black trade union leaders after the State of Emergency since many were avoiding their union offices and homes. They were moving nightly to avoid detection by South Africa's police and security services.

Due to Cannon's ethnicity, there presented an additional avenue to explore to get a South African visa. Cannon was able to secure a Republic of Ireland passport for himself and his family from the Irish embassy in Maseru based upon his heritage. This information was made available to the AALC Executive Director back in Washington. Cannon thought Murphy would grant him approval to re-apply for a South African visa using the Irish passport. Murphy did not grant his approval nor did he ever acknowledge receipt of the Irish passport information.

Cannon set about establishing contacts with black South African trade unions from Maseru. It wasn't too long after his arrival that he was asked to attend an ICFTU conference on South Africa in Lusaka, Zambia. The Zambia conference was attended by representatives from the two main black trade union federations in South Africa: COSATU (Congress of South Africa Trade Unions) and the National Congress of Trade Unions (NACTU).

NACTU was formed in 1986 through the merger of the Council of Unions of South Africa (CUSA) and the Azania Confederation of Trade Unions (AZACTU). Azania was the name used by the PAC for South Africa.

Initially the Black Conscience Movement became involved in helping to organize black trade unions well before the murder of Steve Biko in September 1977. COSATU was a split off federation from AZACTU. It took with it the main large unions such as the Mineworkers Union. It was politically attuned to the ideology of the ANC (African National Congress) whereas AZACTU was politically attuned to the ideology of the PAC (Pan African Congress). The PAC believed a free South Africa should be for blacks. The ANC believed a free South Africa was for all citizens regardless of color.

COSATU wasn't thrilled with the leadership in the USA. President Ronald Reagan and his administration were perceived as a supporter of the minority white apartheid regime through its opposition to communism. Many of COSATU members and affiliated unions also viewed capitalism as the backbone for apartheid. It was widely known that the AFL-CIO's programs overseas used US government funds.

COSATU established a policy not to deal directly with the AALC though they would deal directly with a few of the AFL-CIO affiliated unions. By default, the AALC program in support of the black trade union movement inside of South Africa was almost totally conducted with NACTU.

The AALC Executive Director had hopes that AALC's attendance at the October 1986 ICFTU sponsored conference on South Africa in Lusaka would serve as Cannon's introduction to COSATU attendees. It didn't pan out as hoped. The COSATU persons were civil when introduced to Cannon. The hoped for dialogue stopped after the introductions. On the plane trip back to South Africa, Cannon was seated next to a white South African who was associated with the COSATU's textile workers union in Durban. When the person found out whom Cannon worked with, he changed seats. This illustrates how COSATU viewed the AALC, like pariahs. Alec Irvin later became a Minister in the South African government after the country conducted its first non-racial election in 1994. Additional trips were undertaken in 1986 to Botswana, Swaziland

and Malawi with the hopes of establishing contacts with COSATU unionists. These trips were also unsuccessful.

Cannon established a system to maintain contact with the NACTU black trade unionists possessing travel documents which allowed them to travel within the Southern Africa region: especially the three former British protectorates of Botswana, Swaziland and Lesotho. Many from NACTU represented smallish unions. The larger and more recognized unions were affiliated with COSATU.

Some NACTU affiliated union leaders came to Maseru by road. Cannon would put them up in the Victoria Hotel or give them a per diem if they had relatives they wanted to stay with. Discussions were held in the Victoria Hotel where all could be observed by interested parties-be they Basotho or South African.

If privacy was required, the discussions would be held at the Cannons in the one bedroom flat, which served as an office next to the main house. Sometimes cash was provided for forthcoming union actions to be supported or checks were written in the name of the union. Receipts for previous supported activities were provided or later mailed from South Africa to Lesotho. Monies were then provided to the brothers or sisters to cover expenses to return back to South Africa. The aforementioned was very similar to the system used by Cannon in Kenya with COTU.

One day, Cannon's son was riding his bicycle home after spending the night with his Irish buddy. Marc wasn't aware that he should not place a plastic bag on the front handlebars of the bike. He learned a harsh lesson. While peddling down the street, the bag went into the front wheel spokes. Marc went head first over the handlebars onto the street. The Cannons received a call saying he was seriously hurt and bleeding badly.

The Cannons drove Marc to the Queen Elizabeth II hospital in Maseru. Fortunately the emergency room was empty. It was usually lined with people on both sides of the corridor leading to the ER room. Unfortunately the doctor-on-duty had been drinking. Not only was his breath reeking of alcohol his words didn't make any sense. Cannon called a friend at the US Embassy who said Marc should be taken to the hospital in nearby Ladybrand, South Africa.

Kari, Marc and Chandra had been entering South Africa on their Irish passports for a few weeks prior to the accident. Marc was placed in the back seat of the car with his sister, while Kari drove to the nearby South Africa border post. The police and military questioned her before allowing them to enter the country and to proceed to the Ladybrand hospital.

Marc's sister Chandra along with his mother Kari accompanied him to the Hospital's emergency room. Chandra recalled the ER room had a concrete slab table with an overhead naked light bulb. The on duty Doctor-in-Charge was still in medical school. He overlapped the skin on Marc's face and stitched the wound up with raw hide. Marc was hospitalized for 10 days. Kari, his mother and Chandra were able to visit with him but not his father.

Marc's accident had a profound impact on Cannon. It was the first time Cannon was not able to perform as a father to his children. Cannon felt a sense of complete hopelessness. Additionally, he was dismayed with his employer inaction to allow him to use his Irish passport in applying for a South African visa. Cannon felt his inaction could be construed as placing his work before his family. The only fallback which might justify his inaction was the age old male concept that his work was providing for his family.

In retrospect, this incident was definitely a glitch in the Cannons marriage: whether it played a role in the divorce later remains questionable. The accident was the first time the Cannon children were exposed first-hand to the functioning apartheid state. Cannon believed if he had been driving the car, the South African's would not have allowed Marc into the country

In Cannon's first six months in Maseru, he had an opportunity to witness again first- hand how the insanity of apartheid affected the behavior of all black South Africans including trade union brothers and sisters. The General Secretary and the head of NACTU's Information Department visited Maseru for the day. Maseru was close enough to Johannesburg that one could make a quick road trip in and out in the same day. The visitors had been in Maseru previously so it was easier to arrange a meeting at the Vic Hotel than try to give them directions to Cannons house and office. The meeting was a bit strained initially. The NACTU people had never met Cannon. They seemed leery at first seeing yet another Yank white face. This was completely understandable.

Cannon spent the first half hour giving them an overview of his background, family, work history, etc. which eventually put them at ease. Next, Cannon listened to their problems and their wish list. Many of the NACTU problems were beyond the ability of being assisted by Americans or the AALC. Internal politics with the forces opposing apartheid were along the ideological lines of the liberation forces operating outside of South Africa. Some of the trade union problems facing NACTU were a result of the pulling out of the Mineworkers Union to join COSATU. Cannon indicated he could help them in limited ways predominately in the field of trade union education and work place safety. After agreements were reached and a wade of rand made available, we all walked out to their vehicle parked in the Vic Hotel parking lot.

The first thing the NACTU visitors did was to get down on their hands and knees to examine the undercarriage of the vehicle. They were checking to see whether the breaks had been tampered with or whether a bomb had been placed under the motor. After the inspection was completed, Cannon was told that was standing operating procedures since the apartheid regime wasn't opposed to arranging road accidents for trade union people.

Later on, the NACTU Secretary General was arrested and spent time in jail. While he was in jail, he was fortunate he wasn't thrown out one of the windows of a police station like what happened to Neil Aggett- a white trade unionist associated with COSATU. The white South African regime didn't play by Queensbury's rules.

It was whites who were oppressing non-whites in South Africa. Some in South Africa believed the US had given the white South Africa government information back in the early 1960's that helped in the capture of Nelson Mandela. The US government under Ronald Reagan was very reluctant to impose sanctions against the racist South Africa regime. One could go on and on in quoting examples of the lack of white western government action and pressure against racism in Africa. It all added up to guarded interaction with whites.

Many South African whites tried to curry favor with Yanks thinking they could rationalize the apartheid system. If they were originally of English origin they blamed all the ills on the Boers who were originally from Holland. The Boers were more upfront about apartheid. They had benefited immensely from the 1948 election (whites only) which brought the predominately Boer National Party to power. They also tried to minimize the mess inside South Africa.

The news was always showing a map of South Africa with huge black arrows indicating the "massive communist onslaught" facing South Africa. The news also drew one's attention to the rest of black Africa where things were a bit discombobulated to say the least. However not all white South Africans supported the apartheid regime.

The African National Congress (ANC) had white members of long standing. Some even holding key positions within the party. Whites from the South African Communist party had been very active throughout the decades in seeking the overthrow of the racist government. There were a few whites that were also very active participants in the newly created black trade union movement within South Africa. Yet, if one was honest, these were a very small minority. The remainder of the white population lived very affluent lives in comparison to non-whites and liked it that way.

Most expatriates living in Maseru, including the US Embassy and United Nations staffers, shopped for their daily provisions in South Africa. They also used South Africa for medical situations and holidays. South Africa had first world amenities: an excellent road system; good telecommunication networks; rail and port facilities; good hotels and rest houses; first class medical personnel and facilities; movie theaters; etc.: especially if you were white. Even some of the more affluent Basotho traveled to South Africa for much the same reasons as the whites even if they were treated inhumanly. They had to stand in lines which were for non-whites. They had to use different entrances to some stores. They had different medical facilities. They used different windows to access fast food. The list could go on and on regarding the injustices suffered by non-whites in apartheid South Africa.

Maseru had one movie theater in the Victoria Hotel. There was a tiny shopping plaza, which held a few small stores plus the OK supermarket, part of a South African chain. There were two other small supermarkets; a butcher, a green grocer, a few cafés that sold some dry goods and a few fast food items. It had an outdoor market located in the outskirts of the city and two main hotels plus the original hotel: Lancers Inn. One dry cleaner: the same Andy Anderson the refugee from South Africa who Cannon had met in 1969 and a few South African furniture stores and some small businesses run by people of Portuguese origin.

Living in Lesotho for a second time, Cannon was extremely pleased that his eldest child-Chandra was born in Roma, Lesotho back in 1969 and not in South Africa. Many children of white parentage living in Lesotho were born in South Africa. In the years to come, having South Africa as your place of birth on your passport, one won't be ashamed of one's birthplace as one was during the apartheid years.

The Everett family living in Lesotho had children who were opposed to their fellow white community in South Africa. Cannon knew the Everett family from the 1960's. Maggie Everett's mother, Betty Thompson, worked in the Catholic Relief Services office. The Thompsons had been in South Africa for many generations but were never vocal supporters of white rule. One of the Thompsons, Leonard, fled to the US and became a very well respected academic at Yale University. Maggie's beliefs could be classified as liberal in comparison to her late husband Mike who was more attuned to the prevailing Boer mentality. All four Everett children sought to get away after having completed their educations in South Africa. These were kids who weren't corrupted by the South African lifestyle afforded whites by the apartheid system.

Cannon had no illusions about the tasks of trying to manage the program long-distance. He was aware that his actions would be closely watched by the Basotho military government and by persons acting on behalf of the South African government. This was re-affirmed by a friend of Michael who was an American living in Lesotho-he told Cannon to be careful.

George described himself as an academic with a history of actions against apartheid. Cannon had no way to check whether George was legit or not. Cannon never felt too comfortable with whites in Africa until he had an opportunity to get to know them over time. This was especially true for George.

When George departed Lesotho, he obtained a teaching job at a South African university. How was it possible that a South African university would hire someone like George- an opponent of apartheid? This seemed strange, even during very strange times in Southern Africa. After George left Lesotho, Cannon never saw him nor heard about him again.

It wasn't too long after George's warning that Cannon spotted a car parked outside of his house with South African license plates. Cannon became concerned about the welfare of his family who knew his job was to help South African black trade unions, but they weren't aware of the details. Cannon was also concerned his union visitors would face added scrutiny when they returned to South Africa. These courageous men and women had enough on their plates without additional burdens.

Cannon asked to return to the USA office to update the Executive Director on these developments. He had hopes that the Executive Director would authorize his use of his Irish passport to try to gain South African access. Getting into South Africa himself would help remove the risk for the trade union brothers and sisters traveling to Lesotho as well as removing his family from the day-to-day activities carried out in the office next to their living quarters. It took Cannon two days to get into the office of the Executive Director in Washington, DC, a sure sign he wasn't too concerned about Cannon's worries. When Cannon did meet with the Executive Director nothing came out of the meetings.

Cannon returned to Lesotho and continued as before the trip. Nevertheless Cannon needed to find a means to obtain South African rand outside of the normal banking mechanism if he was to become more effective in getting financial help to the trade union brothers and sisters in South Africa.

Drawing on his experiences in Kenya, he explored the small capital city of Maseru to see if there were businesses with which he could establish an informal banking system to change US dollars into South African rand. Some might call this process laundering. Some might even call it laundering for justice. Was this a former idealistic US Peace Corps volunteer using a creative solution in the fight against apartheid or had Cannon just turned into a realist?

There was one Italian restaurant across the street from the Victoria Hotel. It was only one of two decent small places to eat out in the city-the other being the Auberge. The Cannons became familiar with Gino the manager of the Italian restaurant. Gino was an old hustler from Italy who came to Southern Africa some years back. He ran a few small businesses in Johannesburg before moving to Lesotho and coming into contact with Pino who owned the Victoria Hotel.

Gino introduced Cannon to Pino. Rumor had it that Pino was connected to the Italian mob though that was questionable. Cannon had seen the gun he carried in his waist band, but thought he was showing off for his numerous ladies. Cannon changed his mind after being introduced to him. There were two other Italians in Pino's office that had the staring cold eyes of "hard" men. There was a rumor the Vic was a place to chill out, while things were being sorted out in Italy, became more of a possibility. This was later verified to be true by Gino.

Pino said he'd be happy to change US dollars into rand at a rate above the bank. He preferred cash, but he would also be willing to give the same rate with US dollar checks. Cannon now had his informal banking system in place which had worked so well in Kenya.

Cannon met some wonderful trade union brothers and sisters although there were a few who were obliviously only out for the money. When Cannon raised questions about these few individuals with Washington, he was told they were OK since Michael vouched for them. It soon became obvious to Cannon that the Executive Director paid more attention to what Michael was telling him about South Africa than Cannon who had many more years of experience living and working in Africa. South Africa was rapidly changing, was it wise to rely on a person sitting in Washington or your field representative?

A second aspect of Cannon's job was to work with the trade union movement inside of Lesotho. Over the years, Americans had supported a faction led by the nephew of the former Prime Minister Leabua Jonathan. This faction was aligned with the Basutoland National Party (BNP) while other factions were more attuned to the Basutoland Congress Party (BCP) who was in exile after the debacle of the 1969 election.

Simon Jonathan first came into contact with the AALC back in the early 1970's. Throughout the years, he was groomed by the AALC in spite of their being very few legitimized unions in the country. Simon was a friend of the West and acted accordingly in various international trade union forums. For his efforts, his trade union federation, the Lesotho Trade Union Congress (LTUC) was an annual recipient of AALC funds; basically Simon was on the AALC payroll. Another benefit of the Jonathan relationship was easy access to residential/work permits for AALC representatives in Lesotho. The Cannon/Jonathan relationship worked well on the social level but gradually became frayed at the trade union level.

AALC/W added a third component to Cannon's assignment: work with the General Secretary of the Southern Africa Trade Union Coordinating Council (SATUCC). SATUCC was created to give trade unions in the Southern Africa region a forum to meet in the fight against apartheid. Prior to the creation of SATUCC, trade unions in individual Southern

Africa countries did not have the capacity to effectively fight and condemn apartheid.

SATUCC would provide the mechanism for black South Africa trade unionists to attend seminars and workshops sponsored by the international trade union movements. Programs could be held in southern Africa more cheaply than bringing the brothers and sisters to Europe or the USA. Additionally, this forum could provide a cover for the South Africans to meet with representatives of their respective liberation movements-the ANC or PAC.

After its inception, it was decided the SATUCC headquarters would be located in Gaborone, the capital of Botswana. The Secretary General would be a Malawian trade unionist in exile Chakufwa Chihana. He was of medium build with a thick head of black hair. When happy he always flashed a great smile. He wore thick glasses which gave him a professorial look. Chihana left Malawi for Kenya as a young man after a run in with the President for Life Dr. H. Banda. After Kenya he moved on to Europe to further his academic career while still maintaining a foot in international trade union politics. Chihana knew how to please whichever trade union organization that supported him.

Prior to Cannon's arrival in Maseru, Chihana ran afoul of the Botswana government and could not get there permission to formally open a SATUCC office. Despite the lobbying efforts of the international trade union movement, the Botswana government basically declared Chihana persona non grata. The only country in the Southern Africa region willing to accept the SATUCC office and Chihana was Lesotho.

Chihana rented a postal box in SATUCC's name and moved to Lesotho shortly after Cannon's arrival. The Vic Hotel became his residence as well as his office. As was the case with Simon Jonathan, SATUCC received an annual grant from the AALC. The Cannon/Chihana relationship would eventually travel the same road as the Cannon/Jonathan one.

Many trade union visitors found their way to Maseru. Some came to attend education seminars sponsored by SATUCC. Some came to attend education seminars sponsored by the AALC. Some came as resource personnel for seminars put on for black South African trade unionists. Cannon was the treasury for the seminars, the logistician, facilities coordinator, and the bank for participating trade union brothers and sisters. Cannon also acted as host and confidant for those needing a respite from their respective countries.

One visitor comes to mind, Fred Chiluba. Fred pitched up periodically in Maseru to get away from Lusaka. Fred was not tall. He had a slight build. In spite of these physical dimensions, Fred was a trade union heavy weight-both in Zambia and internationally. Fred's backing and support on issues carried lots of weight among his fellow trade unionists. When Cannon first met him in Nairobi, he was also known to hoist a drink or two. On a trip to the US, funded by AALC, Fred found religion. His days of partying became a thing of the past, he had found Jesus.

Fred was a thorn in the side of the Zambian President Kaunda. Fred held two key posts in Zambia-President of the Mineworkers Union and Member of Parliament. He was perceived by President Kaunda as a threat to Zambia's one-party system led by Kaunda.

If free and fair national elections were ever held and opened to all candidates, Fred could challenge for the Presidency. Fred used his friendship with Chihana to get himself invitations to Maseru. AALC paid for the visits directly or indirectly. Money was either given directly to Fred or given to Chihana to pass on to Fred.

Cannon arranged for a suite of rooms for Fred in a quiet wing attached to the Victoria Hotel. Ironically, the wing was adjacent to the same office block where Cannon had worked as then CRS director in the late 1960's. Fred loved Kari's cooking and was a frequent dinner guest in the Cannon's home.

Fred's kids were named after famous persons regardless of their political bent. One son was named after Fidel Castro. Fred spoke in glowing terms of his family and his wife who gave him a very sizable family. Fred was constantly seeking to improve his knowledge. His reading was a key part of his self-education and his economic books were an essential part of his traveling baggage. When Fred wanted to hold a serious discussion, he asked Cannon to go for a drive in the Lesotho countryside. It was on one of these rides, that Cannon came to realize that Fred held ambitions to become the President of Zambia. Yes he was a threat to President Kaunda.

Cannon wondered what Fred Chiluba's policy towards the trade union movement would be if and when he became the President of Zambia? His government would most likely keep in place the past policies and procedures of his predecessor both internally and towards visiting trade unionist.

Years later, Fred's dream came true when he was elected President of Zambia. His regime wasn't much better than his predecessor. Unfortunately Fred left office under a dark cloud of corruption after his attempt to change the constitution so he could run for another term failed.

During the many seminars held jointly with SATUCC, Cannon frequently came into conflict with Chihana. The conflicting issue was invariably about money. Chihana had at least two families he had to support in Malawi. His original wife and family were located in his birth village in northern Malawi. His second wife and family were located in Lilongwe the Malawian capital. Chihana's salary as the General Secretary of SATUCC was far from what was needed to support two families.

It was only natural that Chihana supplement his salary via the seminar route. If he didn't, that would indicate he wasn't that bright. Chihana was bright. He later returned to Malawi and went into Malawian politics much to the chagrin of the late President-for-Life Hastings Banda. Chihana was instrumental in the demise and eventual removal from office of Hastings Banda. Chihana eventually became Vice President in a free and fair national election after Banda's fall.

Being the treasurer and banker for trade union seminars was a real pain in the arse. The issue of per diem was always a thorn in one's side. The participants wanted more than was payable under US guidelines. They often found fault with the meals provided by the Victoria Hotel. They were unhappy that no funds were made available to cover their social external expenses, such as liquor and women. Often the last thing of interest and importance ended up being the respective seminar itself. Conversely, these seminars were a dream comes true for any trade union politician.

Deals were made, broken and re-made. Some even came to fruition at a later time. One of the key deal making areas pertained to SATUCC elections. Various slates were conceived only later to be re-conceived. Those elected to SATUCC positions were afforded opportunities for international travel with per diems, etc. as well as prestige within one's country.

If being the trade union banker in Maseru was a pain, being host for visiting trade unionists from the USA, Europe or Israel was even worse. Cannon had plenty of experience hosting visiting trade union officials when he was residing in Nairobi. Kenya was a nice place to visit, especially if it was during wintertime in North America. Lesotho was different. The trade union visitors really wanted to be in South Africa where the "action" was, not in Lesotho.

Many of the visitors were competent trade union officers but novices in the international trade union milieu. It didn't take an African trade unionist more than a few minutes to judge whether the visitors could be conned, especially if they were white. Cannon spent a lot of time trying to educate the visitors about what they would be facing in holding their forthcoming seminar. Sometimes they listened to Cannon, sometimes they did not.

If the visitors were black, they often dwelled on the relationship between the trade union movement and the civil rights movement in the US. However Cannon would try his best, without insulting the visitors, to inform them the situation within South Africa was totally different. Most South African trade union leaders had lots of respect for Dr. King, but they were adamantly opposed to his philosophy of non-violence.

They often said blacks in the US were a minority. Hence it was wise of them to form alliances in their battle to gain denied rights and follow a non-violent philosophy. Others were more impressed by the late Malcolm X's views. In South Africa, blacks and other non-whites were a majority being oppressed by a small minority of whites. The South African whites were not about to forgo power to a non-violent movement. Black trade union members believed their movement against apartheid would only succeed if they used violence along with other means, such as, international boycotts of the apartheid regime.

Despite the aforementioned, the issue of the civil rights struggle would be a focus throughout the seminar. If the visitors were black Americans, their philosophy was forgiven and the seminar participants treated them as brothers. If they were white, the participants so be it often fell asleep during their presentations or did not bother to attend. Regardless the seminar attendees would go back to South Africa well fed, rested and with some money to further their struggle against the apartheid regime. The visitors would return to the USA feeling good about themselves only to continue with their respective work which had little if any significant daily bearing on South Africa. Their parting words to Cannon were: "Brother call me when you get to DC the next time." Cannon seldom heard from the visitors again even a few of those he did bother to call when in DC.

The American trade union movement had a very long and strong relationship with Histadrut, the Israel Trade Union Federation. The relationship existed long before the US trade union movement established organs to work internationally. When Cannon worked with AALFI, both bodies did joint-programs which were usually funded by the Americans. Cannon hosted Histadrut visitors in Nairobi, but didn't work on any joint projects or seminars with them. This changed in Lesotho where Histadrut representatives were sometimes seminar presenters.

Many black South African trade unionists were well aware of their fellow countrymen of Jewish origin who were very active in the struggle against the apartheid regime. One name comes to mind- Joe Slovo who died and was given a hero's burial in 1995. There were others who were also very active in their support of the ANC and the SACP in the struggle against the apartheid regime. The state of Israel itself was another issue.

The anti-apartheid struggle received unabridged support from the Palestine people and their liberation organizations. Histadrut was a bona fide trade union federation in its country. Unfortunately it was the country's treatment of the Palestine people that didn't wash too well with black South African trade union people. Cannon understood the Histadrut/AFL-CIO relationship but he didn't understand what benefit this relationship could have in South Africa.

Many seminars throughout the years were conducted in a manner to achieve the political goals of the sponsors. Trade union issues covered in these seminars may have also benefited the attendees from South Africa and Lesotho. If so, that was icing on the cake. Cannon usually didn't wish a seminar to be over before it even started but the one with Histadrut was different. Fears of major ideological conflict never materialized due to the civility of the attendees. Cannon was never given any feedback from AALC/W as to how Histadrut evaluated the seminar.

Getting out of Lesotho to hold seminars in Botswana, Swaziland, Zimbabwe and Malawi offered Cannon a welcomed break from the confines of little Maseru. The majority of these seminars were held jointly with SATUCC. Sometimes funds had to be wired to cover travel costs but mostly the attendees would be reimbursed for their travel costs upon the presentation of airline ticket stubs or proof of other means of travel. Host country participants would get funds based upon the distances they traveled if they weren't able to provide bus receipts. The hotel in which the seminar would take place offered a discount rate for rooms and meals. Multimedia equipment would be rented locally if not provided by the hotel. Seminar topics tried focusing on immediate trade union issues facing the brothers and sisters in South Africa. Occupational Safety and Health at the workplace was one of the more popular topics. Lecturers would be secured from within the host country as well as staff from SATUCC and the AALC. Cannon tried to avoid being the direct paymaster since he wasn't 100% sure what local politics were brewing within the host country's trade union movement. Chihana would handle all direct payments to participants.

It was a given that each seminar would have a representative from the host country security forces in attendance. It wasn't uncommon for security services to have trade union people on their payrolls. Throughout Africa, most governments felt threatened by trade unions; hence either the police or security service watched them closely. In some countries, the security services identified themselves to Cannon. In others, they were a bit more discrete. Either way seminars drew there attention.

The Zimbabwe liberation movements during the struggle years in the 1960's and 1970 sent members overseas for training. Some returnees would become the eyes and ears of the Zimbabwe Central Intelligence Organization (CIO) the security service of the country. This body monitored the trade union movement as well as all international trade union visitors to Zimbabwe.

In the early 1980's, Zimbabwe was the darling of most western international trade union organizations as well as the Southern Africa trade union movement. Many trade union conferences and seminars were booked for Harare, the newly renamed capital, which had first world amenities. Shortly after Independence, the AALC opened an office in Zimbabwe.

An old AALC hand, Charlie Taylor wanted to be the first AALC resident representative. Taylor was married to a woman from Swaziland. She was very active in the anti-apartheid struggle. He had been with AALC since its early days and had paid his dues. His last post was in Kampala, Uganda when it was just liberated from the clutches of Idi Amin. But for reasons only known to the AALC Executive Director, an international novice was recruited and given the plum assignment much to the chagrin of Taylor.

Cannon was instructed to attend an ICFTU sponsored conference in Harare to meet with South Africans from NACTU and COSATU who were guest participants. Unbeknownst to Cannon, the AALC Executive Director sent an African-American from headquarters to attend as well.

The visitors were joined by the AALC representative for Zimbabwe at the conference.

In addition to other foreign guests, three Americans were too many for the trade union dedicated unit of the security services to monitor. Their unit, was part of the CIO, and consisted of five members, more than adequate to oversee the internally trade union movement and monitor the occasional overseas visitor under normal circumstances.

A meeting was held in the AALC Zimbabwe office with CIO representatives at which Cannon was told he had to leave the country since he was the last AALC representative to enter the country. The CIO joked this was only following the trade union principle: last in first out. This was the first and only time in Cannon's career where security services were so openly honest about their monitoring of trade unions especially foreigners from the US.

It was always great to get away from Lesotho and terrific to return home to one's family. In retrospect, this was during the time in which the Cannon marriage was beginning to unravel. Whether work played a part in the unraveling is open to question?

One has plenty of time for reflection living in Africa if one is willing to accept Africa as one's present home instead of an assignment. Fortunately for Cannon, he had accepted life overseas long before coming to Africa in 1969. An interesting observation, which has never been answered, is what role did being an only child play in Cannon's acceptance of life outside of the US of A? One thing is certain, you learned quickly to makes friends as a replacement for the lack of siblings.

It was gradually dawning on Cannon that his work was raising more questions than providing answers. Periodically, the AALC office in Washington would telephone Maseru to give Cannon some instructions that needed implementation immediately. During these infrequent conversations, Cannon started to feel Washington didn't comprehend what was actually taking place in Southern Africa. It seemed there view of South Africa was more important than what was actually occurring with folks fighting apartheid in Southern Africa. It was like the folks in Washington had a certain mindset and Africa was fitted in as opposed to fitting Washington's goals and objectives to the reality of Africa.

If one's mind set only focused on the geo-political scene between the East and the West, then Washington's mind set was understandable. It wasn't understandable if Washington's view was they were assisting in the development of trade union movements in Africa. Influence was a far cry from development.

The role of money, anywhere in the world, is a key ingredient towards the promotion of development and seeking influence. It was a key especially between the haves of the West and basically have-nots found in Africa. To think that assisting developing countries is purely for humanitarian reasons is better left to dreamers, which Cannon was as a Peace Corps volunteer. Any form of aid, from one country to another, has the quandary of "donor" and "recipient" regardless of the words used, such as partners, shareholders, etc. This makes for an awkward relationship regardless.

Cannon continued to evaluate what was actually taking place in the tasks that were a part of his job description. All too often, the people in Washington wouldn't bother to inform the field staff how the voting went in the international forums in which the West and East were confronting each other. How could one know if those one was working with were being influenced, and voted the West way, if one didn't get feedback?

The money being made available through AALC was not making too much difference in the internal development of the various trade union federations and their respective affiliated unions. All one needed to do was look at their growth numbers. Little if any international money and time were being devoted to the services being provided to their members. This might be understandable and acceptable in South Africa, where the union movement was the only open and active internal countrywide body threatening the apartheid regime.

When Cannon would visit local trade union headquarters it became obvious that the external material requirements indicating member development were absent. Some national centers didn't have more than two chairs in their main office for visitors never mind computers, and other signs of a truly national functional organization.

Many headquarters also lacked office equipment unless it was donated from an international donor. If they were providing services to their members, one would assume they would have file cabinets to keep copies of correspondence; etc. Most did not have their own means of transport. If one was realistic, one knew most industries in their countries didn't have collective bargaining agreements. Those who were able to have a regular monthly source of income were frequently dependent on factors outside of normal trade union actions.

Most African governments, whether elected or not, were aware of the role trade unions played in their independence struggles. Consciously, they feared trade unions. They knew first hand of the unions' power to overcome ethnic, tribal and religious differences. In some countries, the National Government enacted trade union legislation, which allowed them a direct or indirect role, in the affairs of trade unions. One piece of legislation was the legal wherewithal for trade unions to collect money from their members.

A carrot thrown to the trade unions: automatic monthly dues/subscription deductions by employers who then forwarded said sums to the respective union and a percentage to the national center. This usually applied to industries with over a stipulated number of workers who had opted to join trade unions, regardless of the existence of a collective bargaining agreement or not. The governments' ability to withdraw or amend legislation for automatic dues or subscriptions payments was held over the union's heads, to try to keep them passive.

Compounding the aforementioned difficulties, most African countries in sub-Sahara Africa didn't have many industries or employers who offered the potential for trade unionization. If such industries and employers did exist, they were almost exclusively located in the capital. It was easier to unionize workers in densely populated capitals, as opposed to an industry located in a sparsely populated rural area.

It was a dream to think that trade unions would develop, especially like those in the US. If one wants to be more cynical, there was never much of a real chance for the actual development of many trade unions except in the public sector. Governments throughout Africa in the 1970's and 1980's were frequently the biggest employer in their respective countries. Two sources of potential trade union members in Africa were civil servants and teachers. Civil servants did not play a role in the development of unions in the United States until after unions were developed in the private sector unlike in many countries in Africa.

If the development of trade unions, as organs, to uplift the welfare of their members wasn't actually being met, why then were the people in Washington always harping about development? A country program would be written annually, in which goals and objectives would be specified to assess accomplishment, if this was actually the case. The wherewithal to achieve these goals and objectives was through seminars and workshops. They were to enhance the upgrading of the host national center.

At the end of the day, one could report that so many workshops/seminars were held for so many trade union members. Receipts which accompanied same proved these activities were held. AALC and USAID seemed to be OK with the process. If Cannon questioned whether paying the salary of Jonathan and Chihana was in fact developing the trade union movement, especially if their salary had been paid for years, he was viewed as not being a team player.

Trying to win friends and influence people has been going on since man first inhabited this earth. It is still going on. What is different is how one tries to influence another outside of your home country. A favorite of AALC was to give trips to selected trade union leaders to the AFL-CIO convention held every four years. These were called educational visits but often were just rewards for being good supporters of the AFL-CIO position at the annual ILO meeting in Geneva.

The AALC field staff did not usually attend the AFL-CIO conventions since they were held in US cities. The field staff had their annual staff conferences in African countries. 1988 was an exception. The AFL-CIO convention coincided with the 25th anniversary of AALC. The staff conference was held at the same time the AFL-CIO convention was being held in Washington, DC.. Among the high profile guests to the convention were President George Bush, Lech Walesa hero of the Polish Solidarity trade union movement, and P. Camay of NACTU from South Africa. Other guests included trade union leaders from South American and Asia. A select group of trade union guests were given about 15 minutes to address the AFL-CIO convention delegates.

Cannon didn't really know Camy well enough since he wasn't allowed inside of South Africa. His contacts were limited to the one Camy visit to Maseru, a couple of international conferences and telephone conversations. The Washington visit gave Cannon and Camy the opportunity to get better acquainted in a less stressful environment. Both were developing respect for each other professionally and getting along well socially until Cannon was asked by AALC Washington staffers to see the draft of the speech he had written for Camy to deliver to the Convention.

Cannon replied he didn't write Camy's speech and couldn't think why anyone would think he would write said speech. To do it, would have been a grievous insult to Camy and all South Africans. Cannon was told that the other AFL-CIO overseas representatives who had visiting guests addressing the convention had drafted the speeches for their guests. Cannon was informed he was not acting as a team player. Cannon later told Camy what happened and both had a good laugh over dinner.

Did the bureaucrats heading up the overseas organs of the AFL-CIO really believe in the basic human right of Freedom of Expression? It was obvious that these individuals were more concerned with their own positions of authority and power than in their acceptance of the brief remarks trade union brothers from the developing world would publically make. Many of the US delegates to the convention were not that interested in overseas affairs and didn't pay too much attention to what they guests had to say, especially since some had to speak through interpreters. The control of speeches insured there would be no unpleasant words spoken. Later, Cannon wondered if disdain towards the visitors would have a more appropriate reason for speech control.

Cannon disillusion with his work grew by leaps and bounds after what happened at the convention. He still was a firm believers in what the AFL-CIO stood for overseas, but he was seeing the AALC leadership had their own interpretation which at times seemed to conflict with the overall AFL-CIO's policy. The AFL-CIO policy on South Africa never waived. It always stood strongly opposed to the apartheid regime in South Africa.

The two major black trade union centers in South Africa, COSATU and NACTU had major qualms with the AALC but not so much with the AFL-CIO, especially COSATU. Many of the leaders in COSATU and some of its main affiliated unions, such as the Mineworkers, were of the belief that the AALC was associated with the CIA in one form or another. NACTU didn't voice their concerns as openly as COSATU did maybe because it needed AALC assistance more than COSATU did.

When the convention was over, Cannon returned to Maseru. His main task still was to support the black trade union movement inside of South Africa, yet he still couldn't travel to the country. As time went on, he became more involved in the affairs of the Lesotho trade union movement and SATUCC.

Workers from Lesotho had a long history in working in the South African mines. Legend had it they were the only Southern African tribe willing to work at the deep depths of the coal and gold mines. These fearless workers were also very instrumental in the establishment of the powerful Mineworkers Union in South Africa.

In 1988, the Mineworkers went on strike in South Africa. The apartheid regime expelled some of the union's leadership from South Africa in hopes of breaking the strike. Three of these leaders returned home to Lesotho. Cannon soon met them while they were paying a social call on the Deputy

Chief of Mission in the US Embassy in Maseru. Cannon set up a follow up meeting at his house/office. The discussions focused on the strike in South Africa and what were the options for these union guys back home in Lesotho?

The infrastructure for Lesotho Highlands Water Project (LHWP) had recently started with road construction. Once the infrastructure was completed, a massive dam and tunnel phase was to follow. This was a golden opportunity to organize a Construction Workers Union in Lesotho! Previously Cannon tried and tried to get Simon Jonathan to establish a Construction Workers Union but to no avail.

The returnees saw their return as a golden opportunity to use their trade union skills acquired in South Africa at home. This would also afford them the opportunity to ensure their Basotho brethren would be treated as proper workers in this massive construction project unlike the Bible used by some white South Africans which made reference to blacks as hues and carriers of water only. Cannon started to devote more time towards the establishment of the Construction Workers Union in Lesotho (CAWULE). He was able to assist the founders in drafting a union constitution. He also served as the union's interlocutor with the Lesotho Department of Labor, which was very suspicious of the militancy of the Mineworkers Union in South Africa. As progress developed with the Construction union, Cannon became more and more estranged from Brother Simon Jonathan.

Likewise differences of opinion were also becoming wider between Cannon and Brother Chihana of SATUCC as well. Cannon was questioning the lack of trade union tasks being undertaken by Chihana. He couldn't see why US money, obtained via USAID, and US workers dues money, obtained from the AFL-CIO, should be used to pay for Chihana's travels, his hotel expenses, his entertainment expenses, and his salary plus per diems when the regions trade union centers were not progressing.

A seminar, funded by the AALC, was scheduled for SATUCC and NACTU in Mbabane, Swaziland. Cannon broke his ankle jogging a few weeks prior to the seminar and was in a cast. He founded it difficult to get about but he was still required to attend the seminar since AALC was funding it. Little if any trade union work was done at the seminar. Chihana used the venue to campaign for his re-election as the SATUCC General Secretary. It seemed the entire (4) days and nights were spent arguing over money.

While in Swaziland, Cannon was able to track down his former colleague Charlie Taylor. Charlie regaled Cannon with stories of things that AALC did before Cannon came on the scene in 1979. From Charlie's stories, it was obvious that he was one of the first American overseas representatives hired by AALC. As such he never should have been passed over for the Zimbabwe post. If AALC treated Charlie this way, what was in store for Cannon now that he was upsetting things by questioning what SATUCC and the other "brothers" were doing with US funds?

Swaziland always struck Cannon as a tiny little place in which the people were laid back as opposed to Lesotho where the people were super active. The Cannon's had 1st visited back in 1987, soon after coming from Kenya, to look at a famous multi-racial boarding high school thinking their elder daughter Chandra might like it. She didn't, but the Cannon's found three excellent little restaurants, which offered great food and ambiance.

Swaziland wasn't completely surrounded by South Africa like Lesotho; hence, it had a more relaxed feeling. There was a couple of decent small hotels in Mbabane and another in Manzini. The two places were about 100 miles apart in a valley. Additionally, there were two tiny game parks, which allowed one to enjoy nature in pleasant small lodges with quaint surroundings. Swaziland also had two gambling casinos and a few small curio shops: one being a glass blowing operation. It just seemed more prosperous than Lesotho.

When Cannon returned to Maseru from the seminar, he found the family situation had changed. His son had gone away to a well-respected boarding school in the United States the previous year. The school was located in the State of Rhode Island where Cannon grew up and was operated by religious. Cannon went to the US to see how Marc was doing. After talking with Marc it was decided he best return to Lesotho and Machabeng High School after the school year was over.

When Cannon returned to Lesotho, he found his wife didn't think Marc's academic shortcomings were his fault but Cannon's fault. Cannon placed too much pressure on Marc. This should have been a wake -up call that the marriage was floundering. Cannon was too involved in the politics of trade unions and not involved enough in family affairs. Little did Cannon know that his dedication to his work would eventually see him get the sack from AALC right around the time that his marriage was breaking? A double barrel whammy!

Out of the blue, when Cannon was jogging, he bumped into an old friend; Jonathan Jenness who he knew from his first stint in Lesotho in the 1960's back then Jonathan was affiliated with the United Nations. This time he was coming to work with the Lesotho Highlands Water Project (LHWP). Shortly after this coincidental meeting, Jonathan showed up on the Cannons house steps. He had just been released from a car- jacking which was quite common in Lesotho and South Africa at the time

After calming his nerves, he and Cannon started calling old mutual well-connected Basotho friends to see whether they could expedite the police to get the car back. These were times when the Lesotho police often lacked available transport, hence the need to call upon well connect Basotho friends. The car was eventually found just outside of Maseru.

While Jonathan was taking up his new duties with the Lesotho Highlands Development Authority (LHDA) under the leadership of his old buddy Ntate Sole, Cannon was working with a private company to undertake a manpower survey of potential blue collar personnel that might possess sufficient skills to get employment on the forthcoming LHWP dam and tunnel phases of the project. One weekend Jonathan set-up a meeting with Sole for him to pick Cannon's brains regarding workers and trade unions. Little did Cannon know this meeting would result in another change of direction in his life!

The visit of the President of the AFL-CIO to South Africa in 1986 marked the start of other visits by US based trade unionists. This should have alerted Cannon that something wasn't what it seemed to be. How was it that they could get into South Africa when Cannon couldn't, despite repeated visa applications which were always rejected?

One of the benefits of living in a small capital city of a country in Africa was the access to a wide variety of persons one normally wouldn't get an opportunity to meet. Mrs. Cannon befriended an American woman who ran the only European-style gift shop in Maseru. Priscilla was married to a Danish businessman. Like the Cannons, this was their 2nd sojourn in Maseru. One day, while in the gift shop, Mrs. Cannon was introduced to the USSR Ambassador, Boris Assorian.

One might ask why the USSR had an embassy in Lesotho. It was because all permanent members of the United Nations Executive had diplomatic representation in Maseru. They all used Lesotho as a listening post for what was taking place in South Africa. This was especially true for the USSR, which didn't have diplomatic relations with South Africa. In the late 1970's, the Lesotho government led by Leabua Jonathan switched sides- going from being a supporter of the West to becoming a supporter of the East. South Africa was the main backer of the Jonathan coup back in 1969. By the late 1970's, Jonathan had established diplomatic relations with eastern bloc countries. He feared the South African government would support a coup against him because of this. To try to buy some insurance against that possibility, Jonathan established diplomatic relations with the USSR, which quickly opened an embassy in Maseru.

Cannon was well aware of the USSR's policy towards trade unions. What came as a surprise was finding out Embassy personnel had befriended his colleague Simon Jonathan. It wasn't too long thereafter those representatives of Simon's federation were enjoying the perks of this relationship such as overseas trips.

USSR Ambassador Assorian was a frequent visitor to the gift shop. His English was first class from his days as a TASS reporter in various African countries Cannon learned later. He didn't have his family with him in Maseru. Some said that keeping his family back in the USSR ensured he wouldn't defect to the West. He resided in a nice old colonial type home in the more affluent section called Maseru West.

The Christensen's and the Cannons were invited for dinner to Boris's house. Cannon was caught in a quandary. What to do? Cannon sought out his jogging buddy for his advice. The buddy suggested Cannon accept the invitation to see what might come out of it. Boris served lots of Georgian wine and even more vodka with each course of food throughout the evening. All that came out of the evening was a great hangover. Cannon's jogging buddy said that was to be expected as he knew from his past dealings with Russians. Should the Cannon's get invited back, he should let him know. This never happened.

At the 1988 AFL-CIO convention and the AALC staff conference, Cannon was informed he was to be transferred out of Lesotho. Egypt and Nigeria were mentioned as possibilities. Another shocker was Brother Nigeria Camy, announced he was planning to resign as Secretary General of NACTU on the 31st of December 1989. His administrative team, who had been with him for years, would also be resigning. This AFL-CIO convention served as another step in Cannon's process in seeing Africa through different lens as previously noted. Just what were international organizations actually doing in Africa besides promoting their own agenda's?

1990 started with lots of rumors of would be major political changes in South Africa. This wasn't the first time that rumors of this nature circulated in Lesotho. South Africa was slowly beginning to discombobulate. The internal anti-apartheid movement along with the black trade union movement was making the country ungovernable by the white minority.

On the 2nd of February 1990, the South African government finally released Nelson Mandela from jail. The government also rescinded the outlawing of the ANC, the PAC and the SACP. The Cannons back in 1969 didn't think this day would occur during their lifetime. At last, true promise for the future of South Africa!

On the 8th of May 1990, a letter dated the 4th, was delivered to Cannon informing him that AALC was closing the Maseru office and that he was to become redundant in August. He was instructed by Washington to depart Maseru in July, which he did on July 6th. He left behind Mrs. Cannon and his son so he could finish high school with kids he knew.

Whether or not this decision to close the office was a by-product of Cannon's refusal to obtain Camy's speech prior to delivery at the AFL-CIO convention or for other issues was never made know to Cannon.

One of the last tasks Cannon had to accomplish before departing Lesotho was to turn the AALC office vehicle to Chihana. Shortly thereafter, Chihana returned to Malawi to challenge President-for-Life Banda in an election: a very courageous undertaking. Unfortunately, Chihana lost his quest for the Presidency, unlike our mutual friend from Zambia Frederick Chiluba. Chihana however did occupy the post of Vice President of Malawi for a brief time before his passing.

Cannon reported to the AALC office in Washington on the 16th of July 1990 as instructed. He believed he would have ample time to secure another trade union assignment upon the completion of his work with AALC. Throughout the years in Africa, the Cannons hosted many, many visiting US trade union senior officers and staffers. All of them always ended up their stay with "Whenever you are in Washington, DC look me up".

Foolishly Cannon took them up on their offer only to learn that if you are not still an active trade union player then nothing can be done for you. Basically Cannon was told-"good luck but there isn't anything I can do to help you". The 14th of August 1990 was Cannon's last day of work with AALC.

While Cannon was in Washington, he wasn't aware the Lesotho Highlands Development Authority (LHDA) had submitted a request for funds to USAID/Lesotho to conduct an industrial relations study on their infrastructure road building contracts. This was to take place before construction would begin on the dam and tunnel aspects of the LHWP Phase I project activities.

The LHWP proposed Phase I major items to be constructed were: 1) Katse Dam- 185m high and 710m long, 2) Excavation of 46 km of about 5m diameter of underground tunnels, and 3) Muela hydroelectric power station. There were to be 9 separate work sites. Over 4,000 persons were to be employed. This was a massive project whose goal was to supply water to South Africa's industrial powerhouses in the Pretoria-Witwatersrand-Vereeniging (PWV) area.

USAID contracted with a private US based consulting firm to undertake the study. Management Systems International (MSI) who's President had worked with in Lesotho as a Peace Corps Volunteer. While in Lesotho, L. Cooley worked together with Ntate Sole in the Lesotho Planning Office. Cannon was selected and approved to do the study. He arrived back in Maseru on the 30th of August 1990.

1990 LESOTHO CONSULTANCY

It was strange arriving back in Maseru some seven weeks after leaving. Mrs. Cannon had secured a job with a Norwegian consulting firm which was involved in small construction projects outside of Maseru. She was able to rent a townhouse next to her boss. This change afforded her the opportunity to re-connect with her Norwegian heritage that had been subsumed, especially after Mrs. Cannon was sworn-in as an American a few years previously. Cannon wasn't aware of it at the time, but this new occurrence would be the final step towards the end of their marriage.

It was easy for Cannon to commence with the one-person industrial relations study since many individuals involved in the LHWP infrastructure roads project were previously known to Cannon. It was easy to set-up meetings with the Ministry of Labor officials; the LHDA officials; the trade union officials; and the Association of Lesotho Employers. The easiest was CAWULE who knew Cannon well from his trade union years.

The major contractors who were responsible for the infrastructure construction were foreign based. One operated out of France and the other out of South Africa. Getting access to data from these two firms wasn't easy. After Cannon secured an introduction from his old friend Labor Commissioner Fanana, things became much easier. The fact that the two contractors had different wage systems: one for Basotho hire and the other for those hired from South Africa was a major issue. This along with complaints of discrimination by South Africans resulted in numerous work stoppages.

About halfway through the study, LHDA announced it would open negotiations with the tender winners for the construction of the Katse Dam initially and later the Tunnels. Cannon was approached by his friend Jonathan Jenness who told him that LHDA's Chief Executive Ntate Sole wanted to see him. At the meeting, Cannon was asked whether he could be a part of the LHDA negotiating team, as its expert in industrial relations.

Cannon contacted USAID Lesotho and MSI Washington who were told of the LHDA offer. MSI said it would need a separate contact for Cannon to be affiliated with LHDA. USAID Lesotho wasn't opposed to a second contract as long as its original contract with MSI stayed within its time frame for completion of the study. Cannon was thrilled with this additional assignment.

On the 1st of October 1990, MSI and LHDA entered into a contract allowing Cannon to join LHDA's negotiating team. The team leader was a very experienced Canadian engineer from the Canadian consulting firm (ACRES) hired by LHDA to oversee the forthcoming negotiations and the construction projects thereafter.

The tender specifications for Phase I contracts of the Lesotho Highlands Water Project (LHWP) were derived from the "bible" of civil engineering construction- Federation Internationale Des Ingenieurs-Conseils (FIDIC). FIDIC standards make mention of the laws of the country in which the civil engineering construction project was to take place.

The Katse dam, FIDIC based, tender specifications served as the foundation for all negotiations. What were to be negotiated were the responses of the winning construction consortium to the pages and pages of engineering construction specifications. The specifications' responses of the contractor consortium made reference to existing Lesotho legislation relative to wages and other industrial relations matters.

Labor laws in countries such as Lesotho were usually out dated carry overs from colonial days. The stipulated minimum wage for unskilled labor was approximately US $ 92 per month very low in comparison with developed countries. Frequently these minimum wage laws became the maximum wage for everyone except a few highly skilled workers. Work place safety, if covered by the Labor Law, was basic. Labor law payments for death or disabling injury were usually minimal. It was cheaper to pay for deaths on the job or disabling injuries on the job according to law stipulations, than to establish employer comprehensive work place safety and health standards.

Departments of Labor, in developing countries, looked terrific on paper modeled after their former western colonial country. What didn't show on paper, was their ability to enforce the labor laws. In many cases, the officials who were poorly paid became susceptible to bribes. Frequently they lacked needed transportation to visit work sites forcing them to rely on erratic public transport. They were often not trained in workplace health and safety issues. Until the aforementioned labor laws are changed according to international norms and standards, Cannon believed labor issues need to be dealt with in tender specifications the same as FIDIC deals with materials to be used in construction process.

Representatives of the South African government were the overseers of the negotiations. They were the paymasters for the project and were joined by representatives of the Lesotho government who were the potential sellers of the project water needed to generate electricity in South Africa. These two bodies had very opposite views and tasks in the negotiations and subsequent project. The South Africans' job was to get Lesotho's water as cheap as possible: the Basotho's job was to try to get the best deal possible.

The majority of the negotiators and overseers where white folks with terrific international engineering experiences, but had little prior experience living and working in Lesotho. The exception was the LHDA Environment Division. Cannon's old friend Jenness was a part of the Environment's division negotiators. This friendship with Jenness made it easier for Cannon to gain immediate credibility with Basotho who had not previously worked with him.

The construction contractor consortium for the Katse dam was the Highlands Water Venture led by Impregilo (Italy) with Bouygues (France), Hochtief (Germany), Stirling (UK), Concor (South Africa) and Group 5 (South Africa).

The design and supervision engineer for the Katse dam was Lesotho Highlands Consultants with a South African group HWDC made up from Ninham Shand, WLPU, Keeve Steyn, MJ Mountain, SRK and VKE. The foreign component was made up from SOGRAECH (France), Coyne & Bellier (France), and Sir Alexander Gibb & Partners (UK).

Prior to the opening of dam negotiations, Cannon and Jenness were told by the LHDA Chief Executive to make sure Basotho workers would get a decent deal regarding wages and other industrial relations issues and to negotiate strongly on these with the Dam contractor.

Throughout Cannon's Africa career, international multinationals used the prevailing minimum wage in an African country as their maximum wage. They informed workers they were being paid according to standards established by their governments. If they wanted more money, the workers should get their government to increase the minimum wage. All too often, indigenous trade unions were too weak to negotiate collective bargaining agreements for wages above the minimum.

The Highlands Water Venture construction consortium that won the tender to build Katse dam was led by the well experienced Italian dam building company Impregilo. Its responses relative to tender specification for personnel, wages and other associated industrial relations points were based upon the prevailing legislation of Lesotho.

Unfortunately, the prevailing Lesotho legislation was not relevant to a massive first world construction project. Frequent strikes on the infrastructure road projects revolved around the poor wages (Lesotho minimum wage) being paid to Basotho workers. If the Katse dam was to be built on time, Basotho workers needed higher wages than the prevailing Lesotho monthly minimum wage of approximately US $ 92 for unskilled construction work.

Negotiations were conducted in a large spacious room in one of the local hotels in Maseru. The main negotiators for LHDA, HWV and the supervising engineers were allocated seats around the oval table. Supporting staff were seated behind their employer. Business suits were the preferred attire. Sessions were conducted twice a day broken by coffee breaks and lunch.

When the issue of industrial relations came up for negotiations, Cannon was the LHDA spokesperson. Previously Cannon sat away from the table alongside Jenness. If either wanted to make a point, it was written on a piece of paper and passed to the Chief of the Environment Division. The HWV participants and the supervising engineer negotiators had no idea of Cannon's background. He was called to a seat at the oval table by the LHDA Environment Division Chief.

The study of the infrastructure road contractors by Cannon, unbeknown to the HWV negotiators, showed the use of the prevailing Lesotho minimum wage resulted in numerous work stoppages which were to be avoided if at all possible at the Katse dam. It became obvious that the contractors' plans to employ Basotho and what they planned to pay them was not acceptable to the LHDA team, mainly as the result of Cannon's negotiating interventions.

Throughout the dam negotiations, the Contractor's negotiating team consisted of only two persons: the lead negotiator and the man who would become the Project Manager on the construction site. Cannon had the opportunity to watch, and at times lock horns with, the best negotiator he had ever crossed paths with: a true professional.

A compromise was eventually reached in which a contractual minimum wage and overtime pay would be established, well above the prevailing Lesotho minimum wage. It was also agreed that the contractor would reduce the number of semi-skilled South Africans they planned to hire as well as other related industrial relation issues. All of these issues and some related to occupational safety and health were to be covered in a Contractual Memorandum of Understanding (MOU). This would take precedence over prior tender specifications and original tender responses. Cannon drafted the LHDA language for the MOU which was later negotiated until all parties agreed on the wording in the MOU. One of the MOU's provisions was that any South Africans hired would be required to have Lesotho work permits before commencing work. Later, it was learned that for each strike day lost, the Italian dam contractor would submit a claim for more than US $ 1 million as the cost for missing one day's production. At the end of the dam negotiations, the Basotho participants told Cannon they were pleased with his performance and his unwillingness to back down in supporting decent provisions for Basotho workers.

Mrs. Cannon was invited to visit Cape Town she asked that Cannon accompany her while the dam negotiations were on-going. Cannon explained that he was unable because the LHDA negotiations were very important and who knows, they might eventually lead into a job at a later date. Mrs. Cannon didn't buy same and voiced her displeasure. She departed Maseru with their son Marc for Cape Town without Cannon. One more nail in the marriage coffin.

Within a few weeks of the completion of the dam negotiations, negotiations opened for the connecting tunnels project. The construction consortium which won the tunnels tender was Lesotho Highlands Project Contractors. It was led by Spie Batignolles (France) with LTA (South Africa), Ed Zublin (Germany) Balfour Beatty (UK) and Campenon Bernard (France).

The design and supervision engineer for the tunnels was Lesotho Highland Tunnel Partnership. It comprised LMJV with Lahmeyer (Germany) and Mott MacDonald (UK) linked to HDTC (South Africa) whose members were VKE, Ninham Shand, Keeve Steyn and SRK all from South Africa.

Two of the tunnel contractors had previously worked in Lesotho. Spie Batignolles (France) previously worked on a small construction project in Maseru. LTA (South Africa) was involved in one the infrastructure road projects. Both contractors had many industrial relations problems previously while adhering only to prevailing Lesotho labor laws, and paying only the legal required minimum wage.

Whereas there were only two dam negotiators representing the construction consortium, there were quadruple the number of whites at the table representing the construction consortium for the tunnel negotiations. Their tender responses relative to industrial relations matters were much the same as the dam contractor relative to the minimum wage, work permits, etc. When industrial relations matters came up for negotiations, the South African partners were the spokespersons for the consortium. Due to their work experiences in South Africa they were adamantly opposed to the creation of a contractual minimum wage in spite of all the points raised by Cannon.

Cannon went to see LHDA's Chief Executive during the stalemate over wages. He said LHDA will have nothing but problems if workers on the tunnels are aware that their brothers working on the dam are being paid wages well in excess of the Lesotho minimum wage. If there were to be two groups of Basotho workers on the LHWP receiving different starting wages only trouble would arise.

The issue of wages on the infrastructure roads project caused numerous strikes and work stoppages as was well known by Ntate Sole. He agreed and prevailed in getting the support of the South African government project overseers to agree that the dam and tunnels needed the exact same contractual minimum wage and matters relative workplace safety and health.

Upon the resumption of the wage issue, a negotiated compromise was reached in which the tunnel contractor agreed to the establishment of a contractual minimum wage the same as that of the dam contractor. Cannon drafted the LHDA language for the Memorandum of Understanding (MOU). Eventually what appeared in the tunnels MOU was only slightly different than that for the dam.

In December, Cannon returned to the original industrials relations study and was able to wrap it for submission by MSI to USAID within the designated time frame. Cannon spent the Christmas holidays in Maseru. It wasn't the happiest Christmas for the Cannon family. Mr. and Mrs. Cannon were drifting away from each other day-by-day. Mrs. Cannon was still upset that Cannon didn't go to Cape Town with her back in October.

Prior to Cannon's Lesotho departure, LHDA inquired whether Cannon would be available for an industrial relations position on its staff to oversee the forthcoming dam and tunnels construction projects. The inquiry was premised upon the agreement by the South African government representatives to agree to the position and the World Bank's willingness to fund the position. Cannon indicated a willingness in principle to accept a position if it was offered, subject to contractual negotiations. Cannon departed Lesotho on 3 January 1991 for Washington, DC.

While in DC, Cannon was taken into the home of a former colleague he worked with from his days with AALC. Ernie and Marietta Yancey's home was very close to the AFL-CIO George Meany Labor School in Silver Spring, Maryland. Cannon still had hopes that he could secure a position with one of the AFL-CIO affiliates.

Ernie Yancy had a very varied career. He was a US military officer before becoming injured. Later Ernie opened numerous small businesses. He was also a Peace Corps Director for Malawi. Ernie was fired by the administration of Ronald Reagan for being too liberal according to

Ernie. It was after his stint with Peace Corps that AALC hired him as a consultant. Ernie did consulting work for AALC in Uganda just after the overthrow of Idi Amin. Whenever Ernie was in Nairobi, he had stayed with the Cannons before heading back to Kampala. The LHDA contract possibility would remain as a bird in the bush until Cannon received a fax confirming same, before becoming a bird in hand.

Cannon arranged for roses to be sent to Mrs. Cannon on their wedding anniversary day the 21st of January 1991. Mrs. Cannon telephone Cannon on the 21st to inform him that their marriage was over. She wanted out and had found another man, her Norwegian next door neighbor who was also her boss at work. Cannon was shattered by the news. In retrospect, he should have seen it coming, especially after the time spent in Maseru doing the consultant work associated with LHWP. The signs of a marriage break down were there Cannon was again too involved in his work for them to hit home.

Fortunately for Cannon his friends, the Yancy's and the Davis's from their days in Kisumu, offered him strong moral support: as did the Bernardini's in Calais, Maine. Daughter Chandra at Bates College hid her feelings well. It is hard for a child to state their true feelings when their parents split. It would take a few years for the divorce to occur.

Cannon was shattered by Mrs. Cannon's telephone call. He didn't think the marriage was beyond redemption. Maybe his belief had its basis in his Catholic upbringing. Down deep Cannon dreamed he might convince Kari to give it another go, especially if he got a job with LHDA back in Maseru. This dream never came to fruition even though the LHDA job did come to fruition.

11

Too Many Cooks in the Kitchen- Lesotho Highlands Water Project

After negotiating, via faxes, LHDA and Cannon agreed to a personal services contract of employment for two years commencing on 21 February 1991. Cannon would be the LHDA industrial relations specialist. He would be reporting to the Deputy Chief Executive Wolfgang Rohrback but was told the door of the Chief Executive Ntate Sole would always be open to him. Cannon would average over 1,500 miles of driving each month in performing his duties as LHDA's industrial relation specialist and later as its workplace safety specialist covering the works sites for Katse dam and the tunnels

The entire country of Lesotho is at least one mile above sea level. It's also completely surrounded by its neighbor South Africa. In 1991, there were two main tarred roads leading out of the capital Maseru. Both were two lane highways passing either through or just on the outskirts of towns to the south of the capital or to the north. The remainders of the roads in the country were dirt except for the newly constructed tarred road leading to future tunnel construction sites and the future Katse dam.

At the same time infrastructure roads were being built for the first phase of LHWP, simultaneously an entire electrical construction project took place. The planned construction sites required vast amounts of electricity to power the massive construction equipment needed to excavate some 65 kilometers of tunnels and built the 27 story dam.

While driving it was not uncommon to see Basotho men, women and children riding ponies alongside of the roads. They sometimes rode their ponies on the road itself. If it was winter-time (summer in the northern hemisphere) snow could often cover the ground in higher elevations. The common clothing used by most Basotho was a blanket with a pin used to close and keep the blanket from falling off their shoulders. The Basotho people were one of the few tribes in Africa that could live and work in snow: they were very hardy.

Except for small stretches of agriculture land in the lowlands, some of the country side was used for animal grazing and the larger remainder was basically barren and extremely rocky. There were infrequent clumps of trees usually surrounding a small village, or a trading store or a religious mission. After the snows melted the earth would be covered with a plethora of wild flowers for a few days before reverting back to its normal brownish color.

The planned Kate dam was located almost in the middle of Lesotho high up in the Maluti Mountains. Normally a visit encompassed a five-hour drive to and fro over the newly paved infrastructure road. The construction site was totally isolated. Residential accommodations were built to house the entire dam workforce including engineers as well as laborers. All supplies, be they for dam construction or food stuffs had to be trucked to the site.

Once completed the Katse dam would be the same height as a 27 story building. The width of the dam, from one river bank to the other was more than a half mile. The Basotho work force would average close to 2000.

The Tunnel project initially had three separate work sites. Each site was located off the newly built infrastructure road in very rural areas. The furthest of the sites was some 75 miles from Maseru while the others only about 50 miles. Each site required accommodations to be built the same as for Katse dam. The Basotho work force averaged close to 2000 workers. Likewise all construction materials as well as food stuffs had to be trucked in. The main headquarters for the tunnel consortium was located just outside of the town of Leribe about a (2) hour drive north from Maseru.

Each tunnel site had its own massive tunnel boring machine (TBM) built overseas. Each machine had to be shipped through South Africa ports and then sent be rail to a railhead in the Orange Free State in South Africa before being trucked to Lesotho. Once in Lesotho each TBM had to be re-assembled. All three TBMs had diameters of about 5m. Each was designed to achieve a theoretical advance rate of 6 m per hour. If drill and blast technology were used, the optimum advance rate would be 6-9m per 24 hours-no competition to the TBMs.

Every tunnel site had its own mini-railroad which was used to transport workers inside the tunnel to the workface. Each TBM was followed by a conveyor belt which transported the excavated rock to rail cars for the drive out of the tunnel. The excavation materials were disposed outside of each tunnel.

MARITAL SITUATION

Fortunately for Cannon some mutual friends, the Christensen's', offered him a room in their home in Maseru. The Christensen's' didn't think there was any possibility of reconciliation with Mrs. Cannon. According to them, she had changed from when they were friends not that long ago. This placed a damper on any hopes which Cannon had when he returned to Maseru for reconciliation. The Christensen's' felt Mrs. Cannon had become arrogant since her employment with the Norwegians and impossible to talk with in spite being her friends before the marriage broke up. The Cannons met once for a walk and talk. Mrs. Cannon was adamant in her verbalization that their marriage was over and she wanted a divorce.

The Cannons thought it might be possible to obtain a divorce in Lesotho. Mr. Cannon also thought he might be able to get the marriage annulled by the Catholic Church in Lesotho. Mrs. Cannon hired a white South African lawyer as her representative while Cannon was advised by a terrific anti-apartheid white Catholic priest-Joe Faulkner.

After a while it became apparent, the Cannons couldn't get a divorce in Lesotho nor in South Africa. Mrs. Cannon then started procedures to get divorced in Norway. The Cannons had their civil marriage ceremony in Norway and Mr. Cannon resided in Norway while attending post-graduate school in the 1970's. On the 25th of September, the day after Cannon's birthday, Mr. Christensen, who was in-charge of the Danish Consulate, was given a package by the Swedish Embassy (they represented Norway in Lesotho) with divorce papers drawn up in Norway. After reading them, Cannon informed Christensen he wouldn't accept said papers because as an American was not subject to the laws of Norway. Hence, the divorce process went into limbo for a few years.

Insofar as the annulment was concerned, Cannon filed the appropriate papers with the Catholic Diocese of Maseru. There was only one Catholic priest in Lesotho who was qualified to deal with annulment matters. Fr. Nqosa. He had studied Canon Law under which the annulment application would be processed. Unfortunately, Fr. Nqosa was killed in a car accident and an annulment couldn't be applied for before a civil divorce was issued. The annulment process wasn't tried again by Cannon until 1998 when he had returned back to Calais, Maine.

MOBILISATION

Due to the change of employer, Cannon easily obtained a multi-entry/exit visa for South Africa shortly after his return to Maseru. A complete change from Cannon's effort to obtain a multi-entry/exit South African visa while employed by the AFL-CIO's African American Labor Center.

A few visits were made to nearby South African mines to obtain information regarding industrial relations, especially relative to the Basotho likes and dislikes regarding food. The purpose of the visits was to help gather information, which could assist the dam & tunnel contractors with the feeding of their future Basotho workforce. South African mine owners learned early that without proper food, the black mine workers wouldn't be too productive. Hard strenuous manual labor requires a fit person. Food is a key factor in one's fitness.

The two contractors' initial staffing was heavily weighted towards the hiring of South Africans. In retrospect this made sense, since they were nearby and had adequate skills to begin the mobilization of their workforces needed to commence construction.

Both contractors' hired white South Africans to staff their personnel/ human resources and job safety positions. Although Nelson Mandela had been released from jail, many, many South African whites didn't neither care for nor respect non-whites. The LHWP wouldn't succeed if South African whites employed on the construction sites exhibited their racial attitudes towards the local Basotho workforce.

According to civil engineering norm, monthly meetings would occur at the respective construction-work site. The purpose of these meetings is to review whether construction progress is being adhered to according to the entire project plan and to address any problems which, could arise and effect progress. The attending representatives of the contractor and the supervising engineer who chaired these meetings. The client's (LHDA) representatives also were in attendance usually as observers but sometimes with speaking privileges.

From the meetings at the 1st site meetings, each contractor had their own interpretation of the Memorandum of Understanding, especially as it pertained to industrial relations and other ancillary related matters. The tunnel contractor started off by giving its Basotho laborers a small daily cash allowance to be used to purchase food from nearby local vendors. Unfortunately many of the Basotho were purchasing beer instead of food. This resulted in them being fired. Cannon was very forceful in his opposition to the contractor's lunchtime method of feeding. Not only was this a poor industrial relation practice, but more important it was a job safety hazard having workers drunk on the job. Eventually the contractor came around to preparing box lunches for its Basotho laborers. This change greatly increased the workforce production and reduced job safety hazards.

One of the major changes which Lesotho and in particular Maseru underwent in the late 1970's and early 1980's encompassed the influx of Indian and Chinese traders and business people. Few if any businesses in Maseru were owned and operated by Basotho. Basotho were hired for menial tasks in the service sectors. The major exception in the private sector was the banking sector where they held managerial positions.

As the dam and tunnel projects were undergoing mobilization, rioting broke out in Maseru on the May 20th 1991 when a Basotho female killed a Chinese shop keeper who was accused of over pricing. Whether the accusation was true or false, the public reaction to the killing reflected built up extremely strong antagonism towards Chinese and Indians.

The Government of Lesotho imposed a nationwide curfew on the 22nd of May from 11 PM until 5 AM. This affected both projects since they were on a 24 hour work cycle. However, Cannon was able to secure a curfew pass which afforded him the wherewithal to continue to travel to the main construction areas. The curfew lasted until around the 19th of June.

The dam project had its own shortcomings during its mobilization process. After receiving complaints over the preferential hiring of South Africans, the Ministry of Labor, under the auspices of the Labor Commissioner Fanana, had one of his inspectors visit the Katse work site on the 11th of September 1991. (15) South Africans were arrested because they lacked the agreed upon Lesotho work permits. The following monthly site meeting for October was quite heated, but eventually the Contractor's personnel manager came to respect the MOU and the importance of obtaining work permits for non-Basotho staff.

There was labor unrest elsewhere in Lesotho. Strikes broke out in October in various foreign owned textile factories, predominately Chinese. Workers were striking for better wages and working safety conditions. Cannon was able to use the labor unrest as a tool to convince the dam and tunnel contractors that it would be wise to seek out CAWULE for discussions. They would find it easier to communicate with their Basotho workers if they had a recognized structure to work with.

Without a structure, the only available structure to deal with labor disputes was the Ministry of Labor which was under staffed and lacked adequate vehicle transportation for its labor inspectors. The Ministry of Labor received a shot-in-the-arm, in late October, when the United Nations International Labor Organization (ILO) expert Mr. Terry Southam arrived in Maseru. He was an Australian expert on safety. He was also deeply opposed to apartheid and had the potential to become a thorn in the side of both the Dam and Tunnel contractors who were slow in providing safety equipment to their workers. There were instances when Cannon found underground workers without a functioning light on their helmet, unacceptable in any underground situation.

Here again Cannon was able to convince both contractors that it was in their best interests to initiate a preventative pro-active safety program. They needed to acquire internationally accepted safety equipment for their laborers, hire a qualified Safety Managers, and appoint safety officers at all of their work sites.

While Cannon was adjusting to his new job, he decided to enter into counseling with an Irish counselor to try to come to grips with the termination of his marriage. Counseling started in early March 1991 and ended in June, when the she and her family were transferred out of Lesotho. The counseling sessions were very helpful for Cannon. He was partially able to come to grips with the knowledge that his marriage was truly over.

Cannon's son, Marc completed high school in June and departed Maseru. He enrolled as a first-year student at Rhode Island School of Design (RISD) in Providence, Rhode Island in September. Daughter Chandra entered her junior year at Bates College, Lewiston, Maine that September.

Both the Cannon children were now enrolled in private institutions of higher learning in the US which were very expensive. He was very fortunate to have the job with LHDA to meet these schooling expenses (since Mrs. Cannon refused to financially contribute towards their education).

The dam and tunnel contractors' holiday shut down, from the third week in December until the 2nd week in January 1992, afforded all staff the opportunity to spend the holiday with their families if so desired. Likewise the offices of LHDA and the supervising engineers' were also closed. This policy would prevail throughout the life of both projects.

NEAR DEATH EXPERIENCE

Shortly after re-commencing work, an industrial dispute at Katse Dam developed into a half-day wildcat strike. Without warning workers dropped tools and walked off their jobs Workers were uneasy at the Tunnel work sites as well. Cannon was driving via South Africa for a tunnel site visit on the 19th, of February 1992 because of the unrest. His pick-up truck skidded off the highway and flew in the air for some 30 feet before hitting a tree and being upended. Fortunately, there were some Basotho employees of Mr. Christensen passing who were able to drag a conscious Cannon out of the completely totaled vehicle.

Cannon was taken by ambulance to a small hospital in the nearby town of Ladybrand. The hospital had a small portable x-ray unit. The x-rays didn't indicate anything serious. As a precaution, they put a neck brace on Cannon and recommended he go into the city of Bloemfontein; the provincial capital of the Orange Free State, which had proper x-ray facilities. There was only one problem: Cannon had to arrange for a ride to get there.

Cannon couldn't call Mrs. Cannon since they were no longer on speaking terms. He was able to get contact with Jette his new Danish friend who was free to drive the 100 miles or so to Bloemfontein. Throughout the drive, Cannon was smoking and making small talk thinking he had a pinched nerve in his neck. Upon arrival at the Hydromed Hospital's x-ray unit, Cannon was given a number to await his turn to be x-rayed.

The x-ray technician removed the collar and pushed his shoulders forward closer to the x-ray machine before beginning the x-ray. The unit was fully computerized. Once the pictures appeared, the next thing that appeared was a wheel chair, more nurses and a Doctor! It seems Cannon had suffered a fracture of his pillar (broken neck in laymen terms) in the accident. This was verified later when a CAT scan was completed. Plans were made to operate on Cannon the following day to fuse his 6th and 7th vertebrae on the left side of his neck.

Cannon was very fortunate that the accident took place in South Africa where there were first world medical facilities and professionals, especially if one happened to have money. When Cannon awoke after the operation, the performing surgeon, Dr. Johan Wilkinson, informed him that he was a very lucky person. It seems the fracture was extremely close to his cervical cord. Anything closer would have turned Cannon into a quadriplegic.

Dr. Wilkinson later performed spinal related surgeries on three other persons working on the LHDA project in Lesotho. Cannon's situation was a piece of cake compared to the others. This doctor truly had a God-Given gift in his fingers and hands.

The entire operation, ancillary services, surgeon fees, plus the 7 day stay in a semi-private hospital room, came to approximately US $ 3,000.00. Cannon's Blue Cross/Blue Shield health insurance coverage was through a policy of his union in the US, Rhode Island's American Federation of Teachers. He paid all expenses locally in South African (RSA rand) and was reimbursed upon provision of receipts when he returned to the USA. The BC/BS folks in the USA thought there was a mistake in the costs because they were so low in comparison to the US costs for a similar procedure. A similar procedure would have run into 6 dollar figures at least.

When Cannon returned to Lesotho from the hospital, he wasn't able to move into the apartment he had rented after moving away from the Christensen's. Again Jette came to his rescue and allowed him to move into her apartment. Cannon wasn't the best patient in following directions and recuperating instructions: very thick headed.

Cannon tried to walk daily in the neighborhood. The little kids were perplexed with the neck brace Cannon had to wear twenty-four hours per day. One day a small kid yelled out: "Why are you walking with a telephone around your neck"? Cannon said something to the effect of so he could talk with people from outer space. The kids thought Cannon was just another crazy white man.

Industrial unrest broke out both projects culminating in a strike which, shut down tunnel construction during Cannon's recuperation process. Cannon was called in by LHDA to provide advice relative to the strike. Before he knew it he was back to work before the month of March was over: way before the 60 day period prescribed by Dr. Wilkinson.

Once Cannon returned to work, Jette threw him out of her apartment. She was a very strong person and a firm believer in following doctor's orders. Jette believed Cannon was actually a bit crazy also going back to work against Doctor's orders.

USA DIVORCE

In May 1992, Cannon went on home-leave. Daughter Chandra was to graduate from Bates College on the 25th. Cannon and Mrs. Cannon were barely speaking. Hence, what was supposed to be a happy family day wasn't. After the graduation both Cannon's returned to Rhode Island. Mrs. Cannon called an Italian Uncle of Cannon hoping to see him since they had previously gotten along so well. Uncle Stanley told her to forget it and to forget about any future contact since she was no longer part of the extended family. Blood is thicker than marriage.

A compromise was reached regarding the divorce. Cannon learned that he could use his US voting address in Rhode Island as the basis to seek a divorce. Mrs. Cannon, through a friend of hers, was introduced to an Italian lawyer who was willing to accept her as a client. Cannon had three lawyers in his family to choose from to represent him. Negotiations were entered into. The major sticking issue was money. At the end Cannon was advised to offer Mrs. Cannon a lump sum in two payments: one upon the signing of the preliminary papers and the 2nd after the divorce was granted on December 10th, 1993.

What was difficult to fathom for Cannon was that, after being together from 1969 until 1991 as a married couple with two children, nothing mattered but money. Cannon was left as the sole financial supporter for both children's education which didn't seem quite fair at the time. So goes life. Cannon wasn't able to obtain a Catholic marriage annulment until December 3rd, 1999. The decision of the Tribunal of the Diocese of Portland, Maine was confirmed by the Metropolitan Tribunal of Boston, Massachusetts on March 29th, 2000.

BACK IN LESOTHO

Cannon and Jette were invited to spend the Christmas holidays in Namibia. A close friend of Cannon from his days working in Lesotho with the trade unions was working in the US embassy in Windhoek, Howard F. Jeter. It was decided that driving to Namibia would afford them an opportunity to see parts of South Africa not seen previously and experience the desert atmosphere of newly independent Namibia.

One experience that will forever remain in Cannon's mind took place in a small pension in downtown Windhoek. One afternoon Cannon and Jette were sitting by the pool when in walked a white person with a leopard on a leash. Cannon couldn't believe his eyes! What happened next was more unbelievable! The leopard broke away from its minder and jumped over a big wall into the next compound belonging to the Chinese Embassy. At this time Cannon better understood what some of his Basotho friends have told him for years: white people are crazy.

A once in a lifetime experience was undertaking a drive south of Windhoek to visit the port city of Swakopmund with the desert sand dunes along one side of the highway and the Atlantic Ocean on the other. Driving into the desert before returning to Windhoek for New Years' Eve we experienced car problems. Fortunately we were able to find a mechanic in a small nearby town to fix the vehicle. He amazed us by telling us he was born in Eldoret, Kenya-not many whites were born there. We gave him the New Years' drink we were carrying. He deserved the single malt more than we did.

Cannon was thrilled in February 1993 when LHDA renewed his contract for another two years. The dam and tunnel contractors felt just the opposite. They viewed Cannon as a thorn in their sides and firmly believed he only looked after the interests of the Basotho workers. They viewed him as a trade unionist in LHDA employ not as an industrial relations expert.

While the major aspect of the two MOU's focus was on industrial relations, each did have a job-training element. The element which was inserted with the hopes that capable Basotho could rise into semi-skilled and skilled positions as the projects progressed. The tunnel contractor had a formal three-day training program for each Basotho they hired before the individual was allowed to proceed to the construction site. The dam contractor's pre-employment training program wasn't nearly as proficient.

The first major training success story entailed a Basotho mechanic. He was employed on one of the three tunnel boring machine crews. All the crews were headed by white Europeans who were paid according to international wage standards. The Basotho mechanic underwent five months of on-the-job training and was promoted to a tunnel boring machine operator on April 3rd, 1993. He received a great salary increase, but wasn't paid as an "international" employee. A few years later he went overseas with the French contractor and was paid as an international ex-pat. As the years progressed, due to the LHDA's position in original contract negotiations in 1990 articulated whenever possible by Cannon, more Basotho were promoted to better paying posts thereby reducing the number of overseas ex-pats (including South Africans) needed on the project.

1993 was the year in which both contractors started discussions with CAWULE. The first to open discussions was the tunnel contractor in June.

The dam contractor followed in September, the same month as Cannon's birthday. Unfortunately, both contractors required CAWULE to show it had obtained written proof from 51% of their respective workforces before they would be willing to open recognition agreements. This was a perquisite to the commencement of collective bargaining negotiations.

After the initial discussions, the General Secretary of CAWULE Justice Tsukulu won a one-year scholarship to study industrial relations at Warwick University in the UK to start in September 1994. Cannon served as a reference for Tsukulu. In many ways, Cannon was happy to see people he formerly associated with, progress as trade union leaders. In other ways, Cannon knew it was only a matter of time before Tsukulu and other CAWULE leaders would flex their muscles and lead the tunnel and dam workers on strike. Then Cannon's work load would increase further.

Each contractor had its own safety department and each supervising engineer had a designated staffer responsible for job safety. Each contractor was required to have a licensed medical practitioner either at its headquarters or on site. Each site had a mini-hospital or a health clinic. Yet the issue of workplace safety fought for in the 1990 negotiations wouldn't go away.

Undertaking work place safety inspections was relatively new for Cannon. Initially it was fairly easy since it the greater part of the dam preparation took place above ground. Each specific work area was inspected at least monthly. The inspection team usually consisted of Cannon, the Dam Safety Officer and occasionally, a representative of the supervising engineer. If there were safety hazards, they were noted and brought up for discussion at the monthly site meeting.

Monthly site meetings were chaired by the Supervising Engineer. In attendance were the Construction Manager, the Financial Manager and Safety Officer for the HWV consortium. There were numerous engineers from the supervising engineers' consortium. There were senior engineers from ACRES representing LHDA as well as Cannon. Cannon was granted speaking privileges only on matters covered under the Memorandum of Understanding.

When the dam wall started rising, safety inspections were no longer relatively easy. Steel ladders were attached to the dam wall. This provided the only access to workers who were atop of each bloc installing steel rebar or pouring concrete. Climbing the ladders was tricky if one wasn't well balance as was the case after Cannon's broken neck. If Cannon did not make the climbs, how could he have done his work overseeing safety on behalf of the Basotho workforce? Cannon had to force himself to make the climbs initially: after a few weeks it became easier.

Initially the tunnels' safety inspections were also fairly easy since the work was above ground. Once ground was broken and work commenced underground it was not easy. Initially Cannon and the tunnel safety officer could walk to the face where the blasting was taking place. Cannon's balance went a bit off after the broken neck hence there were times when he would slip much to the chagrin of the safety officer. The safety officer felt was too slow thus wasting his precious time.

Once the TBM's were installed it became more complicated. The inspection had to be coordinated with the schedule of the underground train. While there were no ladders to climb, crawling in front of the TBM to inspect the massive cutters was scary initially. Cannon would have the stone face at his back and at his front was claustrophobic. Over time Cannon adjusted.

Whereas the monthly site meeting for the dam was in Katse, there were three separate site meetings monthly for each tunnel work site. The participants were basically the same as noted previously for the dam. Likewise Cannon faced the same speaking restrictions.

Key quantitative indicators as to whether a major construction work site was safe were reflected in the disabling injury frequency rate (DIFR) and the injury severity rate (ISR). During the six year period Cannon was associated with the dam and tunnel projects which in 1994 were joined by another smaller dam and tunnel project, the 4,000 Basotho worked 57.8 million man hours. The six year DIFR averaged 20.55 and the ISR average was 2.97. These averages were comparable to averages in western civil engineering construction projects. Not normally seen in developing countries.

In 1993, Lesotho consolidated its labor laws into a new Labour Code with the help of the International Labor Organization (ILO). It was easy to read, clear and concise, but its compensation provisions were Lesotho based. While the code was excellent, the Ministry of Labor and the Labor Commissioner still lacked the personnel and support services to monitor the new code and enforce its standards.

Lesotho had very limited compensation requirements pertaining to job related injuries and deaths. The maximum payout for an injury causing death was approximately US $ 5,400. Payment for a permanent total incapacity injury ranged between US $ 5,400 down to US $ 720. Temporary incapacity was 75% of a workers monthly wage. If an employer did not have injury insurance the fine levied was approximately US $ 120 followed by a daily fine of approximately US $ 8 until insurance was acquired.

Unless these injury and other specific safety requirements were specified in construction tender documents or covered by negotiated memorandum of understandings, it was usually cheaper for contractors to pay death benefits/or serve injury benefits than it was for them to establish proper pro-active job safety programs for their work sites. Safety equipment, safety personnel and ancillary safety provisions for numerous work sites and thousands of workers for 5 to 7 years were much costlier than payments required by law.

As 1993 ended, Cannon and Jette went to visit her sister's family in Argentina. They were able to visit the beautiful and majestic Iqacu Falls in Brazil and nearby Ascension, Paraguay. New Year's Eve was spent in Buenos Ares with rich folks, friends of Jette's sister. It was a very different experience for Cannon who worked with the working poor in Lesotho.

For whatever reasons known to man, it seemed to Cannon that the month of January in Africa produced some interesting and surprising occurrences. In 1994 on the 23rd of January while out jogging on the streets of Maseru,

Cannon heard loud noises accompanied by bright flashes. Mortar fire was occurring in downtown Maseru. Cannon immediately proceeded to Jette's townhouse. The Lesotho Army discombobulated and had started fighting amongst itself. Jette's flat overlooked a small army base. Looking out one could see the incoming fire wasn't accurate at all. Once the firing ceased the exchange of mortar fire only resulted in the killing of a cow before a truce was declared on the 25th.

Cannon was paid a visit from two old friends, originally from Cape Town, prior to the military uprising. The Weber's fled apartheid South Africa in the early 1960's for Lesotho. They eventually re-settled in Canada. The Weber's departed Lesotho right around the time the ex-Prime Minister Chief Leabua Jonathan pulled off a coup after losing a free and fair democratic election in 1969. Was it ironic that their first trip back to Lesotho since their departure, they were able to witness yet another military insanity? As quickly as the trouble commenced, it disappeared, just as rapidly. The Weber's visit after the 25th proceeded smoothly even if too many libations were consumed.

At the start of 1994, young Basotho engineers, mostly schooled in North America, were starting to assume leadership roles within LHDA. The older more experienced ACRES hands reverted to support positions advising the Basotho. In March 1994, the South Africans decided Cannon needed a LHDA Basotho counterpart.

There were not many applications for the Industrial Relations counterpart position initially. Maybe the reason had something to do with an internal Basotho staffer, from another division, who had connections which were supposed to guarantee him the position. Cannon in reviewing the connected application, noted reference to a Canadian University whose name sounded strange. A list of Canadian universities and institutions of higher learning was secured and it didn't contain the name listed in the application. Cannon was able to convince the LHDA leadership to drop their "connected" applicant.

Among the original applications, there was a young Basotho university graduate who did graduate studies in Holland. His field was industrials relations. After a brief interview, Cannon also learned Mr. Khetsi was the goal keeper on the Lesotho national soccer team. Cannon supported his application and he was hired on a three month probationary period prior to the December 1994 break.

Work continued on the dam and tunnels. It was obvious to Cannon in his work site visits and discussions with shop stewards and CAWULE officials, that the Basotho workforce needed a unified voice to deal with management from both consortiums before it could enter into collective bargaining agreements.

Unfortunately both contractors' were using stalling tactics over who could be a trade union member in a union bargaining unit. It was traditional trade union practice to establish which workers were considered management, thus not eligible to be represented by the trade union. It was also natural that management had a say in who was considered management. Until this issue could be resolved, there were no official recognition agreements signed between the contractors and CAWULE.

A major snow storm hit Lesotho mountains on the 20th and 21st of April 1995 Cannon had spent the previous couple of days visiting Katse dam and then one of the tunnel work sites on his way back to Maseru. He was shocked to witness such a winter snow storm in Africa. The storm dumped at least two feet of snow in many areas. The roads were closed for a day. The Lesotho government didn't have snow plows surely not a rarity in Africa! The roads had to be cleared by road graters supplied by the Contractors. Cannon's small Toyota had to be pulled up one mountain pass by a four wheeled truck. Too bad skiing wasn't a popular sport in Southern Africa because the Lesotho mountain areas received snow annually. Not many people in Providence, RI would believe Cannon when he told them it snowed in Africa.

The first free democratic national election for all citizens of South Africa was set for the 27 and 28 of April 1995. Both contractors used the period for their month-end shut down and wage pay out. This gave their South African workers the opportunity to return home to vote in the historic election. As expected, Nelson Mandela was elected by a great majority as President. Cannon watched South African television coverage of the election with almost disbelief reflecting back on his first visit to southern Africa in 1969. This was truly one of the most memorable happenings in Cannons life.

Shortly after the South Africa election, members of the Lesotho police force staged a nation-wide strike on May 9th. Only after the entire police forces were granted big wage increases by the government, did the strike stop. This would further infuriate the Basotho workers working on the LHDA project who always felt they were underpaid. It was not too long after the police strike that a two day 27-28 June, wildcat strike hit the Tunnel contractor over the issues of wages and overtime compensation.

The contractor used the office of the Labor Commissioner to get a meeting with its striking workers. Cannon was granted observer status after receiving concurrence from management, CAWULE, the supervising engineer and the Office of the Labor Commissioner. The contractor's negotiating team consisted of an old white South African with many years of experience in the construction field. He was joined by a black South African from their major partners' headquarters in South Africa.

Workers demanded that representatives from CAWULE should attend the negotiations as their representatives. Meetings were held in the boardroom of the contractor in Leribe, about 45 miles northwest of Maseru. CAWULE was assisted by a Danish volunteer, who was seconded by the Danish Volunteer Service, to their Maseru headquarters office. Workers returned to work on the 29th after management and CAWULE agreed to enter into direct wage negotiations.

These negotiations started an industrial relations equivalent to an ongoing chess match that lasted until Cannon's departure from Lesotho in 1997 and most likely until the project ended in 1999: brief work stoppages, negotiations and work resumption.

Upon returning from the June 1994 months-end break, the Basotho workers at Katse Dam downed their tools in a strike on the 11th of July. The wildcat strike at the dam illustrated the management's problem in not having a collective bargaining agreement within which negotiations could commence. Instead, management was faced with conflicting grievances by workers without any negotiating experience. The situation became so desperate that the managements' key staff had to call in the Lesotho Army for help to protect the millions of dollars of equipment on site. Communications between management and its workers completely broke down. Immediately upon hearing the news, Cannon left Maseru to drive to Katse.

On the 14th of July, the entire work force held a massive meeting at the base of the future dam wall without the presence of the Lesotho Army. The Labor Commissioner, Mr. Fanana, accompanied by his Labor Officer responsible for the Katse area and Mr. R. Ramollo, the recently appointed LHDA Deputy Chief Executive (formerly the assistant to the Mr. Rohaback) flew to the construction site in a chartered helicopter.

Pick-up trucks were borrowed to drive the visitors and Cannon to their meeting with the entire Dam contractors' work force numbering close to 2,000. The visitors had to climb up to the roofs of a few containers in order to be seen. The Labor Commissioner and LHDA's Mr. Ramollo spoke to the strikers seeking their return to work. They were unsuccessful.

While the wildcat strike was technically illegal, the Government couldn't arrest the strikers- there were too many of them. Hence any threats by the Labor Commissioner fell on deaf ears. The visitors from Maseru couldn't convince the workers to return to work because they were not able to resolve two outstanding key issues: low wages and too many South Africans being employed by the contractor.

LHDA and Government officials were briefed not to become party to any wage matters to avoid possible future Contractor claims. If the contractor could provide evidence of Government involvement in the wage dispute to arbitration, the LHDA could find itself paying the costs in the settlement.

The high-powered visitors flew back to Maseru the same day, the dam workforce remained off-the-job.

Cannon stayed behind and using a backdoor channel of communications, He was able to convince representatives from CAWULE's headquarters, including Secretary General J. Tsukulu to meet with the Contractors' Site Manager and Industrial Relations Manager late at night. The dam contractor and CAWULE representatives agreed that Cannon could act as a facilitator in trying to cobble together an agreement as long as LHDA headquarters and the dam contractors' office in Italy gave their approvals. After a series of phone calls to Maseru and Italy, an agreement was reached that Cannon could serve as the facilitator.

Before real negotiations could begin, Cannon needed to convince the CAWULE representatives that Mr. Sole, the LHDA Chief Executive and the Dam Contractor's headquarters both agreed he could play a pro-active role in seeking a settlement. Once convinced the CAWULE folks agreed to appear before the workforce recommending a return to work while negotiations were on-going. CAWULE was to report twice a day on negotiations progress. Because of mistrust by both parties, it took many private meetings before joint meetings could be held.

Hours were spent haggling over an agenda. Once an agenda was agreed, progress was slow since the dam contractor needed the OK from its headquarters before making any firm commitments: ditto CAWULE, which needed the concurrence of the workforce. On the 22nd of July 1994, the dam contractor signed a recognition agreement with CAWULE.

At said meeting, both parties agreed to a timetable to bargain collectively and to negotiate wages and look into the issue of the number of South Africans employed on the job site. Cannon returned to Maseru on the 23rd to report back to Mr. Sole. Mr. Sole must have been pleased with the results because he presented Cannon with two six packs of beer at his home: a Basotho sign of appreciation.

The government representatives of Lesotho and South Africa, which made up the Joint Permanent Technical Commission (JPTC), requested a briefing from the LHDA Chief Executive regarding the wildcat settlement. The meeting was attended by supervising engineer, the dam contractor's industrial relations manager and Cannon on July 25th in Maseru. In driving back to Katse on the 25th, Cannon and the dam IR manager were caught in another big snow storm which forced them to return to Leribe and spend the night in the Tunnel contractor's guest house. The road to Katse re-opened on the 26th.

LHDA postponed Cannon's planned August leave to the USA. Cannon had problems with his son attending the Rhode Island School of Design (RISD) in Providence, Rhode Island. RISD regularly sent tuition bills to Cannon but didn't send Marc's academic results. Their rationale was that the student was over 18 and it was the students' responsibility to inform the parents. Marc was asked to leave RISD prior to his anticipated graduation because of failing grades. RISD received four years of tuition payments. Marc was cast adrift.

What could be done for Marc? Cannon had a bright idea to call Lawson Mooney in France to inquire whether he could take Marc and tutor him individually in painting and sculpting. Mooney agreed to host Marc after a stipend was agreed to cover his room and board. Marc had a place to go to after his departure from RISD. In the long run it was questionable whether this was a positive development for Marc. What isn't questionable is Marc had a great time while with Mooney, especially socially.

The industrial relations situation was far from being stable even after the settlement of the Katse Dam wildcat strike. The Tunnel contractor and CAWULE were not making any progress in their negotiations concerning a recognition agreement and a wages negotiation agreement. Things became so bad that CAWULE requested assistance from the International Federation of Building and Wood Workers Federation (IFBWW). Mr. Walter Mucaza, an old friend and former colleague of Cannon's, arrived from Zimbabwe.

The Labour Commissioner appointed his representative M. Khotle as conciliator for the tunnel negotiations, but he too is unsuccessful. Negotiations come to a halt by late August. During the same period, which was the winter season in Lesotho, LHDA and its engineers were reviewing tender submissions for the building of another dam in Muela.

Cannon was part of the Muela dam review process relative to industrial relations and workplace safety. Cannon was required to prepare a briefing paper for the South Africa/ Lesotho Joint Permanent Technical Commission (JPTC). The purpose of the paper was to give an honest & concise picture of industrial relations on both the Katse dam project and the tunnel project. In August, the LHDA Deputy Chief Executive, Mr. Romollo was departing Lesotho for greener pastures in South Africa. Mr. Romollo would be replaced by Les Fabian who Cannon would reports to. Mr. Fabian had very limited work experience in Africa.

The Dam contractor's manager from Italy arrived in Maseru on August 10th: the day after wage negotiations deadlocked with CAWULE. The Italians requested the service of the Labor Commissioner to conciliate the wage negotiations. Deputy Labor Commissioner M. Mandoro was appointed on the 11th. He too wasn't successful. Negotiations remain at loggerheads. Another dam wildcat strike is feared.

While these labor issues were being unsuccessfully negotiated, the political landscape in Lesotho was in turmoil. On August 17th, the King of Lesotho dissolved Parliament: a constitutional crisis. Shootings erupted in Maseru leaving four people dead. A 7 PM to 5 AM curfew was put in effect. A nation- wide stay away, to protest the constitutional crisis, took place on the 22nd and 23rd. By this time, events of this nature seemed almost normal to Cannon.

September is Cannons birthday month. CAWULE held an election Congress to select an interim Secretary General. The former Secretary General Mr. J. Tsukulu went off to Warwick University on the 1st. His replacement was M. Tseuoa, another former colleague of Cannon, but with less negotiating experience than Tsukulu. Cannon convinces Tseuoa to reopen negotiations with the tunnel contractor. He even provided transportation for the CAWULE negotiators from the Maseru headquarters office. On the 12th of September, the tunnel contractor and CAWULE sign their first collective bargaining agreement.

At month's end, Cannon accepted another contract renewal to February 1997. Cannon was asked to try to use his influence with CAWULE to get dam negotiations back on track. The dam contractor agrees to have Cannon act as a facilitator again. Negotiations recommence on the 14th of September and continue daily until the 17th when their first collective bargaining agreement is signed at 6 PM.

An engineering feat took place on the 2rd of September 1994 at 8:30 AM when two tunnel boring machines met coming from opposite directions. Both had been inserted into two different tunnel heads when excavation first started. This occurrence raised Cannon's esteem for the profession. Most engineers are comfortable with everything associated with massive construction feats except with the workers. It just goes to prove how complex humanity really is.

Cannon finally moved from his small Qoqolosing town house apartment complex nearby the railway station. A bigger apartment in the Friebel Townhouse complex became vacant when Jette and her daughter Line moved back to Denmark. This flat was located next to the biggest hotel in Lesotho, the Lesotho Holiday Inn. In a nearby townhouse resided the Safi family. Monica and her sister Kavita were of Sri Lanka origin and terrific cooks. With much patience, they taught Cannon how to cook curry properly. Great friends!

Throughout 1994 workers on both projects were still getting hurt and dying on the job. In November, negotiations opened on the 18th with the LHPC tunnel contractor who also won the tender to build Muela Dam. The main dam would be north of Leribe which would serve as the last water point transfer in Lesotho before the flow of water from the Katse Dam reached the territory of South Africa.

Prior to the opening of these negotiations, the main Paris based person responsible for all LHPC activities in Lesotho arrived. Daniel Gasquet was a very charming person. He said he was surprised that Cannon played a very positive role in the settlement of the problems with CAWULE in September. He thought Cannon was only a "union" man!

Negotiations often became very contentious especially regarding on-the-job safety. In spite of the statistics gathered by the safety staff of the tunnel contractor, they were unwilling to beef up their staffing for the Muela Dam. They wanted to use their existing tunnel safety staff to oversee this project. Cannon was able to secure "unofficial" support from Terry Southham, the Aussie ILO hired to work out of the Labor Commissioner's Office. Eventually, the tunnel contractor saw the light (Cannon felt Gasquet told his negotiation team to give in to LHDA demands) and said they would set-up a separate safety department for the Muela Dam project.

Cannon traveled to Denmark during the Christmas project break to visit Jette and her family. They had returned there after completing her assignment with the Danish Volunteer Service. Cannon's son Marc was to spend a few days there before going on to Norway to visit his mother. He missed his original plane and arrived in Denmark a few days late. The former Mrs. Cannon blew a gasket, blaming Cannon for her son's irresponsibility. When Marc made poor decisions in future decades, the former Mrs. Cannon's would continue to blame Cannon for her son's poor decision making.

1995 opened in Lesotho with the reinstatement of King Moshoeshoe II to his throne on the 25th of January. He was first exiled by his uncle Chief Leabua Jonathan back in the early 1970's. The reason given was interference in internal politics, the same reason given for his 2nd exile.

The office of the Labor Commissioner, thru the efforts of Mr. Southham, conducted a safety audit at Katse Dam. The results were disputable depending upon which body one was affiliated with. Some Basotho thought an audit would shut down the site because of unsafe working conditions. This didn't occur fortunately, because it would have cost the

Lesotho government millions of dollars in claims that would have been submitted by the Dam contractor who would claim force majeure arising out of an action by the host government. Shortly thereafter, Southham departed Lesotho. His contract was over and the ILO didn't replace him.

In March, a strike of a different nature hit the Katse Dam. The cement and fly ash used to make concrete was imported from a close-by South African rail head. The trucks who delivered the cement and fly ash to Lesotho were South African owned. The drivers were black South Africans. They struck for higher wages and eventually received same. When this happened Cannon knew it was only a matter of time before the Katse Dam workers would strike again for higher wages as well.

Was Cannon a seer? No, anyone with basic trade union experience would know that if selected people are rewarded with pay increases after a strike, it is almost automatic that union workers will use this precedent to strike themselves. The Katse Dam workers dropped tools on May 8th. The strike lasted three days. Cannon again served as a facilitator between the parties. It could have proved a great learning experience for Cannon's counterpart if he had been hired by then. He was hired only in the middle of November. CAWULE negotiated wage increases based upon the truck drivers' strike and settlement as was expected

Insanity was not restricted to Lesotho and the LHWP. It was rumored that a buddy of Cannon, who resided in Lesotho, was able to convince the old apartheid government in South Africa, to subsidize the construction of a large sailing vessel? Cannon never found out if this was true. Regardless, the yacht was competed in March and was big enough to sleep a crew of 12. Cannon was invited to join the crew who were scheduled to sail out of Cape Town for South America on the 14th of April.

It's amazing what can take place in Africa. Millions of black South Africans subsist on pittance wages. Yet, was it possible that a business person was able to get the apartheid South African government to build him a yacht at a very subsidized price? A price from which he would recover at least three fold when he later sold the sailing yacht in the Caribbean where it would be permanently berth after sailing from South Africa. Cannon refused the invitation because of his job with LHDA. In retrospect, Cannon lost a chance in a lifetime to experience a once in a lifetime invitation.

A long distance relationship isn't easy to keep up. Cannon and Jette stopped their relationship in May. This was very hard to do since Jette was a fantastic human being. Cannon believed Jette's future would be better served if she could become involved with a Dane. Was Cannon being a coward or was this belief based upon his own experience with Kari his former wife from Norway?

In July two friends from the US trade union movement visited Maseru as part of a working visit to South Africa. Evelyn was with the National Education Association (NEA). Cannon first met her while in Kenya. Greg was with the Laborers International Union. Cannon first met him when he was part of the teaching staff in the labor education program at the University of District Columbia in Washington, DC. Evelyn and Greg were two great people.

MOONEY REUNION

After their visit to Lesotho was completed, they drove Cannon to the Johannesburg airport at month's end. Cannon had planned a vacation to Europe to visit old friends. Stops were to be made in Sweden and France. While in Sweden Cannon was able to spend time with his old Peace Corps friend Elaine and Buko even though they were no longer together. It was good to break bread. It was even better to realize these old friendships were as strong as when first made years back.

Cannon's entire purpose for visiting France was to see Lawson Mooney. He lived in St. Antonin Noble Val, close to the border with Spain. Mooney met Cannon at the Toulouse airport. After a warm embrace, Cannon told Mooney he was very appreciative of his hospitality shown his son Marc. The drive to his village took about (2) hours. Mooney lived on an old farm outside of town with his youngest daughter Lauceen.

The property was located on a hill top with a wonderful view of the valley below in which the village was located. The main house must have been beautiful in years past. It had gone to seed, maybe after Lisa died. Mooney had a cold case of Pete's Belgium beer waiting. Cannon didn't bother to unpack before story telling commenced with beer drinking. Both continued until the wee hours of the morning and only stopped when the beer was finished.

The following day Cannon was given a tour of the farm. In the garage below the main house was a Mercedes on blocks. It was covered with dust and likely had not been on the road in years. Throughout the garage were pieces of art from Zaire/Congo. They were everywhere except inside the Benz on blocks. Had Mooney become unstable? Mooney moved Cannon into a twelfth century old monastery he owned in the village that had been rehabbed and was used as his art Academy and studio. It had a self-contained flat as well as a dorm area that could sleep six people.

Mooney had not lost his charm. The entire village knew him, especially those town's people, he would frequently meet in the two village pubs. Days were spent lounging around exchanging family happenings since we were last together in Kinshasa. Mooney's politics had moved very far right-he told stories about his new close friends in the US such as Cheney, Rumsfeld, Brady, etc. Cannon decided to forgo speaking about his changing political philosophy.

Cannon had a couple opportunities to speak with Lauceen. She believed that once her mother Lisa died, Lawson became a bit discombobulated. Lisa always took care of the practical things, like paying bills, overseeing the farm, etc. Lawson had no experience with these things hence was a bit lost concerning the family financial situation. Lauceen said Lawson seemed to be living more in the past than in the present.

One of the highlights of the visit occurred when Mooney drove Cannon outside Of the village to a tiny eating establishment operated by a former French Foreign Legion soldier who served in Vietnam as well as in Africa. Cannon had a great meal with excellent wine. Unfortunately he could barely understand the French being spoken nor could be he hardy join in conservation.

It was a good thing that Cannon visited with Mooney because a few short years later, Mooney went to join his wife and ancestors. Cannon was not able to speak with Lawson before his passing. He conveyed his prayers for Lawson's next sojourn to Lauceen a day before Lawson's exit. Lawson was a remarkable character and human being. Was he a spook for the CIA? Or wasn't he?

Back in the late 1950's and early 1960's, Catholic Relief Services (CRS) offered a unique cover should Mooney have been a spook undercover. Mooney's assignments with CRS took him to some interesting places that were of interest to the CIA. On the other hand, CRS headquarters could have provided information to the CIA based upon Mooney's reports. Mooney's dealings and his work with the late Mobutu regime makes one wonder about a possible direct CIA connection. After decades of overseas work, Cannon feels Mooney had dealings with the CIA: whether they were direct or indirect does not matter. Living and working overseas places people in the arena in which the CIA operates. Mooney lived and worked overseas for decades before he died. Does it really matter in God's eyes whether Mooney was a CIA spook or not?

Meeting Mooney in South Vietnam when Cannon was an idealist had to have an impact on Cannon. At that time both were helping to fight communism by supporting programs designed to win hearts and minds of the South Vietnamese people. History will judge whether joining the fight was right or wrong even though the fight was lost. After decades of overseas living and working, Cannon's path never did bring him into contact with a person of the likes of Mooney.

LIFE IN LESOTHO ROLLS ON

Life in Maseru was still a bit tenuous. The problems between the police and military were not yet resolved. The political situation was still confusing, especially the role of the King. One evening Cannon and a female guest from the US Embassy were eating dinner in a small Chinese restaurant when some drunken plain clothes policemen pulled out guns to get some free food and beer. Fortunately, Cannon and the guest had had previous similar experiences elsewhere and were able to complete their meal after a resemblance of order was restored (by giving beer & food to the plain clothes policemen). For a tiny little capital city in a small country, life was seldom boring.

The dam contractor hired a new Industrial Relations manager, another smooth talking South African. Unfortunately, he wasn't as "cool" as his predecessor and soon started to personalize things with CAWULE. So much so, that he terminated the recognition agreement. It seems this was a tactic he found successful previously. Unfortunately CAWULE would not negotiate further until he re-instated same. A wage settlement agreement was signed on the 24th of August 1995 as part of the collective bargaining agreement between the two. A month later, CAWULE was able to sign a wages collective bargaining agreement with the Tunnel contractor. Industrial relations couldn't have been better between CAWULE and both contractors.

In early October a massive crane collapsed at one of the tunnel working sites. Four Basotho workers were killed. Due to fast action of the contractor (he established an inquiry team of experts, which included representatives from CAWULE) their findings were made public before a major work stoppage could occur. Later in the month, the old Secretary General of CAWULE, J.Tsukulu returned from the UK after completing his year of study at Warwick University.

When the LHDA project closed for the year-end break, Cannon embarked on a great holiday vacation. He stopped off in Dublin to visit his cousin Joe: met some great friends of my cousin and acquired a taste for Guinness. Joe had migrated from the US back to Ireland in the mid-1990's and calls Ireland home. Unfortunately both Cannon and Joe are a bit thick-headed. Eventually two strong personalities clash. The easiest way to deal with cousins clashing is for one to move on.

From Ireland, Cannon went to the USA and onto Vancouver, Canada. Cannon visited with a lady he knew while a graduate student at St. Francis Xavier University decades ago. New Years in North American was very different from New Years in Africa-COLD!

The lady, who Cannon hadn't seen since 1975, had become a lawyer with a public sector union. Connie turned out to be a terrific host. A fantastic time was had by all. Cannon returned to Maine in January 1996 to visit the Bernardini's. On his way to Calais, Maine he stopped off at a florist in Bangor, Maine to wire forty-three roses to Connie for her birthday.

1996 started off badly for the people of Lesotho. On the 15th of January, King Moshoeshoe II died in a car accident in the Lesotho's mountains. On the 25th, two underground locomotives collided in a tunnel. This accident raised the job safety issue with the tunnel contractor again just shortly after the crane collapse. The tunnel contractors job safety problems would take another turn for the worst again the following month.

Cannon had the opportunity to personally meet with Johnnie Cochran the famous US lawyer that defended O'J. Simpson. Cannon met him at a party given by the US Ambassador to Lesotho. Cochran addressed the attendees regaling the crowd with tidbits from the Simpson trial. The attendees applauded Cochran frequently and it was obvious they were awed by this very successful lawyer.

After the formal reception was finished, the Secretary to the Ambassador asked Cannon if he would be available to meet in the Ambassador's residence privately with Cochran and Maureen Kindle who were in Lesotho to lobby LHDA on behalf of a Los Angles engineering consulting business firm. Cannon agreed. He knew the visitors wanted to pick his brain regarding LHDA because he was the only Yank still working on the project. Cannon answered a few basic questions while he consumed a soft drink. After a polite few minutes of inane give and take, Cannon took his leave. Cannon's loyalty was to his employer, not to his fellow countrymen. Unfortunately for Carson and Kindel, they never did obtain any work for their USA client with LHDA.

February 1996 was a very interesting month. On the 7th of February, the late King Moshoeshoe II son was sworn in as King Letsie III. Radio Lesotho started airing claims of safety hazards and poor labor practices against the tunnel contractor. The claims were made by CAWULE and some of their individual members. The South African press reported on the Radio Lesotho claims without substantiating the allegations. Allegations unsubstantiated eventually drops out of the news. Allegations change rapidly and accelerated public awareness after an underground worker was killed on the night shift in Pelaneng on the 22nd. Towards the end of the month, there were numerous rumors of another coup attempt. One never knew what happened, but the military did not or could not take over the government. A military coup would have upset South Africa under their new leadership of President Mandela, since Lesotho is completely surrounded by South Africa.

LHDA's Disputes Review Board (DRB) was conveyed on the 26th of February to look into multi-million US dollar claims from the Dam contractor arising out of last years' strikes. Cannon was able to drawn upon his records to provide information which was used by the DRB to contradict the contractor's claim on issues pertaining to industrial relations and CAWULE.

Cannon lost a colleague as well as the best boss he ever worked for when LHDA Chief Executive M. Sole was replaced by Mr. M. Marumo at the end of February 1996. Cannon wouldn't have the close and cordial relationship with the new Chief Executive due to his structural method of administration. If Cannon wanted to meet with the new LHDA Chief Executive, he had to go through Les Fabian. Cannon's counterpart Ntate Khetsi was getting a quick introduction to the machinations of the job he started the previous month.

The tunnel contractor brought unfair labor practice cases against CAWULE and individual workers to Lesotho's newly established Labor Court throughout 1995 and into 1966. Some government officers were getting tired of the tunnel contractor's use of the court as opposed to the collective bargaining agreement provisions agreed upon to settle disputes

It was not that long after Radio Lesotho started broadcasting allegations against the tunnel contractor, officials of the government were forced to act. On the 23rd of March, the members of the Lesotho Work Permit Board, under the auspices of the Labor Commissioner, visited Pelaneng. CAWULE was drawing upon the expertise of the International Federation of Building and Brickworks Workers (IFBBW) to assist them in their confrontations with the Tunnel contractor. Things were getting completely out of hand. All semblances of industrial relations and job safety professionalism and trust normally associated with collective bargaining agreements had been broken between tunnel employer and their employees.

On the 28th of March 1996, individual members of CAWULE wrote a letter to the World Bank in which they claimed apartheid was being practiced by the tunnel and Muela dam contractor on the Lesotho Highlands Water Project (LHWP). This unsubstantiated letter created a maelstrom within the LHDA structure as well as the joint Lesotho/South Africa commission overseeing the LHWP. The new LHDA Chief Executive created a LHDA Committee of Inquiry to investigate the allegations. Cannon was appointed chairman of the committee and responsible for heading up a team of Basotho colleagues to gather evidence pertaining to the allegations. Cannon was also tasked with compiling the findings into a report format which was submitted on the 10th of May 1996. The confidential findings contained in the internal LHDA committee of inquiry's report were made available to the World Bank and the governments of Lesotho and South Africa.

In early May, Labor Commissioner Fanana was hospitalized in South Africa. Cancer was discovered. On the 17th of May, work stopped on all tunnel sites as well as the Muela dam. South African mediators were selected to represent both parties: Mr. Curtin for CAWULE and Mr. Weber for the contractor. A basic settlement was reached and work resumed on May 22nd. Peace wouldn't last long.

On the 17th of June, workers on the Muela dam downed their tools. Within (8) hours, all of the Muela dam and tunnel workers were out on strike. One of the strikers' demands was the removal of the South African industrial relations manager, Mr. Vorster. This stoppage lasted eleven days. Despite their ideological differences, Cannon and Vorster were able to work together.

The Muela dam and tunnel contractor decided to get rid of Vorster in July. Unfortunately, they decided to replace him by poaching the smoothing talking Peter Streng from Katse Dam. A real bad move since CAWULE represented the workers of the tunnel contractor and Muela Dam as well. The union officials were familiar with many of his underhanded negotiating tactics which he had employed while working at Katse dam.

Cannon had a surplus of leave days. He took two weeks' vacation in August: after attending the funeral of Ntate Fanana at the Catholic Cathedral on the 3rd of August and the burial reception at his home after the services. It wasn't long before Peter Streng's magic resulted in yet another Muela dam and Tunnel contractor strike in September. Double talk always catches up with the instigator and eventually bites one in the backside: Streng found this out the hard way.

Shortly after the strike, some workers residing in the residential labor camp in Buthe Buthe (BB) were fired and evicted from the camp. The Muela dam and tunnel contractor requested police and military presence to safe guard their property after the evictions. On the 14th of September, shots were fired resulting in three dead and 25 injured inside the camp. Property was damaged.

For the second time in 1996, the LHDA Chief Executive established another internal Committee of Inquiry to investigate the Butha Buthe shootings. Cannon was again appointed chair and given the same responsibilities and tasks to collected data and write a report for the LHDA Chief Executive. The report was submitted on the 26th of September 1996.

The Government of Lesotho established a Commission of Inquiry, consisting of three High Court Justices, to write a report on the BB disaster. Their report, separate from the LHDA report, was presented to Prime Minister Mokhehle on the 21st of January 1998, after Cannon had departed Lesotho.

A couple of days after Cannon's birthday on the 24th of September, Cannon had the CAWULE Secretary General and two of his key aides to his house for food and drink and to talk about possible ways to get work restarted. CAWULE agreed it would be in the best interests of its members to get back to work. In the afternoon, the Muela dam and the tunnel contractor's Mr. Daniel Gasquet arrived from Paris. Cannon invited him and his South African colleague to his flat for a beer. While Cannon didn't disclose the major findings of his report, he did indicate that the newly hired Mr. Peter Streng was responsible for all major communications breakdowns with CAWULE. On the 31st of October, Mr. Peter Streng was fired.

Prior to the 1996 year end shut down in December, the Lesotho High Court issued a ruling that the September 1996 Muela dam and Tunnel contractor dismissals were legal and the resulting CAWULE strike was illegal. Throughout the insanity of events in 1996, Cannon's understudy Ntate Khetsi was learning the ropes of trying to promote a middle position between the LHDA contractors' and CAWULE while remaining neutral. If one of the LHWP contractors could prove LHDA staffs were siding with CAWULE they would submit financial claims against LHDA. This would be interference with their workforces, a major violation of FIDIC principles.

While working behind the scenes, Cannon's job was always to be in direct communications with the Labor Commissioners' Office, CAWULE headquarters, the contractors' human resource and safety managers and the various supervising engineer's personnel station at each construction site. With the start of the Muela dam project the number of construction sites covered by Cannon rose to eight. Khetsi proved he was more than capable to replace Cannon as all three of the Phase I construction projects were drawing to a close.

As Cannon's understudy became more involved in assuming more and more tasks associated with the position, Cannon was freed up to commence with the closing up of business and personal matters after some (10) years of living and working in Lesotho. Additionally, time was spent sending out resumes seeking new employment. The most difficult was saying goodbye to close friends and colleagues knowing that this might be Cannon's last time in Lesotho.

1996 ended with the first death in the Cannon family of a cousin in Cannon's age bracket. This helped one to understand that this sojourn on earth doesn't last forever. It also saw Marc Cannon enrolling in the University of Rhode Island hoping to complete his undergraduate degree in Fine Arts.

Before Cannon departed Southern Africa in the beginning of February 1997, he made a quick journey to Swaziland hoping to land a job with a massive construction project being undertaken between the countries of Mozambique, South Africa and Swaziland: without success.

Cannon first stop on his journey back to the USA was in Kenya to see his old jogging buddy and other friends. Welch and Cannon visited retired jockey Frank Morbey on Wasini Island on Kenya's south coast. A visit was also made to the Tom Mboya Labor College in Kisumu to see former colleagues. At the time who could have guessed in their wildest dreams and imagination that some twelve years later the son of a Luo from the Kisumu region would be sworn in as the 44th President of the United States?

Cannon's daughter Chandra had settled in Norway, her mothers' homeland, a few years after graduating from Bates College in Maine, USA. While visiting Chandra, Cannon learned he was to become a grandfather in October. This had to be God's gift to an only child. Further stops were made in Belgium and Denmark to visit old friends. Then, it was onward to Ireland to visit Cousin Joey. There Cannon had his first experience of celebrating St. Patrick's Day in Dublin as well as having a very clear sighting of Haley's Comet on the 26th. Cannon arrived back in the USA on the 5th of April 1997.

Cannon had no idea what life would be like in the US. If he had no idea about life in the US, what would life be back in small Calais, Maine? One thing was certain about Calais; Cannon would have a roof over his head, even if that roof covered a barn whose loft was transformed into a self-contained flat.

12

Overseas Consultant Assignments-USA Living

So much had changed since Cannon lived and worked in the USA in 1979. Almost two decades had brought about many significant changes. Cannon had his first culture shock when trying to purchase a computer from a Chinese businessman in North Providence, Rhode Island who's English was very limited while Cannon's Mandarin was non-existent. Cannon was like a baby speaking his first words because he had neither previous computer experience nor any idea what the sales person was saying about computers. Fortunately the sale was made since both parties were familiar with US dollars in cash

Next step was arranging the purchase of his first privately owned vehicle at age 57. Cannon was able to make contact with an old childhood friend the late John Coleman. One of John's numerous kids was a car salesman. Mike was a big help even though he only sold trucks. He contacted a colleague who sold Cannon a well maintained used Ford Escort. Cannon surprised the salesman by paying cash for the vehicle.

On April 10th, 1997 Cannon arrived in Calais, Maine to take up residence in the converted barn loft. The barn loft was a complete difference than living in Africa. While locals thought the temperatures were warm for that time of year in the upper 40's, Cannon thought they were more like winter. Cannon's airfreight from Lesotho was delivered on the 28th. Time had come to start unpacking goods that had been in storage since 1979. While moving furniture up the barn stairs, Cannon tore up his meniscus which would require surgery later.

Cannon spent May and June visiting his mother and son in RI as well as some old friends in Nova Scotia, Virginia, Maryland and New York. Cannon was also seeking work in the US without success. What were the chances of someone hiring a 57 year old who only had international work experiences, except for some four years working domestically? Zilch!

Cannon underwent surgery for his torn meniscus in July. He recuperated in the Bernardini's summer cottage overlooking beautiful St. Croix River which separated Calais, Maine, USA from St. Stephen, New Brunswick, Canada. In August, Cannon had the pleasure to experience the International Festival jointly co-celebrated by Calais and St. Stephen. Adjusting to life in Maine during the summer was easy as well as being very enjoyable.

Later in August, Cannon undertook his first car vacation in the US. He planned to drive out west to visit old friends from Lesotho. Cannon first met Tom and Carol while he was still married to Kari. They worked in the US Embassy in Maseru behind doors Cannon couldn't enter. Both couples socialized on a regular basis. What was memorable were the New Years' morning parties thrown by Tom and Carol-plenty of great food and the entire liquor one could consume. When they retired from US government service they located to North Dakota.

Cannon knew Tom worked in communications at the Embassy in Maseru-this was well known. Carol would tell people she was a secretary in the communications section. It was only when Cannon was reading plaques on their Recreation room wall that he saw one commending Carol for her 20 years of service with the CIA. This trip to North Dakota was Cannon's first car trip ever to the interior of the US.

On the way, Cannon stopped off in Chicago to visit a friend who he hadn't seen since the Peace Corps in 1964. Jane came from an Irish family who resided in the northern suburbs. She was a very attractive young woman who dropped out of college to join the Peace Corps in the early 1960's. While in the Philippines, she fell in love with an Italian guy from Brooklyn. Unfortunately in those days, both families were opposed to a potential marriage.

A few years after leaving the Peace Corps, Jane fell in love with a guy who was commissioned a Marine Corps officer just prior to their marriage. She became pregnant. He shipped out to South Vietnam and was killed in action. Jane's only child never met her father. Poor Jane never got over the death of her late husband. It was great to go back in time and laugh a lot about being young and idealistic.

North Dakota was brown in the summer. The hills, when they appeared, reminded Cannon of the Orange Free State in South Africa. Wide open spaces, which are very different from vista's in the east coast of the US. Tom and Carol ran a restaurant and had a new home on a lake. We had lots of boating and beer drinking and discussions about Africa.

Cannon decided to take a different route back to Maine. He drove north into Canada and headed back towards Toronto to visit with the Weber's, his old friends from Lesotho. They were retired and operated a small motel during the summer season. While there, Princess Diane died. We couldn't get over how much television time was devoted to her death. We agreed a similar amount of time would not have been allocated if she was a black Princess from Africa. Life in North America wasn't like life in Africa.

After Toronto, Cannon drove to Ottawa to visit with more old friends from Lesotho. The Lederman's were in Lesotho during Cannon's first time in the country. Bob was with UNDP and Maggie was a volunteer with the UK- based Volunteers Overseas Organization (VSO). They later spent time in Nigeria before they were married. It was great to re-connect even without the ex-Mrs. Cannon who was a favorite of Bob.

Cannon had one more stop to make to see another old friend in New Hampshire. Mike Kerper worked with Cannon back in the 1970's with the Asian-American Free Labor Institute (AFL-CIO). After a couple of years in Washington, Mike left to go to work with the A. Philip Randolph Institute in New York city for a few years before joining the staff of Senator Patrick Moynihan. Mike said after being a part of the political scene and the trade union scene, his skills would be better used in serving God. So he decided to become a Catholic priest. Mike was happy to see Cannon who in turn was happy to see Fr. Mike Kerper as well. Cannon arrived back in Calais in the middle of September.

On Cannon's 58th birthday on September 24th friends from Lesotho eldest daughter Oona, delivered a baby boy. As Cannon was getting older, it was good to know not everyone was old. Cannon had thoughts of becoming a Peace Corps volunteer again. He was interviewed in Boston. During the interview it became apparent that Cannon's African experiences weren't too impressive to the interviewee. They were looking for volunteers with small business experience to go to the former USSR, Russia. Cannon recalled that old axiom "You Cannot Go Home Again".

On the 14th of October 1997, Chandra Cannon delivered a baby girl Laila Isobel Cannon in Norway. Cannon had become a grandfather. Cannon's son Marc visited Calais with a girlfriend for Thanksgiving. Cannon cooked up a turkey with all the fixings only to learn the girlfriend was a vegetarian. No problem-It only took a few minutes to whip up a quick pasta sauce.

Chris Bernardini dropped by the barn to visit with Marc. Within a few minutes they had put on their winter jackets and were out the door heading to a party. Marc's girlfriend didn't accompany them. The next couple of hours seemed like days to Cannon trying to make small talk with a young woman he had only met briefly once before. The flat became very animated when Marc rolled in around 2 AM. The animation continued until they headed back to Rhode Island around noon.

Marc later returned to Calais alone to celebrate Christmas with his father. Cannon didn't have to cook two meals. Father and Son had a good time before Marc headed back to Rhode Island to celebrate New Years' with friends.

UGANDA CONSULTANT ASSIGNMENT

Prior to Christmas, Cannon entered into discussions with Professor Michael Horowitz of the Institute of Development Anthropology (IDA) about the possibility of undertaking an environmental impact assessment study focusing on resettlement and compensation for a potential dam project in Uganda. The study would be in conjunction with ENSR Engineering, the World Bank and with the American firm AES as the potential client.

Cannon departed the US on the 20th of January 1998 for Uganda with a stop-over in Norway to visit his daughter and new granddaughter who was to be baptized in Stavanger's only Catholic Church during Cannon's visit.

Cannon was thrilled getting to hold his granddaughter in his arms as she was being baptized. After close on 20 years, Cannon's comprehension of Norwegian had diminished profoundly though this did not make the ceremony any less beautiful. Truly a memorable time! The memories and images will last Cannon a lifetime.

Unfortunately, the visit only lasted for a few days before it was time to fly onwards to Kampala, Uganda. Is the reader discerning a pattern by now? Cannon always seemed to be working even when there were family matters which should have had precedent over his professional work. By this time in Cannon's life, he still had the view if he was providing for his family, the other family duties would take care of themselves.

Like so many international construction projects, the proposed Bujakali Dam caused many concerns to many people within Uganda and externally. Within Uganda, major opposition came from a South African white-owned company which ran a white water rafting operation on the Nile; a few environmentalists; and some Ugandans who would be displaced should the project come to fruition.

Externally the key players were the World Bank, the ICF, and the US Import/Export Agency. All three would be deeply involved with the financing and insuring of said proposed project. AES, the proposed client with the Government of Uganda, wanted international support and financial backing needed for a mega construction project.

Cannon was part of a group of expatriates whose main task would be to gather preliminary data for the project's Environmental Impact Assessment. The assessment was one of the requirements before project funding could be secured. Little did Cannon know that he would be called upon to serve as the point person for the foreign organizations in their meetings with local communities?

The meeting participants were the persons who would be forced to re-locate if the proposed project became a reality. Preliminary work on crop compensation had been initiated by the Government as part of the AES preliminary assessment. The offerings were inadequate from an international point of view. Based upon Cannon's interaction with the local communities, he believed the issue of crop and land compensation should be a negotiable part of the entire project.

If compensation funds were part of the entire projects estimated costs, the effected persons would be fairly compensated. If not, compensation values would be set by the Ugandan government. In all likelihood these values would be infinitesimal compared to international standards.

Compensation funds should be incorporated into the project documents with specific line items specifically allocated to compensation. AES was opposed to this concept. They wanted the issue of compensation to be a separate project item in line with the standards established by the Government of Uganda. If crop values and relocation costs were set by the Ugandan government and troubles arose during the project, AES could wash its hands of this major issue.

Cannon returned to Binghamton, NY the home of IDA to write a report based upon the Uganda findings while anticipating a return to Uganda in mid-February to undertake the assessment. After much internal discussion, IDA informed ENSR it couldn't be a partner to the proposed Bujagali Dam environmental impact assessment unless AES committed itself to a specific sum of funds within the proposed project contract that would be specifically earmarked for crop compensation, land compensation, family relocation, and job training and small business training for the potential effected population. ENSR disagreed with the IDA recommendation thereby removing IDA from further association with the proposed Bujagali Dam project. Cannon didn't get back to Uganda.

WINTER IN CALAIS, MAINE

February and March in Calais aren't the best months of the year weather wise. It took Cannon a while to get used to shoveling snow again. The driveway to the entrance to the garage and barn seemed to get longer with each snow storm. The long winter begins to wear on people and tempers become a bit short as the snow continues and the temperatures remain just above zero.

Cannon decided he wasn't cut out to do a 2nd stint with the Peace Corps and withdrew his application. Cannon came to realize that his years overseas, particularly in Africa, had led him to see how the Peace Corps had become more and more an arm of official US government foreign policy.

At its inception, Peace Corps directors served at the pleasure of the President of the United States. Cannon became fully aware of the political nature of this reality when his buddy Ernie Yancy was removed as the Peace Corps Director in Malawi because his politics differed with President Ronald Reagan. The political ideology of the reigning US President had its effect on the Peace Corps. Presidents approved overseas Peace Corps Directors who reflected their ideology. The original primary goal- win friends and influence people stayed the same throughout the years. It is likely when Cannon was a Peace Corps volunteer soon after its inception, his youth and idealistic world view blocked a realistic assessment of how the Peace Corps was part and parcel of the US government's foreign policy.

Cannon knew the prospect of finding employment in Calais, Maine was impossible and likewise, throughout the State of Maine. Cannon's skills and experiences were not too relevant to the employment situation in the US. Catholic Relief Services were seeking a consultant to undertake a six-month assignment in Africa. The assignment area was completely new to Cannon. Monetization of US donated food commodities as part of PL-480 Title II.

Originally PL-480 Title II commodities could not be sold or exchanged. They were to be distributed free of charge to their intended overseas recipients. Sometime in the 1980's the entire PL-480 Title II element of the USAID program overseas was revised. Provisions were made for the sale of the commodities by recipient Non-Government Organizations (NGO's), as long as the NGO could prove to USAID the host country had port and storage facilities to handle them and that the proposed sale would not interfere with the local commercial market.

Monetization was a new concept for Cannon. In his first tour with CRS, the food made available to NGO's, PL-480 Title II (US surplus grown crops) was prohibited from being sold. There were a myriad of rules and regulations associated with Monetization. It was obvious to Cannon, that Monetization was a mechanism created to cover a cutback in foreign assistance. Yet it was being made to look like a foreign-assistance add-on. The Reagan administration's view that big government was the cause of major problems in the US and that only the private sector could right things found its way into the US foreign assistance program.

Financial monies were decreased for NGO development activities overseas. At the same time NGO's were told they could sell (monetize) PL-480 Title II commodities commercially overseas to obtain monies which then could be used to fund their respective development activities.

The rules and regulations governing the monetization process were so convoluted that they required full-time NGO personnel. The catchall for monetization was to ensure it did not interfere with the US private commercial sale of bulk commodities overseas nor overload the limited port facilities of the country in which the monetization might take place.

CRS CONSULTANT ASSIGNMENT IN AFRICA

In April 1998, Cannon found himself back in Africa. Harare, Zimbabwe was where CRS had its regional office for Southern Africa. The office was run by a former colleague from Cannon's days in Vietnam in the mid-1960's-Francis Xavier Carlin.

It was Cannon's good fortune to meet with Mr. George Menegay. George was retired from the NGO- CARE and was quite familiar with monetization. Cannon was to accompany George to Malawi where they were to investigate monetization possibilities. Another surprise: the CRS Malawi Director was Mr. Steve Otto who Cannon had worked for when he first arrived in Lagos, Nigeria back in 1968 during the civil war. Truly a small world! Nothing firm arose from Cannon's visit to Malawi except to meet another terrific person.

Desmond Nkhoma was employed by CRS Malawi. Prior to his work with CRS, Desmond and Cannon had a mutual colleague, Chukufa Chihana. When CC was Vice President for Malawi, Desmond was his Press Secretary. We were able to exchange stories about working with CC. Unfortunately during Cannon's stays in Malawi; he was unable to meet with CC who was living in northern Malawi his home region after his political retirement.

At the time, any monetization study in Southern Africa required a visit to South Africa which was the economic and agriculture engine for the entire region. Menegay and Cannon flew into Johannesburg and teamed up with the Save the Children (SCF) monetization guru Mr. Ron Shaw. Cannon underwent a one-on-one tutorial with Shaw before heading to Kenya to participate in a Monetization Workshop. Menegay returned to Malawi. After completing his assignment for CRS, George was hired by World Vision to undertake a monetization out of Mozambique.

While in Harare, in between monetization trips, Cannon crossed paths with an Italian commodities salesperson for the giant Andre Cie, Switzerland. Christian was so smooth. He talked so confidently about commodity sales, it was almost possible to envision he could cut butter without a knife. Cannon now had another potential player in the monetization game. Little did Cannon know that later the Government of Zimbabwe would arrest Christian for currency violations?

Carlin soon left Harare after Cannon's arrival to assume a senior position with CRS in their Baltimore headquarters. His replacement was completely opposite: all according to the book. Some of the CRS regional staff was terrific, especially a young guy by the name of Ian MacNairn who would become a friend back in the US of A. Another was originally from Argentina, by way of Uruguay-Gino Lofredo. Others aren't worth mentioning.

Out of the blue, Cannon was informed that he was to go to Egypt and join-up with George Menegay on a joint monetization inquiry. Cannon was to represent a consortium of NGO's in Ethiopia led by CRS, while Menegay was to represent a consortium of NGO's in Mozambique led by World Vision. They were to see if it would be possible to monetize (sell) 63,000 metric tons of bulk hard winter wheat in Cairo.

The monies from the hoped for monetization would be split by the two consortiums' and be used to fund development activities by the consortium members in the respective countries. Egypt was the second largest recipient of US assistance in the world after Israel and one of the world's largest importers of wheat.

Cannon was checked into the old Shepherds Hotel in Cairo, close to the Nile. It was the preeminent hotel back in the 1950's and played a role in the Egyptian uprising against the colonial British back then. The rooms were massive, with high ceilings and floor length size windows. The bath was from the 1950's, quaint, but getting a bit worn out. Menegay had completed an assignment in Egypt back in the 1960's with CARE, hence was familiar with certain sections of the city, especially the older ones. It was he who recommended the Shepherds hotel to Cannon. Menegay arrived in Cairo a few days after Cannon.

Prior to going to Egypt, Cannon had contact with the US Wheat Association in South Africa who was willing to contact their counterpart in Cairo. This contact was familiar with most of the big wheat importers and buyers in Cairo. The Egyptian government subsidized its local bread making industry since bread was the basic staple of its citizens. Egypt was also the biggest importer of wheat in the world. Cannon and Menegay had a small list of companies that might be interested in purchasing the hard winter wheat. Hard winter wheat is the key mixing ingredient in the making of bread.

Prior to Menegay arrived, Cannon was allocated office space and access to a computer in the CRS/Cairo office which was within walking distance from the Shepherds hotel. After ensuring a place to operate out of, the next step was to arrange a meeting with the US Wheat Association representative in Cairo. He provided Cannon with a list of potential contacts and suggested who might be seen first.

Cannon met with five potential buyers. Only one expressed an interest in the monetization. An additional positive result of these meetings was names and addresses of other potential buyers who were not on the list provided by the US Wheat Association were given to Cannon. By the time Menegay arrived some of the ground work had been initiated.

Cannon and Menegay's first stop was the offices of USAID in Cairo in order to introduce ourselves and to outline the results of the preliminary investigation for the monetization. Without the USAID/Egypt authorization, no monetization could be done in-country. Another reason for the visit was to obtain the name of the US Embassy Agriculture Officer who would accept or reject the Bellmon Analysis that was required to ensure the potential sale wouldn't disrupt the local wheat commerce and to show the port of Alexandria had the capacity of receive and store the wheat.

One potential buyer who met Cannon and Menegay in the Shepherds hotel relayed a very interesting story. He said a few years back he had been approached by a male who had some 30,000 metric tons of wheat for sale at a reasonable price. After arranging all the financial requirements in Cairo, the buyer later learned the potential seller was a con man from Israel. Fortunately no money had changed hands. The Egyptian said to Cannon and Menegay he thought they were also con men.

Cannon and Menegay spent a few days gathering data on port storage capabilities, yearly wheat import tonnages, and commercial wheat import prices to write the Bellmon Analysis. It took another day working out of the CRS/Cairo office to complete the paper work before it could be submitted to the US Ambassador via his Agriculture Officer. After a week, the US Agriculture Officer said the submitted Bellmon Analysis was approved.

While awaiting the decision of whether the Bellmon Analysis was accepted, Cannon and Menegay continued meetings with potential buyers and did a bit of sight-seeing on the side. One of the potential buyers Cannon had previously met was a Canadian, Wayne Becon, who represented a company called ORIAC.

After another meeting with Wayne and some hard bargaining, it was agreed a further meeting could be useful for a potential sale. Next step was to report back to the consortiums and ensure they both were on board with the possible sale price. This was done. The only one remaining step was to present a Monetization Plan of Action proposal to USAID whose approval was required before the sale could be finalized. Once USAID gave its approval, Cannon departed Egypt for Ethiopia to brief the consortium members and Menegay departed for Mozambique. Eventually, Menegay returned to Cairo to finalize the monetization for a sales price of US $ 45,000,000.

Cannon eventually returned to Harare, Zimbabwe to resume his consultancy for CRS. In July 1998, Cannon flew to London to be interviewed by the Association of Commonwealth Universities for a position in the Papua New Guinea technical school system. While in London, he was able to renew contact with Ted and Jane Irving who he first met in 1969 in Lesotho and had last seen in Hong Kong after he had completed a temporary assignment in Bangladesh. It was great seeing Ted and Jane again. We all had turned into gray headed older folks. Cannon was eventually told he was "over qualified" for the position in Papua New Guinea. Whatever "over qualified" means?

Next, Cannon was informed he was to undertake a monetization study in Liberia. Before flying to Liberia, he needed to go to Ghana to obtain an entry visa for Liberia. Also Cannon was to work with a young CRS person who was recently hired to oversee the CRS/Ghana monetization process.

Liberia was like a Mad Max movie: insane to put it mildly. The arrival lounge at the airport was order less. There were people everywhere shouting, pushing, trying to grab ones bags. Liberian customs officials were not in uniform hence you could not tell if the person asking for your passport was an official or a crowd member. It seemed everyone was asking Cannon for money. Fortunately a CRS staff member arrived to bail Cannon out of the insanity.

The ride into the city of Monrovia was an eye opener. The physical effects of years of civil war were evident everywhere one looked. Buildings had windows damaged, some had had been looted of their tin roofs, yet people were still living in them. Young unemployed people were wandering the streets. There were few vehicles using the streets.

The CRS office compound was a different matter. It had a very tall wall completely surrounding the compound topped with razor wire. There were guards at the two entrances/exits who opened and closed the steel gate doors. It had its own generator for electricity. This would be the location Cannon operated out of while on assignment.

After meeting the CRS/Liberia Director, Cannon was taken to a compound on the outskirts of the city. CRS and another NGO had rented houses for their expatriate staff. Once unpacked Cannon was told the brewery that produced the excellent Club Beer was still functioning fortunately.

One of the potential buyers for soybean oil was the Bridgeway company. The person in charge, George Haddad, had trunks full of US dollars in his office-sort of like an "informal" bank. Rumor had it that Haddad was one of President Charles Taylor's main men. Haddad wasn't interested buying soybean oil unless CRS would pay him in US dollars outside of Liberia. The monetization study didn't result in any sales. More than monetization was needed for poor Liberia.

Getting out of Liberia was worse than getting in. There were armed soldiers at some 6 to 7 places along the departure walk to the airplane They all asked to see the airport departure receipt ($ 20) trying to supplement their meager wages. It wasn't too bad being an expatriate, but if you were Liberian you needed to "dash" each soldier before he would allow you to proceed to the plane. No "dash" no entry onto the plane even if one had a valid ticket. The last check was at the foot of the airplane stairs.

Cannon fulfilled a promise made previously in Lesotho to attend the wedding of Christensen's daughter in Sienna, Italy. Cannon took a few days leave and departed Harare for Rome. Cannon took a bus from Rome to Sienna. The wedding was held in one of the seven or eight mini churches in the old city. A beautiful ceremony followed by a terrific wedding meal. Cannon stayed a few days after the wedding to relax before heading back to Zimbabwe.

Cannon traveled to Madagascar and Malawi to conduct monetization studies before his consultancy with CRS was completed in early October 1998. Monetization was and could possibly be a good idea. Unfortunately, it has too many USAID rules and regulations that make it almost impossible as a regular source of development monies for NGO's. It was a great learning experience.

Cannon stopped off in Norway to attend the baptismal of his granddaughter Laila Isobel Cannon who came into this world on the 14th of October 1997. After Norway, Cannon visited Denmark to see his old girlfriend Jette and the Christensen's. Then it was off to the US. Cannon was unable to attend the funeral in France for his former mentor, Lawson Mooney, who passed away on the 27th of October.

SOUTHERN AFRICA MONITISATION ASSIGNMENT

Cannon was back in Harare, Zimbabwe before 1998 ended. He was rehired to undertake a monetization study, for the Southern Africa regional office of CRS. First stop was Zambia. Cannon was accompanied by Ian MacNairn who was to become the CRS monetization person for the Southern Africa region. Unless one was willing to contribute to the fortunes of the family of President Fred Chiluba, it was unlikely that one could do monetization. This was especially true with soybean oil since Chiluba's uncle ran the state owned oil mill in Lusaka which also happened to be the only one with the capacity to process any monetization oil.

Years later Cannon's former trade union colleague and frequent home visitor, Fred Chiluba, was charged with stealing millions of dollars from the state coffers during his years as President. What good beliefs and intentions Fred had while leading the Zambia Trade Union movement seemed to have gotten lost when he became President. Maybe the trappings and temptations of office were too much for a person of poor and humble origins?

Christmas 1998 was spent on lovely Lake Malawi as well as 1999 New Years' Day. After the holidays, it was back to Zimbabwe to undertake a soybean oil monetization study there. While in Harare, Cannon was able to reconnect with Martin Doherty who he knew from his working days with the AALC. Next was South Africa after the Zimbabwe study.

The purpose of the trip to South Africa was to explore the possibility of selling wheat and soybean oil. Cannon was required to travel to Durban, the home of the major food oil process plant. There he was able to have dinner with Alan Vorster who worked on the LHWP for the tunnel contractor. Then, it was onwards to Swaziland and Lesotho to speak with management of two flour processing factories. Whether or not CRS followed up further on these studies is unknown.

While in South Africa, Cannon was able to re-establish contact with the NGO monetization guru, Mr. Ron Shaw who was still with Save the Children. Cannon traveled to Cape Town along with Shaw and Ian MacNairn to attend a monetization conference sponsored by the U.S. Wheat Associates at the lovely Victoria Albert Hotel on the Cape Town waterfront.

What a cast of characters attended the conference. There was Ed Smith who headed the U.S. Wheat Associates (USWA) office in Cape Town (nicknamed Fast Eddy); Joe Barbberri, who handled monetization for the NGO Winrock, and was doing a monetization in Angola with USWA; Andrew Sims and Carlos Ferreira from Angola, whose company TONDO were doing the monetization. A couple of religious persons were representing World Vision. Attendees also included Shaw, MacNairn and Cannon plus Fast Eddy's local Cape Town staff. Cannon felt like an outsider as all the aforementioned all were on first name basis. Little did Cannon know that this conference would result in another monetization consultancy later in 1999?

In Swaziland, Cannon was able to see old friends. Jonathan Jenness, who Cannon worked with on the Lesotho Highlands Water Project, was employed on a Southern Africa private sector project for Mozambique and Swaziland. Cannon touched base with Delores Taylor, a native of Swaziland, who was formerly married to Charlie Taylor. Taylor was a colleague of Cannon's back when he was with AALC. Delores had been very active in the late 1970's in the South African underground with the ANC. This was well before the South African government lifted their ban of the ANC, PAC, and SACP in the late 1980's.

Charlie lived up the road from Delores. Cannon had previously visited Charlie on the farm. At that time the house and surrounding were well kept. This time it was a completely different story. Charlie's Mercedes was up on wooden blocks-two wheels were missing. The front door to the house was off its hinges. Parts of the roof were missing.

Charlie's clothes were tattered and he appeared disheveled. He had let the farm go to seed and was basically losing touch with life on the outside. Even with this unpleasant finding, it was still great to talk with Charlie about the old trade union days in Africa long before Cannon's time. Cannon departed Charlie's farm with a heavy heart knowing it was likely he would never see Charlie again.

After Swaziland, Cannon went to Lesotho for a day. Cannon did not have sufficient time to touch base with his former colleagues at LHDA. He met with management of the only flour mill in the country. Management told him they were not interested in a monetization with CRS. Unfortunately, Cannon was unable to conduct a monetization in Southern Africa in which Delores Taylor could have participated.

A monetization study was conducted in Madagascar. CRS/Madagascar asked Cannon to study whether it was feasible to monetize soybean oil. The factory processing edible oil had a monopoly throughout the country. It was run by a future President of Madagascar. After reviewing data, especially shipping costs to get the soybean oil from the US, monetization was not economical. This was a situation in which CRS couldn't fight city hall.

Cannon traveled to Denmark and Ireland on his way back to the US. While in Denmark, his daughter and granddaughter came over from Norway. Jette and Cannon talked again about Cannon moving to Denmark. Cannon said yes, but later Jette said she knew it was no before Cannon left. He had behaved as an African: giving her a yes not to upset her, but really meaning no. In Ireland, it was good to see Cousin Joey even if we had our usual falling-out after a week or so.

May and June were spent visiting old friends in New York and Washington, DC; flogging resumes; taking in ball games; seeing my Mother and Son in Rhode Island; pulling lobster traps in beautiful Calais, Maine with my buddy and drinking beer.

WORLD VISION ANGOLA ASSIGNMENT

Out of the blue in July, World Vision contacted Cannon to inquire whether he was available to undertake a monetization consultancy in Angola. Cannon agreed and ended up in Luanda where he was able to see Andrew Sims and Carlos Ferreira again and interview a contact from Christian Fillipinni in Zimbabwe as a potential buyer. USAID cancelled the monetization study.

Before departing Luanda, Cannon attended a fantastic beach party thrown by Sims & Ferreira: great food, plenty to drink, beautiful ladies, and crazy men. One of the crazy men was a Cuban who didn't return to Cuba when Fidel pulled out the troops in the late 1970's. He liked dancing naked while drinking Johnny Walker straight out of the bottle.

CHANGING NGO'S

Cannon's recent work with NGO's produced some unexpected results. First off, there was a new breed working with and for NGOs, especially on the ground in their overseas operations. It was refreshing to be exposed to new faces and more important to different ideas. International development work had become more institutionalized since its inception after World War II in Cannon's view.

Back in the late 1950's and early 1960's, major NGOs were able to derive a good percentage of their operating costs from private donor sources while they received commodities from the US government. Come the 1970's, the NGO scene expanded greatly when European countries became active overseas. In their early stages of formation, they drew their major support from private non-government sources. They sometimes referred to American NGOs as overseas arms of the US government due to the increased financial role of the US government. Yet some of the European NGO's served as organs to employ their unemployed citizens who had little if any previous development experience or skills. They were frequently sent to Africa to "advise" Africans on how to develop their countries.

Cannon didn't pay too much attention initially to the relationship between his NGO employers and the US government since his first overseas assignment was with the US government's Peace Corps in 1963. Living and working overseas one focused on development tasks with the people one worked with in local organizations.

It wasn't until Cannon went to work for the overseas arm of the AFL-CIO that the close tie between NGO and US government became very apparent. Close to 100% of funds used to work with trade unions overseas was derived from the US government. Was this very different than using US government donated food to provide assistance to needy infants and mothers and using food aid to facilitate development projects?

One forum in which the Western and Eastern influence and ideology clashed was at the annual meeting of the International Labor Organization (ILO) in Geneva, Switzerland. The ILO is the only international body in which there are representatives drawn for government, employer organizations and trade union (labor) organizations. Opposite views and positions were openly debated and voted upon at each annual ILO meeting. Countries in which the AFL-CIO had overseas representation were expected to adhere to the position put forth by the West deeply influenced by the US government and the AFL-CIO and vote accordingly.

As long as the Cold War between the East and West remained "cold", battles were waged to win hearts and minds. It wasn't that troubling to Cannon's views on international development. When Cannon became involved with the private sector in the start of the decade of the 1990's, his views regarding international development began to change.

The LHWP opened Cannon's eyes to power relationships between smaller developing nations, the capitalist private sector contractors and the World Bank. The major donors were more interested in protecting their organizations than promoting the views of a small developing country.

The international construction companies, who made up the consortiums who built the dam and tunnels, were interested in making a profit. The international engineering companies, who made up the consortiums which monitored the project, were looking forward to additional projects in the future. The host country who possessed the natural resources (water in this case), which were being developed, had very limited say internationally. They had even lesser control over what took place daily on the project. Yet it was their resources and their citizens who were the most affected by the project. It became obvious to Cannon, that the aforementioned players didn't act and behave in Lesotho as they would have in Europe. A question arose: are there dual standards, one for Europe and another for Africa?

Cannon's Catholic belief and faith remained consistent. If anything changed, it was Cannon's realization that his view of the structure of the Church had undergone a dramatic change from his days growing up in Rhode Island. Initially, Cannon saw priests as the manifestation of the church itself. Throughout the years in Africa, Cannon witnessed deviant behavior from priests, especially those who openly consorted with females. Over time Cannon could accept such strange behavior because he realized priests were human beings subject to short comings like any other human being. Cannon had no right to judge priests behavior that rested with God alone. Cannons Catholicism was no longer intertwined with priests' behavior but totally focused on his relationship to God.

Cannon's disillusionment regarding international development work, especially in Africa, was growing. The monetization assignments illustrated the limited policy input afforded recipient countries. Likewise the input of local citizen's was limited. Donor bodies often conducted their programs as if they knew what was best for the recipients.

New questions arose in Cannon's mind. What historical and/or moral right did westerners have to think they know what is best for developing countries and people? Was the main purpose of US government supplied development aid's to assist the host country people or to promote the growth of its NGO movement? Did following western development administration procedures, rules and regulations take precedent over local control of the developmental process?

Will there be western international developmental programs in the year 2050? If so, it's likely they will not be operated in a similar manner as they are presently. Host governments will have a much larger say into potential 2050 programs, if they still exist then? Would Cannon have additional opportunities overseas to seek answers to the aforementioned?

BACK TO THE REAL WORLD!

Cannon's son Marc was still trying to get his university degree after being bounced out of RISD. He was enrolled part-time as a student at the University of Rhode Island while laboring in construction industry and living in the city of Providence. The main URI campus is located in Kingston in the southern part of RI, not too far from the beaches, but far away if one does not own a car.

Cannon, at the time, thought he had a brilliant idea. He would see if he could rent a summer beach house from his Cousin Vinnie. If successful, he could offer Marc a place to live free so he could enroll in URI as a full-time student. Also being in RI would offer him the chance to spend more time with his ailing Mother and surrogate aunt Evelyn.

Cannon's cousin Vinnie had not rented out his summer cottage in the fall of 1999. Once a rental agreement was reached, Cannon's son Marc moved in first. Drama! His girlfriend from Providence visited and either caught him with another woman or thought there was another woman in the cottage. She proceeded to rip off the cottage screened door. Cannon arrived a few days later and should have realized then that living together with his son for the 1st time in almost ten years would be trying. Both parties agreed to try to make the best of the situation.

On the 24th of September 1999, Cannon celebrated his 60th birthday. Prior to the birthday, Cannon had re-established contact via the internet with a girl friend from Lesotho. Denise was in Washington attending language school before proceeding on her next State Department assignment.

Cannon received a phone call from Denise indicating a willingness to fly to RI on Cannon's birthday. Cannon picked Denise at the Green Airport and drove to the cottage where she met Marc for the first time. Marc and Denise were closer in age than Cannon and Denise.

It was good to see Denise after a few years. We had a torrid affair but short lived affair in Lesotho before going separate ways. Both thought that the other had changed since Lesotho. The affair renewed itself and after a few months it was obvious that neither had changed too much. The 2nd time around followed the same course as the first: torrid but short lived.

In October, Joe and Barbara Davis, friends from Cannon's days in Kenya, came to Rhode Island to visit with one of their best friends. It was impossible, due to their short visit, to arrange a time for all to get together. Their friend was willing to invite Cannon to a dinner she was hosting for Joe and Barbara and another couple. The hostess lived not too far from the beach cottage so it was an easy drive for Cannon. The introduction to Gudrun would change Cannon's life.

In November Cannon committed himself to drive to Washington, DC to pick up Denise and bring her back to New England to celebrate Thanksgiving. On the way to DC, Cannon stopped off in central New Jersey to spend a couple of days with his old jogging buddy from Kenya, Bob Welsh. As was the custom, Cannon cooked a couple of Italian dinners and Welsh supplied the libations.

Denise knew about Cannon's place in Calais, Maine. She didn't believe Cannon that he had rehabbed the old barn/carriage house and was living in it and not in the main house proper. She was pleasantly surprised to find the barn flat was a very comfortable, well- conceived and furnished residence for one person. It proved too small for a couple.

Thanksgiving was spent with the extended Bernardini family in Calais. Denise spent a lot of time in the kitchen with the men regaling them with experiences from some of her assignments overseas in South America, India and Africa with the State Department. Most of the Bernardini men weren't used to listening to a well educated and well-spoken African American woman. They could not picture the international background of her experiences. In mid-December, Cannon drove to Washington to say goodbye before Denise left for the Congo

Then it was back to Rhode Island for the holidays. Cannon spent Christmas with his son Marc, his Mother and Aunt Evelyn. We all went out for Christmas lunch at a cozy inn in nearby Jamestown, RI. The two older ladies had a great time. Aunt Evelyn started her meal with the dessert-something she said she always wanted to do. Mother thought the inn was a boat. She was starting her journey back to being a child- the Alzheimer's disease. All in all it was a great Christmas.

Fear was in the air as the year 2000 was due to arrive. The 2K fear mongers were forecasting the possible disintegration of the computerized systems throughout the country. Cannon and Gudrun, after a fantastic cooked meal in RI, went outside at midnight. The sky was full of stars and the end of the world had yet to arrive. All slept peaceful since the doomsayers had been proven wrong again.

Cannon spent the first four and one-half months of 2000 actively seeking employment, both internationally and domestically. Wayne Newell, an old friend from the days with Maine Indian Education (MIE), David Dorn and Joe Davis with the American Federation of Teachers (AFT), and many others were contacted. At one time, Cannon's bags were packed for a consultancy for the AFT in Kosovo only to hear from Dorn that he cancelled same.

Gudrun and Cannon visited with their mutual friends the Davis's during Easter. A month later disaster struck. Gudrun learned she had developed a cancer in her ovaries. Cannon returned to Rhode Island from Calais to be available as Gudrun's primary health care supporter in her home. Her two kids were far away pursuing their careers in academia: one in California and the other in Pittsburgh.

She underwent surgery on the 19th of May to remove the cancerous growths. Surgery was successful. Gudrun proved to be a fighter and terrific house patient. Cannon's skills that he developed as an only child when his Mother was a full-time worker back in the 1950's came in handy: cooking, cleaning house, etc. Gudrun was recovering well when Cannon left for his next overseas assignment.

NIGERIA CALLING

Old friends from his days with the African American Labor Center (AFL-CIO) now renamed American Center for International Labor Solidarity (ACILS) short for Solidarity Center (SC) inquired whether he'd be interested in taking a consultant assignment in Nigeria. Cannon accepted the offer and departed for Lagos, Nigeria on the 15th of July 2000. Nigeria had changed since Cannon was there last in the late 1960's during the civil war. Oil had forested massive infrastructure development, especially in Lagos and the new capital city Abuja. The Solidarity Center office was run by an old colleague: who was in the process of being transferred to Kenya. Cannon was to serve as acting-director until a replacement came out from Washington and to undertake a feasibility study as to the pros and cons of moving the office to Abuja.

It was uncomfortable for Tom Medley, Cannon's former colleague, who thought he was being evaluated. It was worst for Cannon since Medley ran the office like a one-piece band. Trying to get a grip on funds, equipment, staff and other office matters was time-consuming and unpleasant. The worst occurred when Medley decided to take the office lap top and cam recorder to Kenya as his own personal property.

While in Nigeria for the 2nd time, Cannon was fortunate to tie-up with Ben Edherue. Ben had previously worked with the Nigerian Labor Congress (NLC) for many years before he was poached by the African-American Labor Center. The AALC needed a local trade unionist well versed in politics as a guide for Tom Miller its first American resident representative to Nigeria.

Tom Medley did not have sufficient time to brief Cannon on the trade union situation in Nigeria since he was too busy making arrangements to move to Kenya. Although Cannon had not been directly involved with the trade union movement since he was employed by AALC, he know he needed a quick tutorial on the Nigerian trade union movement if he was to function properly as a consultant.

After meeting individually with each Nigerian staff member in the SC/Nigeria office, it was clear to Cannon that Ben Edherue was the only competent person to provide the detailed trade union briefing he needed. Cannon asked Ben to undertake this task. At first Ben was shy and reluctant. Cannon later learned the reasons: Tom did not bother to confide with Ben nor did he utilize his vast past experience with the NLC. Ben was given a week to prepare same since Cannon wanted historical information, the roles of the USSR and USA in the development of the trade union movement, the tribal composition of union leadership, numerical strengths, collective bargaining agreements, dues structures and collection mechanisms, labor college potential, roles of other international donors, etc. Ben blossomed with the assignment.

A schedule was established with a two-hour time frame set aside for Cannon's tutorial on the Nigerian trade union movement. At first Ben wasn't sure exactly what Cannon was seeking nor was he sure Cannon was serious about this. Ben was shocked to see Cannon taking notes during their first session. Later he told Cannon he was very impressed with the questions he raised which illustrated an insightfulness previously missing in his relationship with Tom. How does one describe a fellow human being who was a work colleague and later a very close friend?

Ben wasn't a big man physically. He was about 5 feet 8 inches. He had a full head of hair which was beginning to recede. His face was more rounded than square and he was starting to develop a slight paunch. His eyes sparkled and his voice boomed, especially when he would greet friends.

Ben had a cutting sense of humor, especially when he was discussing trade unions' or politics in Nigeria with a non-Nigerian. This sense of humor grew as he talked about the inconsistent actions taken by the US versus their beliefs put forth to the entire world.

At days end Ben would accompany Cannon back to the nearby Sheraton Hotel for a few beers: Nigerian beer is excellent. It was in this informal setting that Ben's personality became infectious. He would regale Cannon with stories about his younger days with the NLC that would have Cannon doubling over with laughter. This setting allowed Ben to ask numerous questions about Cannon and his background. It was inevitable a friendship would blossom.

Ben and Cannon were invited as guests to participate in a workshop upcountry in Jos. The workshop was sponsored by a German donor and run by a couple of South African trade unionists. The German's donor's representative had previously been assigned to South Africa before being posted to Nigeria. Cannon felt like an intruder due to the cold shoulder presented by the German and the South Africans. This feeling of being an outsider diminished as a result of Ben's including him in all outside workshop activities. At the workshop, Cannon had the opportunity to meet and establish a working relationship with a few NLC staffers who were Ben's peers when he worked with them at the NLC. Their help came in very handy when the feasibility study was undertaken.

Medley was replaced by a young African-American about six weeks after Cannon's arrival in Lagos. When he arrived in Nigeria, he proceeded to inform the senior leadership of the NLC that he had no trade union background besides his late grandfather having been a union member. Cannon was shocked! So much so, that when he returned to Washington, he questioned the SC Director why hadn't he at least sent the young man to the AFL-CIO's George Meany Center, at least for a few weeks of trade union orientation and training, before placing him in the highly political atmosphere of the trade union movement in Nigeria? No answer was forthcoming. Things had changed in the ten years Cannon was away from the US labor movement overseas.

On Cannon's way back to Washington, he stopped in Norway to see his daughter and granddaughter. He stopped in Denmark to see Jette and the Christensen's; Sweden to see friends from the 1960's; and Ireland to see his cousin Joey. The remainder of 2000 was spent either in Calais, Maine or in Rhode Island.

In 2001, a friend was confirmed as the United States Ambassador to Nigeria. Back in the 1980's while in Lesotho, Howard Jeter was given the choice of the # 2 position in newly independent Namibia or the # 2 position in Nigeria. At the time Namibia had better schooling facilities for younger children than did Lagos-hence Howard opted for Namibia. Upon completion of the assignment, he was appointed Ambassador to Botswana.

His last career overseas appointment was to Nigeria: the culmination of his diplomatic career. As noted elsewhere, Howard made Cannon proud to identify himself as an American in Africa. He was a wonderful representative of all the good the US stood for. Cannon could not say the same for some US Ambassadors he met during his years in Africa.

In April, Cannon's daughter Chandra visited from Norway. Cannon's granddaughter Laila was too small to accompany her Mother. Cannon drove to Boston to meet Chandra's flight which delayed until late afternoon. Instead of getting hotel rooms, it was decided to drive back to Maine. Both Father and daughter were exhausted by the time they arrived back in Calais.

It was Chandra's first time to see the barn/flat which her Father now called home. The flat had two bedrooms but only one bed: the second bedroom was used as an office. Cannon gave up his bed and slept on a blow-up camp bed in the office during Chandra's stay. Chandra re-connected with the Bernardini's and a few other folks. Day trips were taken to the Roosevelt summer cottage across from Lubec, Maine in New Brunswick and to nearby St. Andrews, also in New Brunswick. Great visit!

After a few days, Chandra wanted to head south to Rhode Island- about 430 miles away to visit with her grandmother and brother Marc. Unfortunately, she had to return back to Norway before Marc was to graduate from the University of Rhode Island on the 20th of May 2001.

Graduation Day was a beauty: warm with a clear blue sky. Cannon was accompanied to the graduation by Gudrun who had recovered from her bout with cancer. Cannon felt very proud when the name Marc Erik Cannon was called and to see him walk up to receive his diploma. Only later did Cannon learn that the actual diploma wasn't presented due to the number of graduates. It was to be picked up later at the administration office. A small graduation party was thrown by Marc's girlfriend Jerah in the tiny house they shared close to the university.

Cannon returned to Maine later in May. One day Cannon's post box held a letter from the University of Rhode Island addressed to Marc who was in RI. Cannon wondered why the letter's address was his at 120 North Street, Calais, Maine not Marc's where he was living while attending URI. Cannon opened the letter to read Marc didn't graduate. He was short two courses to meet the Bachelor of Fine Arts requirements. Cannon was furious to say the least.

Cannon was involved in a vehicle accident in June. He attended a wedding of the son of some friends in Calais and after served as the dishwasher at the reception overlooking the lovely St. Croix River which separated the USA from Canada in Eastern Maine. While washing pots, pans, dishes, etc. Cannon nipped on some good Irish whiskey. This proved his downfall. He fell asleep at the wheel driving back to Calais, drove off the highway into a stone ledge.

Fortunately the accident took place late at night and did not involve another vehicle. People living in a near-by house called the Calais police. A private operated ambulance operating out of Calais drove Cannon to the Calais hospital. Cannon gave permission for a blood sample to be drawn. After the blood was drawn, the police office was kind enough to drive Cannon to his barn/flat. Cannon was later convicted of Operating Under the Influence (OUI). This conviction resulted in a driving license suspension for 90 days and a 48 hour county jail sentence and a $ 500 fine. Cannon served his sentence over the Labor Day weekend. Due to jail over- crowding (young male drug offenders) he was released after only serving 24 hours.

In July, Cannon's mother was moved into a nursing home due to her onset of Alzheimer's. She was unable to care for herself. Fortunately her girlfriend and my surrogate Aunt Evelyn joined her in the nursing home a short while later. It was one of the saddest days in Cannon's life. Thank God his son Marc was available to help with the move from her lovely assisted living residence where she spent a great 15 years according to her.

July wasn't all bad. Cannon's buddy from Nigeria, Ben Edherue finally made it to the USA as a recipient of the US Department of Labor overseas visitors program. When speaking with Ben while he was in Washington, DC, Cannon was asked if he had any thoughts about the study program. Once Cannon was informed the visitors were to spend time out west, he suggested Ben ask the sponsors to visit an American Indian Reservation if he wanted to see the worst of the USA. Needless to say the study tour sponsors did not take them to an American Indian Reservation. Could it be they did not want their overseas visitors to see the squalor and under development present in so many of the native American Indian reservations in the US?

After Cannon's road accident he now had to depend on bus transportation to reach Rhode Island. Fortunately there was a small 8 seat bus that went from Calais to Bangor following Route 1 along the coastline. In Bangor, a bus was available to Boston and from Boston one could connect with the Logan Airport bus to Providence. The sojourn took the entire day: about 12 hours. Public transportation in rural America is basically nonexistent.

Cannon's Mother suffered a debilitating fall in early September. The nursing staff recommended she receive last rites of the Catholic Church. They didn't know the inner strength of the polite tiny Mrs. Cannon. Cannon was holding her hand saying a few prayers, while she was asleep during the early hours of the morning on September 11th when disaster struck the USA.

There was a nearby television in the nursing home. Cannon joined the nation watching the images being reported in disbelief. What resulted in more disbelief was hearing the President of the United States recommend the American people a few days later: Go Shopping.

Cannon returned to Maine in late September: reversing his journey taken earlier in the month. Cannon learned what life must be like for rural living folks in the US who unfortunately do not have a car-isolated. In October, Cannon applied for a job in Nigeria that was advertised in one of the headhunters' publications. Within a day of applying, a call was initiated by a Washington, DC consulting firm seeking references. Later in the week, a job offer was made. It took a few weeks of negotiations over the language in the contract before Cannon accepted the offer.

13

Nigeria- Cannon/ Edherue Renaissance

In 1999, Nigeria returned to civilian rule after too many years of being ruled by the military. President William Clinton visited Nigeria and offered varied forms of assistance, sometimes referred to as Presidential Deliverables. One of them under the auspices of the US Department of Labor was to assist in the demobilization of military personnel at the Nigerian Armed Forces Resettlement Center (NAFRC) in Lagos.

NAFRC was constructed in 1945 by the British, former colonial power, to provide demobilization skills to Nigerian enlisted personnel who had fought with the British in World War II. When initially constructed, the base in the Oshodi section was located in the far outskirts of Lagos: not so years later. It was located on a huge plot of land within the city's residential and commercial section of Lagos on the road to the international airport.

Once the WWII veterans were demobilized, the base was incorporated into the structure of the Nigerian Army. It reverted back to a training facility after the 1960's Nigerian civil war ceased. It was used to provide physical rehabilitation and some technical skills training to soldiers set for retirement after having completed their terms of service. Only later Cannon learned that the US government, via USAID, provided technical advisory staff and equipment to the facility in the early 1970's.

Enlisted and non-commissioned officers in the Nigerian Army, Air Force and Navy scheduled for retirement had an opportunity to seek admission into NAFRC six months prior to their retirement from early 1980's onwards. NAFRC conducted two twenty-five week training sessions per year in which they accepted some 2000 trainees per session. Trainees who completed their respective course received certificates which were recognized by both the federal government and each state government as valid technical training certification.

On the 14th of November, Cannon and Gary Curry (he was the former project manager) arrived in Lagos. The following day, they proceeded to the US Consulate compound on Victoria Island. The former US Embassy in Lagos had become the US Consulate a few miles in distance from the apartment where Cannon was to live.

Lagos is famous for vehicle traffic situations. The Nigerian term "go slow" is used when there is grid-lock, with no vehicle movement at all. The usual driving time from Cannon's flat to the nearby Lagos international airport was about 30 minutes for the 15 mile drive. During go-slows, the same drive could reach 6 hours. There were times when it took Cannon two hours to reach the Consulate from his apartment. Normally it took about 30 minutes.

The main support for the NAFRC project was located in the Political Section of the Consulate. Cannon was taken aback when Ms. Barrie Hofmann came out to greet Curry and Cannon. She was an old friend from Lesotho. Her husband Karl was serving as the US Ambassador to Togo which was a few hours' drive from Lagos. Barrie and Cannon both were good friends with Ambassador Jeter in Abuja, who also served in Lesotho back in the 1980's.

The following day, Curry, Cannon and Hofmann drove to the Nigerian Armed Forces Resettlement Center (NAFRC). The purpose was to introduce Cannon as the new project director. NAFRC was commanded by a two star general (Air Vice Marshall) with the Nigerian Air Force. Staffs were drawn from the Nigerian Army and Nigerian Navy as well. Cannon was immediately put on the carpet by the hosts who were demanding answers as to why previous US promises of equipment had yet to be supplied. Cannon responded by asking for a NAFRC picture identity card to get on and off the base and promised to supply answers once he was settled in. Cannon was also shown the small office for the project. It was located in back of the main headquarters administration block and even had a toilet with a wash basin.

After the introductory meeting, Curry left for Europe. Cannon moved into a fully furnished apartment previously occupied by Curry. It was located down the street from the US compound that formerly housed the US Ambassador, before his move to the Abuja where a new US Embassy was in the process of being constructed.

Cannon's fully furnished flat was big enough for a family: two bedrooms, dining room, living room, two bathrooms, stove, fridge, washing machine and dryer, and a kitchen. The flat was located on the upper floor over the apartment of the owner, an Italian business woman. There were two other apartments within the same building. The long tiny outside balcony overlooked the garden of the owner. All the windows were barred on the outside including the balcony. It also included a color television with access to cable programs from a South African network. There was a cleaning person, employed by the landlady, who did laundry. Externally, the compound was surrounded by a high cement wall with broken glass imbedded on the top with razor wire inside. There were also private hired security guards who opened and closed the steel entry gate.

There were two generators for electrical power as backup when the municipal power was off (which was frequent). A private contractor supplied water when the municipal system wasn't operational. A sheltered parking space was also provided a few steps away from the entrance door to the apartment which was very convenient during the heavy down pours in the West African rainy season.

On the 2nd of December, a team of officers from the US Department of Labor (USDOL), accompanied by the Vice President of Aurora Associates-the implementing consulting firm who hired Cannon-arrived from Washington. The team was made up of Dr. Robert Young, Mr. Michael Talbert, and Mr. Eric Ruddek of the DOL and Dr. James Statman of Aurora. As soon as Cannon attended his first roundtable meeting, the realization set-in that these "experts" had their own preconceived views as to where the NAFRC project should be heading and how the NAFRC project should be administrated, especially the DOL persons. They had even picked-out Nigerian persons to serve as the bridge between the DOL and the officers at NAFRC.

Nobody associated with the project was willing to acknowledge the project had problems. Curry the former US on-site project director told Cannon he resigned partially out of frustration with the DOL. One cause of his frustration was the inability of the USA folks to deliver the big-ticket items' promised to NAFRC personnel when they were in Washington on a study tour earlier in the year.

The visitors and Cannon flew to Abuja to meet with the US Ambassador Jeter the next day. The existing Embassy was temporary located in a residential compound until the construction of the new embassy was completed. Cannon was surprised Ambassador Jeter's residence consisted of a series of rooms in the Hilton Hotel which were converted into a small flat.

The US Embassy arranged meetings with officials in the Nigerian government including the Nigerian Minister of Defense (rd.) Lt. General Theophilus Danjuma and the Nigerian Minister of State Defense (Army), the Honorable Batagarawa. The meetings were able to update all parties as to the current status of the project and plans for 2002. After returning to Lagos, the visitors held a meeting with the NAFRC Commandant to brief him on what transpired in Abuja and to outline what they envisioned Cannon's tasks to be in 2002.

Many of the project deliverables were to derive from previous ideas hatched with Engineer Oginni. He was a Nigerian technician from Yaba Technical Institute who the DOL drew upon for project ideas. Later, Cannon was to learn the NAFRC leadership did not sign-off on any of the Oginni identified tasks which were identified as deliverables envisioned for 2002.

Additionally the project deliverables had a component with a local Lagos state government office. Representatives of the Lagos State Government (LSG) were participants in the USA study tour that proceeded Cannon's arrival in Nigeria. Sessions with the Lagos State Government officials were discombobulated. The LSG ideas as to what they were to get from the project were completely different from what was in project documents.

At the final de-briefing in the US consulate in Lagos, Cannon didn't concur with the DOL's assessment, especially regarding the LSG. Cannon was told his job was to follow what the DOL had envisioned and initiated for the project. If he didn't, he could be fired by the DOL. Cannon said he was hired by Aurora and would report to Aurora/Washington not to DOL in Washington. If the DOL and Aurora couldn't concur, Cannon would be happy to return to Calais, Maine. Once tempers cooled, the de-briefing proceeded. The visitors left Nigeria on the 8th of December.

As soon as the visitors departed, Cannon was joined by Ben Edherue at his flat to drink some beer and catch up on what was happening in Nigeria and within the Nigerian Labor Movement. At that time, Cannon inquired whether Ben would be interested in coming to work as his counterpart on the NAFRC project. Ben rejected the offer. His previous experiences with the Nigerian military coupled with the limited duration of the project were the main factors in his rejection. He said he had a kid brother who recently graduated from university that might be a good substitute.

Cannon's predecessor had arranged transportation via a private car hire service which, operated out of the Ekoi Hotel which was close to his furnished flat. There was provision in the project for a project vehicle. If a new vehicle was to be purchased overseas duty-free, the importation process would take forever. If a second hand vehicle was purchased, different headaches would entail. The car hire folks wanted a 100% increase in their daily rate once they realized there was a newcomer to deal with. Cannon had a transportation problem which needed to be resolved quickly. Without transport, Cannon would find it almost impossible to work at NAFRC.

The week following the visitors' departure, Cannon secured his NAFRC military identification card and proceeded to outline the projects plans for 2002 to the NAFRC Commandant and his senior officers. These plans included actions, which would fore fill promises made to the NAFRC leadership when they visited the United States in the summer of 2000. One of the major actions planned was to secure generators from the US promised to NAFRC.

NAFRC held its passing-out (graduation) ceremony for the 2001 second group of military personnel scheduled for demobilization and retirement at the end of the 2nd week in December. Thereafter NAFRC closed for the holidays. It was set to re-open the 2nd week in January 2002 when the first 2002 intake of trainees would arrive.

Cannon's Christmas and New Year's Day were quite. Nigeria wasn't any different from other African countries when it came to year-end holidays. Basically, government closed, as did most private sector establishments. If they were not completely closed, they remained open staffed by a skeleton crew. Major cities emptied as residents returned to their villages of birth to celebrate the holidays with their extended families. For many, this was the only time in the year in which they were able to secure sufficient time off to make the trip "home".

After the holidays, Ben came up with a proposal to resolve Cannon's transportation problem. He proposed that the project hire his 2nd hand vehicle for a flat monthly fee. The fee would include the provision of a driver, insurance and the cost of petrol (gas). The vehicle could be parked nightly inside the compound for Cannon's flat and it was available should Cannon need to drive anywhere during the evening or on weekends. Cannon submitted the proposal to the Aurora office in Washington. They concurred with his recommendation to lease Ben's vehicle. Ben was now a small entrepreneur as well as a trade unionist: a contradiction in the west, but not in Africa where taking care of one's family took precedent over one's profession.

During the period before the vehicle lease was finalized, Cannon confirmed his major suspicions and wondered whether the project was even legal in Nigeria:

(1) Aurora did not have a signed contract/agreement with the Government of Nigeria for the project. This was normally a legal requirement for doing business in a foreign country as well as being a pre-requisite for importing duty-free project goods.

(2) The DOL/US Embassy Nigeria did not have a contract/agreement with the Government of Nigeria for the project. Was it possible the DOL persons thought a contract or agreement was not required because the DOL was a US Government department operating through the US Embassy to Nigeria? Aurora, being a private US non-government entity definitely could not operate in Nigeria under diplomatic protocol without formal legal status.

(3) There was no project contract/agreement between Aurora/DOL and NAFRC. Without a formal contract or agreement, how could any leverage be placed upon NAFRC to live up to its verbal commitments?

Was the project in Nigeria arriving out of a visit by President Clinton created to forester neo-colonialism? Surely the answer to this question would be of course not. On the other hand, what would be the chances of a Nigerian or any other foreign government arm coming into the United States and setting up a project in the same way as the DOL set-up the project in Nigeria? Never in a million years. It is totally impossible to even think of something happening such as this in the US.

In comparison to the Lesotho Highlands Water Project, the project set-up in Nigeria was very amateurish in comparison especially on paper. Maybe this was caused by a lack of working international experience of the USDOL personnel. If so, this is another illustration of western good intensions thinking they know best what was needed to make a project succeed in Africa. Any poorly arranged project usually starts under a cloud with a potential for future disaster and failure in Cannon's African work experience.

Driving to NAFRC daily, required passage through some of the worst sections of Lagos city. Leasing a 2nd hand vehicle went a long way to deter potential car hijackers and crooks who viewed expatriates as easy targets for carjacking. They were interested in new SUVs and similar high priced imported vehicles not a 2nd hand old used passenger car. Even when trouble erupted, such as when the Nigerian Labour Congress (NLC) called a strike over the government enforced petrol price increases, the leased vehicle never drew any attention from the local troublemakers who were called "area boys". Yemi the Driver, hired by Ben, knew Lagos. He was an even a better person than he was a great driver.

Cannon was still familiarizing himself with the NAFRC base and personnel, when two retired US military officers visited NAFRC. They were employed by Military Professional Resources Incorporated (MPRI) a private US defense contractor founded by retired senior army officers. MPRI had the contract for the 2nd component of the Presidential deliverable-retraining of key sections of the Nigerian military. Cannon attended meetings in which they informed the NAFRC Commandant and Deputy Commandant they could easily provide the big-ticket items, such as generators, which Aurora had yet to deliver. Cannon informed Ambassador Jeter about the visit. There were no future visits from MPRI personnel to NAFRC.

While attending the Martin Luther King Junior celebration at the Consulate's residence in Lagos, Cannon was asked by one of the attendees to step outside for a private talk. It was shocking to learn there were Consulate personnel who were actively seeking to get the Ambassador removed from his post. It seemed he didn't give approval for Consulate staff to play volleyball at the residence, he demanded too much work from staff; etc. A sorry state of affairs!

It was obvious to Cannon during the December meetings with the Nigerian Minister of Defense and Minister of State for Defense (army) that the Ambassador was very highly thought of. Isn't one of the main responsibilities of a US Ambassador to develop good working relations with the host country? Or maybe things changed in 2002? Or was it a new major task to pamper the junior officers in the consulate instead?

Later, Cannon delivered a letter of support to a representative in the State Department's Office of Inspector General who had come to Nigeria to look into the allegations regarding Ambassador Jeter. How the US State Department was changing from the days when Cannon first went overseas. Could it be possible playing volleyball on the grounds of the Ambassadors' Lagos residence provoked the investigation? Cannon was dismayed by the treatment Ambassador Jeter was being subject to.

After securing prices from three suppliers (a US government regulation), Cannon purchased computers and printers for the NAFRC senior staff and administrative headquarters-the first big-ticket item the project had committed itself to. The purchases were made with a Nigerian Lebanese supplier who also was willing to offer a training service workshop as part of the purchase price. The installation of the computers and printers was warmly welcomed, especially after a training workshop was held. During the workshop, the electricity was cut- a frequent occurrence in the Oshodi area, illustrating the need for the US promised generators.

January 2002 drew to a close with a loud bang. Literally, on the 27th, the Lagos skies were filled with exploding artillery ordinance flying overhead. Cannon initially thought a coup was underway. Exploding ordinance in Cannon's past experiences usually signaled the military was planning to take power or started fighting among themselves. Based on Nigeria's past history, Cannon ruled out the fight option.

A telephone call was made to the Deputy NAFRC Commandant Brigadier General S. Shaibu- a person Cannon trusted based upon their dealings to date. He said a cooking fire next to an armory at the Army based not far from NAFRC had caused the ordinance to explode. After receiving the aforementioned information, Cannon telephone Barrie Hofmann at the US Consulate to pass along what he heard. Hofmann expressed her thanks.

It was obvious that the rest of the day would be spent inside the flat until the situation returned to normal. Cannon returned to the book he had started reading the previous night. It would be a good day to get in some serious reading. The next day it was learned the armory explosions were caused by cooking fires. The explosions even caused damage to some of the external structures in NAFRC including the small office assigned to Cannon.

One of the hidden gems of NAFRC was animal husbandry in the agriculture wing. Besides office and classroom facilities, there were also mini holding pens for animals such as goats, pigs, chickens, snails, etc. as well as a fish pond. The Agriculture Department often would commercially sell eggs, rabbits, etc.

Cannon purchased rabbits to bring to Togo in February for the Hofmann kids. Cannon was last in Togo in the mid-1970 as part of an evaluation team. Lome, Togo's seaside capital had not changed much. It still had very nice beaches on the Atlantic with good French restaurants. Cannon was put up in the Ambassador's residence in a very nice pool side cabana. Jogging along the Atlantic was a joy in the early morning hours. Togo was a nice break from NAFRC.

Engineer Oginni provided a very good service technician for the computers a young Ibo by the name of Ejike. Ejike was to remain a key person throughout the project's duration, especially once the computer training lab was established. Shortly after Ejike showed up at NAFRC, Cannon hired Ben's younger brother, Oke Edherue.

Now there were two people daily in Cannon's little NAFRC office. It was a joy to be able to speak with a younger civilian Nigerian to get another view of Nigeria and its military. What was difficult to get used was being called Uncle Pete. The terms Aunt and Uncle are frequently used in Africa to show respect to elder persons. Over time, Cannon became accustomed to this term of endearment. Most of Oke's life had been lived under military rule; hence he was very apprehensive initially to convey any NAFRC shortcomings which NAFRC were keeping hidden from the Yankee white man.

Early in 2002, Cannon kept trying to follow up with non-military bodies to explore the potential of establishing civilian training centers which could supplement skill training offered by NAFRC. Numerous visits were made to the Lagos state government (LSG) offices as well as sites they identified as their Job Creation Centers. All Cannon ever found was empty buildings before giving up on the LSG. A visit was made to Ibadan to visit the International Institute for Tropical Agriculture hoping to get their expertise to assist the improvement of NAFRC's agriculture wing. The last civilian body Cannon contacted was the Nigeria Legion as per instructions received from the USDOL in Washington.

The DOL in the US was able to partner with the American Legion for some of its re-training programs offered to discharge US military veterans. Mr. Erik Ruddek, who was a member of the DOL team that visited Nigeria in December, had obtained the address of the Nigerian Legion and thought the NAFRC project, could join forces as was the case in the US. Here again, the lack of international development experience overseas produced ideas that more closely resembled dreams than concrete reality.

The Nigerian Legion's primary function was to administer monies made available by the Federal Government to disabled veterans. The Legion had neither interest nor incentive, to become involved neither with the USDOL nor with NAFRC. They told Cannon so in very blunt words uncharacteristic for most Nigerians.

Cannon received the go-ahead for the next major big-ticket project purchases: four diesel generators which would serve as a back-up electrical supply for the NAFRC workshops and administrative offices whenever power was cut. Power cuts were very frequent. The first task was to construct concrete pads for each generator's location. Work was started by Engineer Oginni in March 2002.

During the Easter season, Cannon was surprised when Ben invited him to spend the Easter holidays with his Isoko village family. Cannon later learned he was the first foreigner who worked with Ben throughout the years that was ever invited to accompany him "home" in the Niger delta.

First stop on the way to Isokoland was Benin City, southeast of Lagos. Cannon had last been in Benin City during the civil war in 1968. It sure had changed in the ensuring years growing much bigger and more disjointed. After checking into a local hotel and showering, Ben and Cannon started out to locate Ben's buddy & colleague Sylvester. After picking Sylvester up at his house, we proceeded to his girlfriend's place. We all joined forces proceeding to a local bar well known for its "pepper soup" and cold beer. After the drive from Lagos over horrible highways the food and drink were a real treat.

After a second days drive, we arrived at night to see some of Ben's extended family in Adah. Even though it was well after dark, the men folk set-up chairs under a nearby tree and we started to consume "local" gin straight. Thank goodness for the ancestors. One could pour out a portion of one's libation on the ground to honor their spirits. At night, it was easy to pour out more than the acceptable amount protocol warranted. Late at night we finally arrived at Ben's senior brother's home in the nearby town of Irri. Sleep came easy.

The next day Ben gave Cannon a few bottles of water. He said this will be his only concession since the local water would surely make Cannon ill. Other than the water, Cannon was treated with the same facilities and provisions as the other male family members. The food was wonderful and the company better. Even drinking warm beer wasn't as bad as one might think.

Cannon was taken to a relative's funeral ceremony. It was completely different from those in the US. Here in Isokoland, there were bands playing, people singing praise for the deceased, and lots of good food and drink to consume. Cannon participated in his first dance in which you placed money on your dance partner's forehead. They money collected helped cover the very expensive cost of the burial ceremony.

Prior to returning to Lagos, Ben drove Cannon to visit with his mother in his birth village of Ikori. Mama Edherue and Cannon conversed using Ben as our translator. Before Cannon knew it, it was time to start the long drive back to Lagos. One treat remained.

About mid-way to Lagos, Ben pulled off at highway into the Nigerian equivalent of a fast food mall. There were stalls offering various Nigerian specialties. The one we went to must have been a favorite of Ben because the cook and waiting staff all greeted him fondly. Their special was fish soup. The choicest portion according to Ben was the head served with fufu (boiled yam pounded into a dough like texture) chased by cold beer. Cannon marveled at the simplicity of the establishment and their excellent preparation of the soup.

The food was more nutritional and better tasting than Burger King or McDonalds. Both of which had yet to become a part of the Nigerian market. Nigerians love food and consume big portions of fresh cooked food unlike American fast food chains where most of the food served is pre-cooked.

The next big-ticket item for the project had to do with the establishment of a computer laboratory, even if the availability of electricity was spotty. Us Yanks thought the arrival of the four generators would go a long way in solving the electrical situation at NAFRC. Initially, parties had to agree to the site for the proposed lab. Should a new building be built (there wasn't any money in the project for the construction of new buildings) or an existing one turned into a lab?

Opposite the parade ground was the club for enlisted men which was in very poor condition but was in an excellent location. All that was necessary was to find another building and location for the club. This was done and the new site only required small renovations. The next question arose as to who would actually do the physical labor to gut the club? Would it be possible to use the construction trades trainees? Yes, if they were given additional pay! Engineer Oginni came to the rescue. He hired a few laborers (later it was learned they were only paid a portion of the sum the project paid). While the work was on-going, Aurora/Washington was negotiating with a US company to supply the generators.

Cannon was recalled to Washington for his input. Unfortunately, the DOL and Aurora had completed the tender specifications thus limiting Cannon's input. Fortunately, Cannon was able to convince the folks in Washington to ship the generators in c/o of the US Consulate in Lagos. Originally Aurora/Washington wanted to ship these to an import/export business they had located. Cannon and Yemi-the-Driver spent hours trying to locate the Lagos address of this business. After much searching it was apparent the business was bogus.

If the generators were not shipped in care of the US Consulate in Lagos, they never would have cleared customs since neither Aurora nor the DOL had duty-free import privileges for Nigeria. On Cannon's way back to Nigeria, he was able to stop-off (at his expense) in Norway to visit his daughter and granddaughter.

Remodeling work for the anticipated computer laboratory was proceeding beyond what was expected. NAFRC hosted some unexpected visitors from the US War College. They were a bit taken aback with the NAFRC base and found the facilities very primitive in comparison to US bases.

These visitors received numerous requests for assistance from NAFRC's senior staff. All they could say was they would inform the US Embassy in Abuja of these requests before they departed Nigeria.

The generators arrived in the port of Lagos and were cleared through customs by the US Consulates agent. The same agent transported them to NAFRC Oshodi and deposited them on their concrete pads under the supervision of Don Greeneville and Lou Myers who representing the US supplier. Two 150 watt diesel generators were to be located next to the administration block and the auditorium/mess hall. Two 300 watt diesel generators were to be located near the planned computer laboratory and in the middle of the workshop area. Don and Lou did a great job hooking up the generators but when it came time to test them a major problem arose. No diesel.

The NAFRC Commandant said the bases fuel storage dump was out of commission. It had been for years. He also said neither Aurora nor the DOL had made any mention that NAFRC would be expected to supply diesel for the generators. To facilitate the generator testing, Cannon purchased a truck load of diesel and filled the generator tanks. The generators worked perfectly.

Don and Lou conducted a hands-on workshop for NAFRC personnel who were to operate the generators. Before departing, Cannon insisted they subcontract with a local Nigerian engineering company to service and maintain the generators while they were covered by warrant. This was a hot point of contention.

The DOL and Aurora had not raised this point in the Washington negotiations. Cannon's previous experience with tender specifications overcame this sticky point. Don and Lou hired Ole Thomas, a local engineer to maintain and service the generators while they were covered by warranty. He would become a good friend.

The refurbishing of the computer laboratory was a Nigerian operation. The supplier was paid from an amendment to the projects original budget. The chairs, tables, storage cabinets, copy machine, etc. to furnish the lab were purchased from the open market after securing three price quotes. The computers, printers, and other high tech equipment were purchased by the DOL from a US minority business. Said firm had another contract with the US Embassy in Nigeria. Hence, there wasn't a problem in bringing in the equipment duty free. The US company's Nigerian counterpart installed the computers at NAFRC.

On the 14th of June 2002, NAFRC held its passing out/graduation ceremony for the trainees. Guest of honor was the Nigerian Minister of Defense (rd.) Lt. General T. Danjuma, who was accompanied by the Nigerian Senate Committee on Defense Chairman and the House Committee on Defense Chairman Senator S. Negele and Representative B. Salmi. The Minister was very impressed in the progress made in (7) months since his meeting in Abuja on the project. He said he wanted to formally dedicate the NAFRC computer laboratory along with the US Ambassador in the coming months. Everyone was so pleased with developments. Nobody bothered to raise the issue of diesel supply. The computer laboratory would not operate during the frequent electrical shutdowns if the generators were also not working. The computers also ran the risk of being damaged by power spikes.

While NAFRC was closed for a few weeks prior to the arrival of the 2nd 2002 batch of trainees in mid -July, Cannon came to realize the entire NAFRC project looked great on paper in Washington. Being implemented, in the field, the project wasn't as good as it looked on paper. It had been poorly planned. It did not have written specifications and contracts/agreements with the Nigerian government and military. Outputs listed on paper were seldom achieved.

Engineer Oginni and Yaba Tech were hired originally at the projects inception to draw-up learning manuals for each of the 29 NAFRC workshops. They did. NAFRC didn't feel compelled to use the manuals. There was not a written agreement requiring them to do so nor did NAFRC have any input into these learning manuals according to the NAFRC Commandant.

The provision of (4) generators looked good on paper. However without a regular source of diesel the only generator that was used regularly was the one that supplied power to the Commandant's Office and the Administration block.

Calling upon the experience of DOL experts from Washington and their consultants to try to twine possible NAFRC programs with similar ones conducted in the US was pie-in-the-sky dreaming. Did the good intentioned US personnel really believe they could replicate US type programs in Nigeria?

Being assigned to NAFRC for many of the senior military officers was viewed as punishment or as their last post before retirement. They were all good people, but they lacked enthusiasm for the project: unlike the politicians and senior military in Abuja.

NAFRC had been limping along for too long and viewed as a dumping ground to expect it to respond to the enthusiasm of Aurora and the DOL. A disconnect existed between what was originally envisioned for the project and the views of the NAFRC officers responsible for implementing the project. Without official project documentation binding the Nigerian government and NAFRC, no one could exert pressure on NAFRC.

After (6) months, Cannon thought the project should focus on only a few of the 29 workshops, the newly established computer lab/workshop, the agriculture wing, trainee publications and introduction video's, limited supplies and equipment for specific workshops, and remodeling of the trainees quarters using the trainees themselves enrolled in the construction trades. Secondary efforts would be made with counseling with emphasis on HIV-AIDS prevention. Efforts would also be made to conduct a mini-survey to identify what recent NAFRC graduates were doing in civilian life to get some baseline data as to what areas/ skills NAFRC efforts were succeeding and those having no bearing in civilian life. Once Aurora/DOL concurred with the aforementioned project change of direction, Engineer Oginni's role was no longer essential.

NAFRC proposed the project provide help with a planned demobilization program for officers from the three services. The NAFRC Commandant started work to construct self-contained apartments on the base for officers. Major emphasis would be the utilization of the computer lab facilities.

Cannon was introduced to Professor Kandi (Ukandi) Damachi by Ambassador Jeter. Kandi had worked previously with the ILO and was very well connected to the upper political and military echelons. Kandi spoke very highly of the work being done by Ambassador Jeter and said he'd be happy to assist Cannon's project with NAFRC if possible

Professor Kandi Damachi drew-up an officers' course which would partially use the dormant facilities of the joint government/NLC labor education center in Ilorin, as well as the NAFRC Oshodi base. Kandi's cost estimates were way beyond the realm of the project. Hence they were never followed up by NAFRC. By the time the DOL project was completed on 1 October 2004, no construction progress had been made beyond the shell of the building for officers.

Likewise another indirect project likewise had a similar effect on NAFRC. The US Department of Defense earmarked US one million dollars to help upgrade NAFRC's main facilities, water, sanitation and electrical. The project documentation was between the US Embassy Abuja and the Ministry of Defense's Joint Services Department with no role specifically for NAFRC.

Internal NAFRC procurement procedures were to be by-passed again by the Yanks thereby cutting off supplemental potential personal income generating activities for senior NAFRC officers. NAFRC senior officers deeply resented Cannons procurement of supplies and equipment for NAFRC workshop outside of the internal NAFRC system.

Initially the Colonel responsible for the education/training aspect of NAFRC complained bitterly regarding Cannon's unwillingness to use NAFRC channels for supplies and equipment purchases. Cannon was accused of taking food out of his kid's mouths. All Cannon could assume from this accusation was the Colonel could not inflate prices for supplies and equipment. This precluded his obtaining a commission/kick-back.

Later the NAFRC Commandant, with his senior staff, called Oke into his office and basically put the fear of God into him regarding the project's procurements. Cannon requested a meeting with the Commandant and senior staff. After he was threatened, he told all present they were never to meet with Oke or any other Aurora staff without Cannon and never to threaten anyone again regarding project procurements. If the threats continued, Cannon would close the project and return to the US. The NAFRC staff would then have to explain to the Minister of Defense why the project was closed while Cannon would leave it up to the people in Washington to find another person to manage the project in Nigeria.

Cannon secured a trip to the USA for Oke and Col. Ibrahim, the NAFRC Director of Training. The purpose of the trip was to gather additional ideas on how the DOL's Transition Assistance Program (TAP) run in the US for discharged military personnel might be used by NAFRC. The Nigerian visitors had a great time even though it snowed during the visit. It was the first time Oke saw snow. Col. Ibrahim had seen snow while undergoing a training program with the US Army previously.

Upon Oke's return to Lagos, disaster struck. He had placed $ 400 in one of his pieces of checked in luggage. Upon opening the bag after clearing customs, he found the money missing along with gifts he had purchased for his family while in Washington. Cannon personally replaced the lost money but was unable to replace the presents purchased in the US.

While Oke was in Washington, fire struck the complex in which Cannon lived. The downstairs apartment, occupied by the Italian landlady, burst out in flames. She and her attack dogs were saved by the gardener who was from Chad and the Nigerian night watch staff. They broke the glass windows to let the smoke escape and forced apart the steel bars covering the window to allow them access into the burning apartment. They were able to use fire extinguishers, including one borrowed from Cannon, to put the flames out. All were shortly thereafter fired by the Italian landlady for reasons unbeknownst to Cannon.

Cannon's second floor flat had only one exit: via the wooden walled stairway, to the outside. Cannon asked Washington to provide him with a portable ladder that could be affixed to a windowsill and thrown out to the ground below. This action was only taken after Aurora offered him another year on the project which he accepted.

2002 ended on a high note. Early in the month, a team of visitors from the DOL arrived in Lagos. The team was headed by Mike Talbert and Patrick White. The later was a young US Presidential scholar who was seconded to the DOL. It also included Kevin Nagel; a decorated career retired US Marine who was working on TAP programs, and Vaune Shebbourn a consultant as well as Jim Statman from Aurora.

The visitors and Cannon travelled to Abuja for briefings with Nigerian government officials and the US Ambassador. Additionally the visit was to confirm their attendance at the NAFRC passing out/graduation ceremony on the 13th of December and to officially dedicate the NAFRC Computer

Lab. The passing out/graduation ceremony went off without any hitches as did the Computer Lab dedication officiated jointly by the Nigerian Minister of Defense and the US Ambassador to Nigeria.

After the official computer lab dedication was completed the NAFRC Commandant hosted a party in his spacious office. Cannon was in the back of the room drinking beer with Kevin Nagel when he was summons by Ambassador Jeter who was seated next to the Nigerian Minister of Defense, Lt. Gen. (rd.) Theophilus Danjuma. Cannon left Kevin and was given a seat to Danjuma's right and was able to mention their paths had crossed briefly back in 1968 when Cannon was with the International Committee of the Red Cross (ICRC) during the civil war. Danjuma was surprised that Cannon had been in Nigeria that long ago.

During the holidays, Cannon had the opportunity to spend a lot of time with Ben. A visit to the outskirts of Lagos to see the house Ben was building was among the highlights of the season. Ben said basically the car hire contract had afforded him the opportunity to start building a house for his family which now included two wives and two children. The hardship of not having personal transport for his family (the vehicle was hired out to Aurora) was well worth it.

The project at NAFRC was starting to become more focused. Time was no longer spent trying to work out possible training activities with the Lagos State Government. Additionally, Engineer Oginni role in the project was coming to a close. Cannon found there were issues over project costs submitted by Oginni on behalf of Yaba Tech. The main reason for Oginni's diminishing role had to do with the fact that NAFRC had not systematically instituted the training modules he had developed and charged the project for.

Prior to the arrival of the first 2003 group of trainees, workshop materials and small equipment began to arrive on the base. Cannon was surprised at the inability of the workshop managers to access the newly delivered items. Military procedures regarding the securing and distribution of goods was cumbersome and very slow. Oke said it was the military's pay-back for excluding them from the project purchasing process.

While goods were gradually getting into the hands of the workshops, discussions were again being held with officials of the International Institute for Tropical Agriculture (IITA) in Ibadan. Ways were being explored as to how their expertise could be used to build a new fish pond and develop a curriculum that could be used with the new batch of NAFRC trainees. Unfortunately, no agreement could be secured due to the high financial estimates put forth by IITA.

The project's refurbishment of a block of empty offices into the counseling block was completed. Meanwhile in the US, sections with the DOL were working on a draft benefit table (pay grades, years of service, rank, etc.) which might be handed out to each trainee at NAFRC to help them better understand their retirement packages.

On the 11th of January 2003, President George W. Bush paid an official visit to Nigeria. Cannon was able to offer scheduling conflicts to avoid traveling to Abuja. He was committed to visiting the newly promoted Major General S. Shaibu at his new posting as the Commandant of the Nigerian Army Logistics College.

The NAFRC Commandant again grew very upset with the project when it didn't award the printing of a NAFRC trainees Joining Instruction Brochure to his wife's printing business. Instead, it was awarded to another printer who was much cheaper, Mike the Printer. The Commandant's anger diminished when discussions opened with the Major-In-Charge of the NAFRC Medical Unit. The medical unit was in shambles. The Commandant realized that if the project became involved with the medical unit, there was a chance refurbishment might occur. The project saw the potential of upgrading the Medical Unit as a precursor to the establishment of a HIV/Aids training activity.

Throughout the project, informal feedback was being received which indicated the Ministry of Defense's Retirement Board wasn't the most efficient body in Nigeria. One complaint heard by Cannon when meeting with a few retirees in Isokoland was they either were getting their retirement payments late or not at all. Demonstrations were held in various cities including one in Abuja, where recent NAFRC retirees were very active in front of the office of the Retirement Board. Unfortunately, this issue was never properly resolved during the life of the project.

The retirees demonstration was the basis for the drafting a questionnaire to conduct a survey. The survey would seek to solicit information from past NAFRC retirees on the usefulness of the NAFRC training. The right person was found to conduct the survey, Tony Okafor. Prior to his hiring for the NAFRC survey, Tony was employed as a night watchman at the former British Embassy in Lagos. Not an ideal job for a university graduate with a degree in English, but a job when there were millions of other Nigerians without work in the formal wage earning sector.

Just after Tony was hired, a TAP delegation visited from Washington. It was headed by Mike Talbert along with Eric Ruddert, Yvonne Gregoria and Jim Statman. When Yvonne started giving away some of her clothes to "poor" Nigerian female soldiers at NAFRC, it further illustrated how unprofessional the project still was. Cannon had to inform her that she was insulting her "sisters" since it was not polite in Nigerian custom to refuse the offer of a gift. Good intentions sometimes result in misunderstandings, especially if it's a person's first visit to a developing country.

In mid-March, Cannon was recalled to Washington for discussions with Professor A. Kruger, (rd.) from the University of Michigan. Prof. Kruger undertook a study of NAFRC in the early 1970's on behalf of USAID. It was learned that many of the NAFRC problems identified in the Kruger study were still in existence in 2003. Thirty some years had passed without NAFRC problems being solved.

When Cannon returned to Lagos, Cannon initiated contact with Family Health International Jacky Conley and Shelagh O'Rourke of USAID/ Nigeria to see if it was possible to use their HIV/AIDs experience and expertise with NAFRC. If possible, could they provide HIV/AIDs information that could be used by NAFRC trainees as well as the dependents' of NAFRC staff who attended the high school on the base?

Right after the start of the Iraq War, the NAFRC Commandant Air Vice Marshall Martins retired. A well-attended passing-out ceremony took place on the NAFRC parade grounds. Air Vice Marshall E. Aquaisua assumed his new assignment as NAFRC Commandant the same day; 31 March 2003, as well as Brigadier J. Onu who assumed his role as Deputy Commandant.

Cannon was now well experienced to know the assignment of Nigerian military officers by the three services to NAFRC was based strictly on rank not their skill and experience to perform the duties associated with their NAFRC title and job.

An example was the assignment of an Air Force Wing Commander, with a university degree in counseling, to the NAFRC transport wing and not to the NAFRC Counseling Wing. Some might say NAFRC was sort of an assignment of last resort and a career dead end.

The project continued to seek out competent professionals to get new ideas on how to improve the delivery of services to NAFRC. It hired on a retainer, Professor Ngozi Osarenren of the University of Lagos to serve as a resource to the DOL people from Washington who were promoting the TAP project at NAFRC. As the project continued, Prof. Ngozi's role was expanded into the media field besides her role with TAP.

Having made Ngozi's acquaintance, Cannon was able to inquire about graduate school at the University of Lagos on behalf of Oke and Tony. They were hoping to get admitted into the Masters of Communications program. Ngozi's contacts at the University of Lagos was very helpful to both of the, as their original applications were a bit late. In spite of their late application, both were accepted. There was much joy in the one-room NAFRC office when the acceptance notices were received by my two colleagues.

With the good news came another hurdle to overcome, how would they pay tuition fees if they no longer could work on the NAFRC project? After much internal soul searching, it was agreed they could stagger their NAFRC (40) hours per week around their course hours. Not only was the DOL project providing assistance to soon-to-be retirees from the Nigerian military, it was also instrumental in assisting two very bright and able young civilians.

Some progress was being made in securing external help to re-design the curriculum for NAFRC's agriculture wing via the University of Abeokuta Agriculture Department. Additionally, Cannon was able to convince the new NAFRC Commandant to plant food crops on various plots of vacant land throughout the base. The project would provide seeds and basic farm tools. The trainees studying in the agriculture wing would provide labor to plant, maintain and harvest the crops. Work commenced to refurbish an empty block into classrooms, a video room and a publications room for the agriculture wing. Trainees from the construction wing would provide the skills and labor. The project would supply the refurbishing materials and classrooms desks and chairs.

DOL officials in Washington were interested in trying to come to grips with NAFRC's future after their aid finished. The project sought the help of three Nigerian experts to promote the concept of a Nigerian study for NAFRC's future. Mike Talbert came out from Washington in early May 2003 and with Cannon, Professor Matanmi, Professor Ngozi, and Retired Air Force Group Captain Canice Nzewunwah visited Abuja for discussions with Nigerian officials to see whether they would be interested in a study to look at NAFRC's future. The Nigerian experts were acceptable to the decision-makers in Abuja and gave the go-ahead to conduct the study.

Cannon was surprised to receive a phone call from the office of Chief Ernest Shonekan in Lagos (he was the former Nigerian Head of State in 1993) asking whether he would be available to attend a farewell ceremony in honor of Ambassador Jeter who would depart Nigeria soon. Cannon was honored to receive the invitation and was surprised to be only one of two Americans invited. That wasn't the only surprise. Aurora Washington gave Cannon the go-ahead to hire Tony Okafor full-time.

Cannon spent about a month in the US for consultations with Aurora in Washington with DOL officials regarding the TAP project. Whereas the Washington people had there concepts of what the TAP component in Nigeria should entail, Aurora's view was more limited. It was based upon NAFRC's ability to follow Washington's concepts. A compromise was reached in which the US TAP materials possibly could be adapted in Nigeria if they were acceptable to NAFRC.

Cannon had the opportunity to visit Chico, California with Gudrun to visit her daughter a Professor at Chico State University. Chico was a delightful little town. On Cannon's way back to Nigeria, he stopped off in Norway to visit his daughter and granddaughter. While there he was joined by his cousin Joey from Ireland. Both had way too much to drink celebrating the 4th of July. This provoked a blow-up with the ex-Mrs. Cannon who said his visit, along with his Irish cousin, brought-on an anxiety attack in his daughter.

Mrs. Cannon didn't stop there. After her divorce from her former boss in Lesotho, she moved to Mozambique with another Norwegian man. She sent a very nasty email to Gudrun in the USA about Cannon's trip to Norway as well. Beware of an ex-wife!

Upon Cannon's return to NAFRC, he was informed by the NAFRC Commandant, that Abuja informed him there was no more new money forthcoming for NAFRC. This decision forced the DOL sponsored project to fall short on numerous goals it was to have achieved. How could (4) donated diesel generators operate without diesel? How could the Computer Lab operate when the electricity failed? These are just two of the paper goals not achievable.

In spite of the NAFRC draw-backs, Cannon continued to plod along trying to keep the DOL project positive since it was promoted by the former President of the United States, Bill Clinton. A Xerox copy machine, along with a hired operator, was secured for the NAFRC facility to print brochures, lesson copies, trainee hand-outs, etc. A contract was entered into with the University of Lagos's Mr. Chima to produce a video on the construction of a 2nd NAFRC fish pond. The video would then be used as a teaching tool for future agriculture trainees.

Jim Statman arrived in Nigeria for a visit in September 2003. He renewed Cannon's contract until October 2004. He gave permission to hire a part-time bookkeeper to ready the books for a forthcoming DOL evaluation. He authorized a 20% monthly increase for Oke and Tony effective 1 October 2003. Cannon returned to the US to undergo a colon procedure on his birthday the 24th of September. A strange way to celebrate one's birthday!

As noted previously, many of the DOL policies and procedures for the project in Nigeria were established prior to Cannon's arrival in Nigeria by DOL personnel from Washington. One procedure was with the bank so that foreign exchange could be turned into Nigerian Naira. The bank informed Aurora it would no longer honor its checks because the sums exchanged were too small. A new bank was needed: resulting in more headaches.

To open a Nigerian bank account, one of the usual requirements is a permit to do business in Nigeria and/or an agreement with the Government of Nigeria to operate as a duty-free non-government organization. Signatories to any account were required to have Nigerian residence and work permits. Persons associated with the DOL project had neither. After many meetings between potential Nigerian banks and Cannon, Cannon and US officials, etc. a letter was written by the DOL which was accepted by Standard Chartered Bank. It became the project's new Nigerian bank.

Prior to the close of 2003, the project's first video "Fish Pond Construction" was completed. Mr. Chima and his team did a terrific job. The job done was so good that it was agreed that he would participate in the production of additional videos for NAFRC. The 2nd video completed was entitled "Transition to Civilian Life". Professor Ngozi's skills in working with senior NAFRC were a welcomed addition to Chima's. The third video entitled "Stress and Anger Management" was to be completed in 2004 before Chima started on the final video "This is NAFRC".

New equipment was procured and delivered for the NAFRC dispensary. The equipment was predominately to facilitate blood testing for HIV/ AIDS if NAFRC trainees wished to participate. Testing was also open to the NAFRC staff and dependents. This was the follow through after the securing of educational materials and video's from the Family Health International project funded via USAID.

The success of the DOL sponsored project was apparent in many areas. Yet, it was becoming more and more apparent that the NAFRC structure, in the overall future of the Nigerian military, was very low regardless of the project success. Some of the NAFRC officers, besides Shaibu, continued climbing in the military hierarchy: including the Director of Training Colonel Katung who was given a star as Brigadier General.

There was no contractual documentation with Nigerian authorities which could give the DOL project any leverage which might overcome NAFRC's low priority within the military headquarters. Yet, the folks in Washington were pushing Aurora and Cannon for long-term NAFRC inputs which would illustrate the success of the project. If two parties are not signatures to a contract and/or other type of formal agreement, the receiving party is not bound by any verbal commitments which may have been made years earlier.

The NAFRC Commandant, after much pleading by Cannon finally did something about the lack of electricity for the Computer Lab. Instead of providing diesel for the generator that was specifically located near to the lab and the nearby high school, he disconnected the original cables and re-connected the lab to the nearby headquarters generator. PROGRESS!

Personally Cannon's life continued with normal ups and downs. He spent the holiday season in the USA with Gudrun. They visited Gudrun's grandchildren who were visiting grandparents in Baltimore which was nice.

One of Cannon's close friends from his youth took a massive heart attack and passed in early January 2004. Cannon's daughter, granddaughter and a friend visited Texas and Rhode Island during the month. Unfortunately, Cannon had returned to Nigeria prior to the visit. Before departing the US, Cannon arranged for the delivery of 60 roses for Gudrun on the 22nd of February her birthday. In Nigeria, Cannon continued to personally provide financial support to Oke, Tony, Femi the Driver, and Grace the apartment maid. Grace said her gift would be used to pay for exams needed to enter university.

The Computer Lab experienced a few early set-backs in 2004. A small fire broke out. The cable that was used by the Commandant to connect the lab to the Headquarters generator was too small to carry the electrical load when the generator was operational. The Air Force officer in-charge of the lab privatized the lab unbeknown to Cannon while he was in the US.

Akeem had cut a private deal with the internet provider. The project had made available funds for internet services, connection and (12) months fees to give NAFRC time to re-position itself and become self-sufficient insofar as the Computer Lab was concerned. Akeem was able to get all the funds originally provided to the server by disconnecting the services.

This only became known after Akeem was transferred out of NAFRC. While he served as the Commanding Officer for the Lab, he kept saying there was no internet service because of the lack of electricity, the poor service of the provider, etc. A different form of small business initiative not normally associated with Capitalism.

Professor Matami and retired NAFRC Air Force officer Canice were making slow progress in their attempt to obtain updated information on the status, condition and future NAFRC plans for each of its 30 workshops. This information was critical for the NAFRC report that was to be completed before the DOL funds stopped on 1 October 2004. While the study was on-going, Aurora in Washington secured the services of four experts from the United Kingdom to undertake an external study at NAFRC as required by the original project document between the DOL and Aurora.

The NAFRC Commandant wasn't thrilled with the study by Matami and Canice, but at least they were Nigerians so he could use his rank to keep them from revealing too much NAFRC negativity. When it came to the expats doing the DOL study his cooperation was limited to say the best. He told Cannon after the experts and Statman left at the end of April that he was very unhappy.

Aurora and the US government (DOL) didn't have the right to evaluate his base since they had no agreements or contracts with the Nigerian government nor NAFRC itself. There were Plans of Action, but these had no official status except for the DOL and Aurora.

As the project progressed, Cannon became more sympathetic with the views of the NAFRC Commandant. Cannon knew that the US military would never allow any foreign civilians on their bases to operate any type of project without specific instructions from the Department of Defense. Surely if there were foreign projects on US bases they would result from formal and legal agreements entered into by the US Government. What gave the DOL and Aurora the right to involve themselves in a foreign country's military operation without a legal agreement between the US government and Nigerian authorities which would spell out both parties' rights and responsibilities?

After some two years, the project-provided generators were still not being used as originally envisioned by the DOL and Aurora. The generator which was supposed to provide power to the main workshops had been used for 162 hours, the generator for the computer lab and school had been used for 269 hours, the generator for the auditorium for 479 hours and the generator for headquarters 1,541 hours.

All was not hopeless. Trainees completed rehabilitation work on two hostels before they had their passing-out ceremony on June 11th. Thus all four hostels were now rehabilitated and over 75 trainees had acquired hands-on construction work experience which would assist them in constructing or upgrading their own homes once they became officially retired.

There were major changes in the US Embassy. The new Ambassador Joseph Campbell arrived in Abuja and a new Consulate General, Bryan Brown arrived in Lagos. Cannon forgot he had met Campbell in South Africa years previously. Brown was a close friend of former Ambassador Jeter. Cannon found Brown a welcome relief from his predecessor.

Aurora held a workshop under the direction of Jim Statman after NAFRC's passing out ceremony in Lagos. It took place during tremendous rains the flooded many parts of the city. Cars were often flooded trying to cross small rivers that developed on roads. How the participants arrived at the workshop venue still remains a mystery to Cannon.

The workshop's focus was to review progress on the study of NAFRC. The workshop would review as well as to plan for a September seminar in Abuja in which a final report on the NAFRC project and the 4th video "THIS IS NAFRC" would be presented to Nigerian government officials and officials from the US Embassy. Whatever short-comings existed, they were ironed out at the workshop.

Cannon took a break and flew out to Paris to attend the wedding of his Cousin Vinnie's son. Was Paris ever different from Lagos! Cannon's cousin from Ireland and his daughter, an artist, flew into Paris to join the festivities. The civil wedding ceremony was held in one of the numerous City Halls which exist for each section of the city. After a great meal was held in a nearby left bank restaurant, the family got together in an apartment Vinnie had rented. The day after the wedding, time was spent visiting a few tourist sites before it was time to fly onwards to Washington for staff consultations and a couple of weeks holiday.

Prior to Cannon's return to Lagos to begin wrapping up the project, a major issue arose which further illustrated the discombobulating nature of the entire project. Throughout 2004, Patrick White had assumed responsibility for the NAFRC project in the DOL/Washington office. That in itself was not a problem. The problem however arose during discussions with the DOL when Aurora was informed White would lead the DOL team to Nigeria for the final seminar and project wrap up. Cannon said if this took place he would resign before the final seminar.

The final seminar in Abuja would be attended by senior civilian Defense ministry officials as well as senior military officers from Nigeria's three services. Surely, the DOL wouldn't consider sending a young junior staff member to be its representative at a similar seminar in Europe. They would send an appropriate senior staffer. For the life of him, Cannon couldn't comprehend the thinking of DOL officials. White was barely 30 years old. While this was not a problem in US culture it would be perceived as a grave insult by the Nigerians.

Can one imagine if the situation was reversed? A young Nigerian coming to the US to head-up a visiting team of experts to participate in a seminar with senior Department of Defense personnel and senior grade officers from branches of the US military! It is so preposterous that it's almost beyond comprehension. Nigerians would never think of something so far- fetched.

The NAFRC project was established as a result of US President Clinton's visit which in itself creates a very high profile. If Cannon was shocked by the unprofessionalness of the project's conception and delivery system, he was now completely disillusioned by the DOL's plan to have a youngster head its team at the project's closing. If things like this were taking place throughout Africa, it is no wonder Africans have started to question their relations with the US.

Upon Cannon's return to Lagos in July, he learned that Oke and Tony had completed their respective Masters' Theses. They had turned them into the University of Lagos on schedule in order to graduate in November 2004. A very proud time for all!

Before the project could be formally closed at the September Abuja seminar, there were two DOL requirements which still needed to be completed? One was a survey of project purchases and the other was a DOL formal evaluation. Aurora was required to initiate a coding system, according to a DOL mandate, for equipment purchased. Initially, Cannon thought this was only for items like the generators, computers, etc. The DOL official Dr. Lucian Smallwood wanted more. The initial coding system was revamped and accepted by Dr. Smallwood who was on his first visit to Africa. Smallwood informed the NAFRC Commandant upon introduction that he was "happy to be home". It was moving to hear an African-American refer to Africa as home.

A formal ceremony was held at NAFRC Oshodi on the 25th of August. The entire US project donated equipment, supplies, films, syllabuses, etc. became the property of the Nigerian government. Dr. Smallwood was the official US Government official who turned over the project purchases to Mrs. Marie Egbe, who represented the Nigerian Minister of Defense.

A DOL contractor hired by the DOL to evaluate the project, Mr. Hurst arrived in Lagos shortly after Smallwood departed. Jim Statman arrived from South Africa a day later. Hurst was joined by Dr. Robert Young of the DOL who was selected to head-up the DOL team at the closing seminar in Abuja.

The evaluator premised his evaluation and evaluation tools on the project documents signed between the DOL and Aurora. From the start of Cannon Employment with Aurora he tried telling Statman, that the project documents were misleading. They contained quantified objectives for NAFRC and the Nigerian government in spite of there not being a contract/agreement with the Nigerian Government nor NAFRC. Any evaluation couldn't be premised upon a misleading set of objectives.

Cannon and the project couldn't force NAFRC to undertake any verbal commitments that might have been made before and after President Clinton's state visit in 1999. For example: NAFRC's Affective Use of the Four Donated Generators. One wonders how this project evaluation assisted the DOL and where it ended-up in DOL headquarters in Washington.

On the 31st of August 2004, a seminar to officially wrap up the NAFRC project was held at the Hilton Hotel in Abuja-the Capital of Nigeria.

Setting up the seminar proved to be another learning experience. There were financial limits associated with the DOL contract regarding local per diems, hotel charges, etc. based upon US Department of State standards. Senior Nigerian military officers and senior civil servants were accustomed to receiving higher financial compensations than the project afforded. In spite of this, there were only a few instances which resulted in disputes.

The Nigerian consultants hired by Aurora were the main presenters at the workshop. They focused on their final report 'THIS IS NAFRC'. The only problem in their presentation was Canice's inability to properly use the power point presentation as a compliment to his verbal presentation. He repeated word-for-word the power point boring folks. However, the participants, including the US Ambassador and the Nigerian Minister of Defense, were impressed with the video showing of the film ***THIS IS NAFRC***. Bound copies of the final project report as well as copies of the ***THIS IS NAFRC*** video were given to the honored guests. A set was also handed over the top the DOL team from Washington. The DOL team and Aurora de-briefed the US Consulate General in Lagos prior to their departure for the US.

Cannon spent the remainder of September packing out; closing up the project office at NAFRC, saying farewell to NAFRC personnel and arranging for the turning over of office equipment to the US Consulate before departing for the USA.

During the packing out period, Cannon had ample opportunity to reflect upon the project's accomplishments. It could be considered a success insofar as material upgrading was concerned. It was likely the Nigerian military would not financially support NAFRC at a level needed to continue its upgrading. It was also highly improbable that the US government would re-allocate monies to the US Department of Labor for NAFRC. Would another thirty to forty years transpire before the US government provided aid to NAFRC or would it be more likely NAFRC would be a relic of the past?

Cannon realized that one major accomplishment of his third assignment in Nigeria was the positive effect it had on the Edherue family. Oke had completed his Master's 'Degree. Ben was enrolled in law school. He was able to finish the construction of his home on the outskirts of Lagos. The Edherue family helped to solidify changes in Cannon's perceptions and attitude towards 'development'.

Cannon stopped off in Ireland to visit Cousin Joe. Cannon hadn't seen him since we attended the wedding in Paris of our cousin Vinnie's son. Joe had moved from Athlone to the west coast. The area was more upscale and closer to major population areas. One of the highlights was a quick trip to Northern Ireland. Yet, old patterns resurfaced and belong too long the cousins were squabbling Like two teenagers. It was time for Cannon to head home.

Next stop was Washington, DC for a project de-briefing. The de-briefing was very short. An illustration the project was history-yesterday's news. Cannon thought the final project report, which included the ***THIS IS NAFRC*** video, would serve as the basis of the de-briefing. The video was hardly mentioned during the de-briefing. It is likely the final report and videos could be collecting dust in some DOL office. It was obvious the US Department of Labor (DOL) was not going to fund any projects with the Nigerian military in the distant future especially NAFRC. Cannon left Washington with a sense of accomplishment. He had completed the Presidential deliverable project of President Clinton and ensured that Aurora International Associates fulfilled its contract with the USDOL as the implementing organization with NAFRC.

14

Transformation Completed

Cannon headed to Providence, Rhode Island to visit with his mother and see his kids and his girlfriend Gudrun. In June 2004, Chandra and her daughter Laila came to the US. Chandra had been living in Norway the past decade. She and her then-boyfriend planned to relocate, but at the last moment the boyfriend backed out. Chandra and Laila were able to move in with her brother Marc and his girlfriend Jerah. They had a spare bedroom available for a few weeks until Chandra and Laila were able to locate a flat. How ironic the flat they located was on Hope Street in Providence-about two city blocks away from the third floor flat his late parents brought him too after he was born. It wasn't too long after the move that Chandra was able to secure a job at the nearby Miriam Hospital.

Cannon's mother's health was gradually declining, especially her intellectual capabilities. As she regressed, it was very difficult for Cannon to cope as an only child. In reality, there wasn't anything Cannon could do besides ensure she was well cared for and pray for her inner peace. My surrogate aunt, Evelyn, was experiencing similar aging difficulties. The two close old ladies could console each other in the nursing home.

Cannon's girlfriend did yeoman work during his absence in Nigeria for his mother and Aunt Evelyn. She constantly visited with them and took them out for rides in the country and to lunch when they were able to get out. Gudrun's cancer was in remission and she was still in the classroom teaching special children in pre-school.

Gudrun had two children from her marriage to her former husband. The eldest, Jennifer was a professor at Chico State University in California and the youngest, Jeff, was a professor at the University of Florida. When Gudrun's former husband passed, the kids and their families came to RI for the funeral services. Before returning to California and Florida, both

Jennifer and Jeff badgered Cannon and Gudrun about getting married. "Wasn't it time to stop the long-distant courtship after five years?" "What was wrong with marriage?" Marc and Chandra felt the same but were not as vocal as Gudrun's kids. At the time both Cannon and Gudrun were still reluctant about marriage since both were burnt in their previous marriages. Marriage was put on the back burner.

Cannon had one more task to accomplish in RI before heading back to Calais, Maine. He needed transportation home. His older Toyota had been given to Marc while he was still in Nigeria. It was time for Cannon to call Mike Coleman the son of an old neighborhood guy who worked in the auto business.

Mike's late father and Cannon stayed in contact since 1963 when Cannon first went overseas. John or Jocko his nickname, had developed heart issues and just after the holidays in 2003 had a fatal heart attack in Florida: he'll be missed.

Mike came through again as he did back in 1997 when Cannon needed a vehicle after finishing the Lesotho assignment with LHDA. Cannon this time purchased a new Toyota from a local dealership. Mike knew the salesman. He sold Cannon the vehicle at a good price! Cannon showed his appreciation by delivering a couple of bottles of Irish whiskey. Once the car purchase was finalized (cash), Cannon said his goodbyes to family and initiated the 450 mile drive back to Calais, Maine.

The drive from RI to Calais followed the usual route I 95 North with a stop in Manchester, New Hampshire. Here, Cannon was able to touch base with Fr. Mike Kerper. Mike's church was located on Route 1 so it wasn't too difficult to locate. After the usual greetings, it was off to lunch to catch up on the happenings since their last meeting. Mike had lost some weight as well as a lot of hair on his head since they were last together breaking bread. Cannon always felt good after being in Mike's presence. After lunch, the next stop was the New Hampshire State Liquor store (no state tax) to pick up some liquor for himself and his buddy, Louis Bernardini.

Once Cannon arrived in Bangor, Maine he was almost home. He had only about 100 miles more to drive. Cannon usually stopped in Bangor to shop for food and supplies as they were a bit cheaper than in Calais before completing the drive.

The drive from Bangor to Calais was mainly through an unpopulated forest region. The two lane road was constantly being upgraded. In places, it had been expanded to three lanes-one used for slow driving and the other for passing on long hills. The autumn foliage was over, but the drive was still pleasant unlike the winter months when it was dangerous if snow had fallen and hadn't melted.

Just before dark, Cannon pulled into the driveway. First off was the walk up the indoor barn stairs to open up the flat. As usual, the Bernardini family had made arrangements to turn on the water and electricity and do a bit of cleaning. After unpacking the car and putting away the food, supplies and clothes, it was time to contact Louis. The flat telephone wasn't yet reconnected.

Cannon put on some winterish clothes and left to find his buddy Louis. Autumn in Calais after Lagos, Nigeria was like winter. Cannon took the five minute walk to a local gin mill run by Dick Davies (nicknamed Dirty Dick's).

The establishment was located on Main Street in an old three story building that was in need of major repairs. When the front windows were clean you could see out across the St. Croix River into St. Stephen, New Brunswick, Canada. If the windows weren't clean, which was most of the time, you looked into Canada only when departing.

Dick was an old merchant marine who re-located to Connecticut after WW II and raised a family. He returned to Calais where he was born after his divorce when he was around 65. He then started a new family and opened the gin mill after previous individuals who leased the premises went broke. Dick had the cheapest beer in town and attracted an older group that he considered his regular customers.

Louis was seated at the bar. It was good to see him and to embrace each other. Handshakes were exchanged with Dick; Mike, a retired Army career man; Neil, from across the river and Sharon, who at times tended bar. Then, it was time to catch up on the local happenings. Most of the catching up dealt with people and things in Calais. Folks weren't at all interested in what Cannon had been doing in Nigeria. This wasn't the first time he had been away in Africa since his arrival in 1997. Plus, Cannon wasn't a native to the area which was the standard by which folks were judged.

Cannon had arrived home just in time to help Captain Bernardini beach the lobster traps for the forthcoming winter. Louis had passed his US Coast Guard test to captain smaller vessels. The traps were scattered along the St. Croix River. First, they needed to find them in low tide. Then, pull them onboard the open air lobster boat. And finally, place the floating lines inside the wire traps. The traps were then beached on high rocks to prevent them from being washed away in the winter. It was hard work, but worth the effort until the coming spring. It would then be time to place new State of Maine tags on each trap, clean them out, place bait in them before dropping them back into the river with hopes of catching many lobsters again.

Cannon spent the next few days getting the telephone in working order, the television re-connected to cable and re-establishing his connection with his local church, Immaculate Conception. The church was about a five-minute walk from the barn flat. Now it was time to get back into the Calais routine.

Cannon's radio alarm clock would go off at 4:45AM in time for him to get the news on British Broadcasting Company (BBC). BBC carried news on Africa which wasn't the case with any of the radio bands Cannon could access in Calais.

After the news was over, Cannon put on some clothes and walked across North Street to the local Dunkin Donuts to buy the Bangor Daily News. It was a while before Cannon learned that the older folks who were in Dunkin Donuts each morning were supporters of the Republican Party.

Cannon asked one of them, Bill Howard, where the democrats hung out. He said at the McDonalds just up the street, who didn't sell the Bangor Daily News.

Cannon read the paper while having breakfast. Many a morning Cannon would walk to attend daily mass at Immaculate Conception at 8AM. After mass, Cannon would try jogging a bit. It was getting harder and harder to jog because of some physical issues which eventually led to a hip replacement in a few years. If the weather was too rotten for jogging, Cannon tried walking. If it was too inclement for walking, Cannon would do some reading before lunch. Sometimes, he tried pecking away on the computer writing this story. Then the story would rest, often for years at a time.

Soon it would be Thanksgiving; Cannon's favorite holiday in the USA. Since Cannon started going out with Gudrun, he would spend the holiday at her place in Rhode Island. Gudrun would invite Cannon's kids or all of us would be invited to Cousin Vinnie's. Driving down to RI seemed to be shorter time-wise, especially after Cannon purchased a transponder (EZ Pass) which allowed the vehicle to pass through the road tolls without stopping. Payments were deducted from his bank account via a credit card.

Cannon would often stay in RI after Thanksgiving for the Christmas season. Gudrun's school would close for a break at Christmas and she did not need to return to work until after the New Year. During Cannon's absence in Nigeria, Gudrun made a decision to convert to the Roman Catholic faith. She had been contemplating this decision for years. After her conversion, it was easier for them both to attend mass where previously Cannon's attendance sometimes cause small hiccups to plans.

After Christmas, the Davises would come to RI to celebrate New Year's Eve at Gudrun's. A big meal would be prepared and served with lots of good wine. Gudrun's best friends often came too. Gudrun first met Bob and Pat Trudeau at the University of North Carolina back in the 1960's. Cousin Vinnie and his wife Mary rounded out the dinner participants. Most of the time, they were in bed before the New Year's celebrations started. Getting old wasn't easy.

During one or two trips to Rhode Island, Cannon sought out guys he had grown up. Like himself, they were mostly retired. A few were still working trying to keep their heads above water. Others had put on a lot of weight as they got old.

This was not the case with Cannon's former grammar school basketball coach Armand Batastini. He was rail thin. When they got together, they found it difficult to communicate unless it was about the old days or sports. Cannon's life experiences held no reference points for the guys who stayed in Rhode Island (except for military service out of the state).

Upon completion of the holidays, Cannon would drive back to Calais. The trip always seemed longer than going to RI and usually took more time. A highlight of the winter was watching Calais High School basketball teams play at their home gym. There was a long tradition of Calais having very good boys' and girls' teams, frequently winning Eastern Maine Class C championships, as well as State of Maine championships.

Cannon's barn was attached to the main house. Originally, it was built around 1870 to house a single family. When Cannon purchased it in 1985, it had been split into two apartments on the first and second floors. There was a fairly long drive way leading off of North Street which was the main road leading into downtown Calais. Cannon was responsible for snow removal. This usually entailed him shoveling. If the snow was very heavy, Louis usually came by with his plow to take away the heavy stuff.

After one big storm, Cannon was shoveling for what seemed like hours when he spotted two kids walking on the plowed area of North Street. Cannon asked them if they wanted to earn $ 50 in helping him shovel. They told him "FU we don't even shovel snow in our own houses." Times surely had changed since Cannon was a kid back in the 1950's! After a snow storm, a kid had to shovel his parents place and any neighbors who were too old to shovel themselves. Then, they would go door-to-door asking if they could shovel the snow for a few dollars.

Cannon's kids and Chandra's boyfriend Vik chipped in and bought him a snow blower. Cleaning the drive way sure became easier thereafter. Cannon did notice that if there was more than 18 inches on the ground, he needed to use the blower on two levels: get the top lawyer removed first before the blower was placed at ground level. Cannon always found it very difficult to explain what snow was to his friends in Africa, except those in Lesotho. The entire country of Lesotho was close to a mile above sea level and frequently was hit by snow, especially in the higher mountain regions.

Cannon usually would undertake a trip to RI in February around Valentine's Day. This usually coincided with Gudrun's birthday which was on the 23rd and with her winter break at school. Driving in the ice and snow was difficult, but once Bangor was reached and Interstate 95 was available, driving became easy. It stayed easy until just outside of Boston when it turned into a cat and mouse game.

Cannon would then return to Calais and wouldn't return to RI until Easter time. Cannon usually made about 8 to 10 trips a year to RI to see his mother, children, his granddaughter and Gudrun. Neither Gudrun nor Cannon would seriously discuss marriage, but a few times the subject would be brought up by friends. Sometimes on his trips, Cannon would stop in Manchester to see Fr. Mike and spend the night at the rectory.

As summer drew closer, anticipation grew for the forthcoming lobster season. Captain Louis would apply to the state for his commercial license and the State of Maine would issue tags for the traps. The license included a provision for a stern man which Cannon filled when he was in Calais. The St. Croix River's water is quite cold so the traps weren't put in the water until Memorial Day-give or take a few days when the water was a bit warmer.

Next up was the purchasing of bait for the traps. Bait consisted of the heads and tails of herring or sardines, which had been removed before the canning process. Over the years as the fish factory industry in Maine gradually died the source for the purchase of bait also died. Fortunately, there was a canning factory in Bucks Harbor, New Brunswick, Canada which was about 30 miles northeast of Calais. After the terrorist attack on the US in 2001, border security changed completely on the US side as well as the Canadian side. Previously, if you were a resident of Calais or St. Stephen's, it was easy for you to cross over. Paper work now had to be filled out with US Customs to get back into the US.

Captain Louis and Cannon would put a large plastic container in the back of the pick-up truck for the trip to Canada. Bait was fairly cheap at about 10 cents US per pound. Sometimes the pieces poured into the plastic tote appeared good enough to eat. Other times it was only heads and tails. An added purchase of fifty pound bags of salt was made at the canning factory. Once the bait was back in the US, it was shoveled out of the tote into large plastic buckets. The bait was salted at layers until the buckets were filled and ready for storage. Salting the bait prevented early rotting.

The traps were taken out onto the river in batches. Once the traps' resting places were reached, a bait bag (a small cloth bag with holes) was filled with the salted bait and then the traps were thrown overboard. The process was repeated until all the traps were in the river. Trips were made, daily or every other day, depending upon the tide to check on the traps to see if lobsters had entered the traps.

Cannon's mother, Lena, joined the ancestors on 23 May 2005. She died peacefully with Cannon at her bedside. Traditionally, Catholics hold a viewing of the deceased before burial called a wake. At that time, some of the guys Cannon grew up with showed to pay respects. A burial mass was held at the church next to the cemetery a day after the wake.

After the mass and service at the cemetery, immediate family and friends gathered at a nearby Italian restaurant for lunch. Mrs. Cannon was buried in the plot with her husband John who passed away in 1977. Unlike John, my late father who died at age 71, my mother died at a ripe old age of 94.

Ben Edherue had seen white colleagues come and go in his work with the Nigerian Labour Congress (LNC) and the AFL-CIO affiliate in Nigeria. Prior to Cannon's departure, he and Ben frequently did not cross paths.

His employer, Solidarity Center, had moved its offices from Lagos to Abuja. Ben moved with his new wife and small children as well.

It was in Abuja that Ben applied to law school and was accepted. Cannon was thrilled with the news but his elation didn't last for long. Ben called one night saying his place in the admissions was "sold" to another person. After the initial shock, Cannon suggested that he seek out the admissions folks and hold a talk with them indicating he empathized with the position they were in. It isn't easy to withstand pressure from the rich and famous. At the end of the talk, Cannon suggested Ben leave a small envelope with Naira (Nigerian currency) as a sign of understanding. Whether that worked or not is unknown, but Ben was given a place in the next incoming class. He continued to work with Solidarity Center and attended law classes at night while his young family grew.

Cannon last saw Ben in Abuja at the NAFRC farewell presentation. Cannon said that once Ben completed his law studies and passed the bar exam, he would purchase him the white wig worn by Nigerian lawyers. Cannon frequently made fun of the hold-over from colonial days, wondering why in such heat, the wig was still standard gear used in Nigerian courts?

When Ben asked where Cannon could buy a lawyers white wig in the US, Cannon replied at Wal-Mart. When asked for further explanation, Cannon said he could purchase a white floor washing mop that Ben could use. Ben laughed. Cannon followed up on this when Ben was called to the bar in 2007. He mailed him a brand new Wal-Mart mop, which was probably made in China.

Nigeria is similar to the US in that it has many, many lawyers. Trying to get a new career started isn't easy regardless of what country one finds oneself in. This was especially true in Nigeria for Ben who was very interested in labor law. Unlike the US, a lawyer focusing on labor law wasn't in much demand. How was he to feed a young and growing family?

Ben never cut his ties with the NLC after he moved over to the AFL-CIO's overseas arm in Africa. First it was named the African-American Labor

Center (AALC), and later renamed Solidarity Center. The NLC and its affiliated unions were constantly fighting to keep their heads above water in the ever changing political scene in the country.

The NLC helped Ben to re-enter the Nigerian Trade Union movement. After a prolonged campaign, Ben got himself elected as the General Secretary of the Communications' Workers Union. He now had a full-time job which would allow him to provide for his family and stay in the struggle for workers' rights in Nigeria. Ben's happiness didn't last too long.

The trade union movement in many African countries helps to promote tribal unity. This is a positive attribute working together for the common good. Many movements are also faced with fierce internal political intrigue and power struggles. Unfortunately, many of the power struggles arise from tribal differences from within. It sort of reminds me of the struggles President Obama faces daily with the Republicans: a constant struggle. In Ben's case, the old guard in the union (their candidate was defeated by Ben) felt he wasn't bold enough in his dealings with government and with the relatively new private-sector cell phone employers. Eventually, Ben was removed as General Secretary of the Communications Workers Union

Reflections

How did it happen that Cannon spent decades living and working outside of the US? It surely wasn't because of his Irish and Italian lineage. It wasn't because he was an only child in a lower middle class family in the US. Cannon's faith, service to country and serendipity moved him from one job to another. Cannon first answered the call to serve his country in 1957. At the age of 17, he joined the US Coast Guard. His second opportunity to serve his country occurred in 1963 when he joined the Peace Corps.

Little did Cannon know that after completing his two-year assignment with the Peace Corps in the Philippines, he would live and work in some 24 countries overseas, namely Angola, Bangladesh, Botswana, Canada, Congo, Egypt, Ghana, Kenya, Liberia, Lesotho, Madagascar, Malawi, Mauritius, Nigeria, Norway, South Africa, South Korea, Sudan, Swaziland, Togo, Uganda, Vietnam, Zambia and Zimbabwe.

In spite of the varying circumstances and economic deprivation which existed in many of the African countries Cannon worked in, the average local would always greet you with a smile and handshake. It didn't matter whether the person offering the greeting was a laborer or a high-up government official. Most conservation's Cannon had, included moments of laughter, regardless of the topic. Yet when Cannon was visiting or back on business in the US, it always amazed him to see so few people smiling-especially those one would see at airports, on subways, trains and buses. What amazed him even more was the almost total absence of laughter. The higher standards of living in the US didn't seem to make its citizens happier than those in poorer African countries.

Regardless of the place, job and circumstances, Cannon believed he was following his path on planet earth as was pre-ordained by God. In bygone days, Cannon was classified as a "cradle" Catholic-born into the religion thru his parents. Cannon was educated in Catholic schools from the 1st grade in grammar school to a university graduate degree. The Catholic church in the US during Cannon's upbringing and early adulthood was conservative. Throughout this process, Cannon was basically a conservative person in his political beliefs'.

Like many Catholics, Cannon wasn't a Bible reader. Christ's teachings were gleaned over the years via the gospel readings at mass. The four evangelists who recorded Jesus Christ's life John, Luke, Mark and Matthew, each in their own way, wrote about the glad tidings proclaimed by Christ. Seldom was a gospel reading devoted to the rich and powerful. In Cannon's view, the most powerful messages focused on the poor, the sick and the outcasts of society.

The Catholic Church, as an institution, might be conservative in the eyes of many people. The gospel portrayed Jesus not as a conservative as some evangelicals believe, but rather as a radical in Cannon's view. Helping the poor, curing the sick, taking on the money lenders in the temple, etc. all went against the existing structure and cannot be seen as being conservative. This view was advocated in the 1971 publication of **A Theology of Liberation** by Gustavo Gutierrez, a Dominican priest from Peru.

As Cannon grew older he juxtaposed liberation theology with Jesus's ministry to the poor and downtrodden. In 2014 capitalism, based upon consumption of goods and services, is best reflected by a publication issued by Oxfam-a UK non-government body. In the 178 Oxfam Briefing Paper of 20 January 2014, the world's richest **85 people** have more wealth than **3.5 billion people** who make up the bottom half of the entire world's population. If this statistic does not justify liberation theology nothing will.

Cannon had plenty of time to catch up on all the reading he missed while growing up. Cannon would at times decide to purchase a book for his mini-library. It was usually a book on history or politics that tended towards the left and liberalism. One book, "**SLOVO-The Unfinished Autobiography of ANC leader Joe Slovo**" which Cannon purchased in South Africa, was often re-read. The introduction was by his wife, Helena Dolny. The foreword was by Nelson Mandela, the first black President of

South Africa, who regarded Slovo as a friend and colleague in the struggle against apartheid.

Over the years, Slovo, became head of the South Africa Communist Party (SACP). He was also a close colleague of Oliver Tambo who was the President of the African National Congress (ANC). Shortly after Mandela was arrested in 1962, Slovo and Tambo both ended up in exile initially in Europe. They were tasked by the ANC, to insure that the ANC was kept alive in spite of their numerous leaders being incarcerated in South Africa's jails.

When Cannon first arrived in Southern Africa (Lesotho) in 1969, the ANC was viewed and portrayed as a communistic front group by most Western countries including the USA. Cannon, at the time, accepted the said view which was also voiced by the late Ted Irving who was working with the intelligence wing of the Lesotho Mounted Police. However, Cannon refused to accept the apartheid ideology of the South African government, but he could not conceive the over-throw of the white minority government then or in the foreseeable future due to the lack of strength of the ANC military wing.

Only over time did Cannon's attitude towards colonialism, communism and capitalism evolved. As noted previously, being raised a Catholic and retaining Catholicism as an adult wasn't too conducive towards leftist ideology. When in the Peace Corps and later employed by CRS, Cannon seldom thought about questioning the overseas policy of the US. In later years, Cannon became a believer of socialism as a more equitable system for mankind than capitalism, which rewarded the successful and left the weak by the wayside.

While living in Norway, most Norwegian students at the University of Bergen were anti-US because of the Vietnam War. Cannon, as the only American living in married students' quarters, was starting to wonder whether the Nixon administration was doing the right thing by bombing the hell out of Cambodia.

When Cannon returned to the US and started work with Americans Indians in Maine, it was obvious life was very different on the reservation than in the nearby predominately white communities. The housing conditions reminded Cannon of conditions in some developing countries he lived in previously. The employment situation on the reservations was dismissal. Living standards frequently were more third-world than North American. What chance did these residents have in the capitalistic world outside of the reservation? It's still a valid question four decades later.

Cannon's overseas work on behalf of the AFL-CIO's overseas arms was portrayed as developmental in the fight against communism. The tasks being funded predominately by the US government were in support of the free democratic trade union movement. The USSR supported trade unions in order to promote its communistic ideology. The mentality of a Cold War warrior fighting communism prevailed.

It wasn't until a stay in Bangladesh that Cannon's eyes were truly opened to see that the work he was promoting wasn't developmental but political. How could it be when he was told by the late Emilio Garza to work with a trade union federation flying the hammer and sickle on its office roof in Chittagong? Had Garza made a mistake or had Garza been conned? Had Cannon been instructed to work with this federation to obtain information that might be useful to other US organizations? Since Garza has died, Cannon will never know in this life.

In Nairobi, Cannon was questioned frequently, mostly by expatriates, why the US trade union movement was involved with the trade union federation (COTU) in Kenya. Cannon would respond by saying that the aid to COTU was being used to promote democracy as well as to educate trade union members on how to bargain collectively, process work, place grievances, and resolve safety issues.

When the shop stewards' programs were conducted on specific trade union tasks they were received very positively by the attendees. In one case, the topic was safety-on-the-job. How ironic that a couple of the participants were later promoted into management positions by their employer? As part of management, they would be on the other side of the table-no longer fighting for their fellow workers well-being.

Obviously, this removed them from their trade union. By all means, who could expect a person to refuse a promotion with more pay? The most ironic thing of all was that the trade union movements were educating persons to the benefit of management and not their respective union.

International trade union politics relative to the cold war continued during this period. Cannon still thought his work was important in keeping the "bad guys" from making inroads with African trade unions. When Cannon travelled out of Kenya to conduct programs in places like Mauritius, he knew the main reason was political and not developmental. The Mauritius Labor Congress (MLC) was a supporter of the pro-western political party in the country. These programs helped the MLC to gain good publicity in-county with their members and the government.

During Cannon's work with trade unions in South Africa, development was also secondary to politics. The major goal was to help the black African trade unions grow stronger. It wasn't easy being an American when dealing with NACTU and their affiliated unions. One might wonder why?

The US government led by President Reagan still viewed the ANC as a communist front. US businesses were still operational which kept monies flowing into South Africa. It was only as a "late comer" that the US government supported sanctions. Most black trade unionists associated capitalism with apartheid because of this. The US, as the largest capitalistic country, was thus viewed as the biggest supporter of apartheid for many years.

It was obvious to Cannon that the ANC was the main organization supported by the majority of black persons in the country. It was easier for their supporters to form opposition groups to oppose the government with support of the black population as a whole. Groups, such as the PAC, found it harder to form opposition groups because of limited support. This remained true until the government unbanned the ANC, PAC and SACP in 1989.

Black South Africans were required to prove they had a right to be in white areas (the pass law). This apartheid system was used to control the access of black's to white areas and was deeply hated. The PAC called for a massive campaign against the pass law. On March 21, 1960 police in Sharpeville shot and killed over 65 people protesting against the pass law. After Sharpeville, the PAC popularity was very high. The PAC's popularity versus the ANC gradually diminished and what little it still had, melted away when Steve Biko was murdered in 1977 while in police custody.

On the 10th of April 1993, another major political disaster struck South Africa. A very intelligent, brave and charismatic leader in the African National Congress (ANC) and South Africa Communist Party (SACP) Chris Hani was murdered by a white former Polish citizen who just hated black people.

According to many people Hani was seen as a potential successor to Nelson Mandela who was expected to be elected President of South Africa in 1994. People braced themselves for an outburst of rage from Hani's followers who were mostly young blacks. Mr. Mandela was able to go on television and radio to defuse a potential bloodbath situation. After the killing, it was learned that a white Afrikaner woman jotted down the license plate of the vehicle used by the killer that helped the police to capture the assassin within hours after the murder. People in Lesotho were also shocked by Hani's murder: especially since he had spent time in Maseru underground in the 1970's and he was married to a Basotho woman.

Residing and working in Lesotho, completely surrounded by South Africa, one couldn't escape from the apartheid South African system of government. There was a long history with both countries. For years, the major travel access to the outside world was via South Africa. Telecommunications access to the outside world was via South Africa.

When Cannon first worked in Lesotho, the functioning telephone system was part of the South Africa system. Under this system there was no need for South Africa to tap phones in Lesotho. 99% of consumer goods for sale in Lesotho were a product of South Africa. There were South African newspapers. The list went on and on.

For decades upon decades, many Basotho men worked in the South African diamond, gold, and coal mines. The South African mines were an excellent example of capitalism's exploitation of labor. The mineworkers from Lesotho could not bring their families to South Africa. They were housed in single sex hostels, which were often located on the mine premises. HIV/AIDS developed into a major health disaster for Basotho mineworkers and their families. At one time in the early 2000's, Lesotho had one of the highest infection rates in the world.

The Lesotho economy was even premised on remittances from the poorly paid mine workers in South Africa for decades. A percentage of the minimal monthly mineworkers' pay was withheld by their employer for remittances. Interest earned on these monies went to the employer not the mineworker. If the aforementioned wasn't a form of capitalism exploitation nothing is.

Living and working in Lesotho, one experienced the reality of "BIG BROTHER". It was almost impossible to escape from the effect South Africa had on Lesotho especially if one was a foreign expatriate. The South African police and intelligence services were always present: either undercover or via their system of informants. BIG BROTHER wasn't a leftwing concept, but a reality that one learned to live with. It wasn't a surprise to Cannon to witness the patronizing attitude of international organizations when they dealt with "tiny" Lesotho. BIG BROTHER wasn't a concept reserved for South Africans only

It wasn't as bad as witnessing the arrogance of the NGO's in Liberia who provided services the government couldn't during the war years and shortly thereafter. It sort of reminded Cannon of the attitude of some US Department of Labor persons in dealing with NAFRC in Nigeria: i.e. **WESTERN WHITE PEOPLE KNEW WHAT WAS BEST FOR BLACK RECIPIENTS.** If this was not a form of neo-colonialism, nothing is!!

The aforementioned is a bold statement. During Cannon's years working with LHDA on the Lesotho Highlands Water Project, representatives of international organizations were frequent visitors to the project. Cannon had minimal dealings with the international financiers, since his work did not directly deal with project finances. Cannon, did however, have many interactions with the World Bank (WB) whose experts were mainly focused on the environmental aspects of the project. At times, it seemed they were always seeking more than environmental information. Cannon's main dealings with World Bank experts arose from the workers discrimination charges. The LHDA findings, resulting from the two internal investigations led by Cannon, were submitted to the World Bank. Cannon never did find out what the WB did with these reports, if anything!

There were very well qualified persons who were either direct WB employees or consultants. The WB experts were well qualified in their respective competencies. However what bothered Cannon was the power which they perceived they held and the manner how they demanded action by LHDA personnel, especially in environmental aspects of the LHWP.

Lesotho is a tiny country with little if any political power in the world. The WB and other international agencies and NGO's operate in poor countries who receive international assistance. When China was to build the Three Gorges Dam, there were numerous environmental issues raised by international bodies. Smaller countries such as Lesotho were required to answer and act on many of the recommendations made by these same bodies. China on the other hand was powerful enough to go-it-alone to build the Three Gorges Dam. One would think there are two standards held by numerous international agencies. One for weak and poor countries and one for the powerful countries!

China embraced massive industrialization in the later part of the 20th century. Africa has been blessed with an abundance of mineral resources, a pre-requisite for industrial development. It was only a matter of time until China entered into bi-lateral trade agreements with individual African countries, to eventually become the world's biggest investor in Africa. This was a gigantic step forward since 1970 when China financed and built the railroad connecting Tanzania to Zambia (TANZAM): it was completed in 1975.

When Cannon joined the Peace Corps in 1963, the US (not China) was the world's biggest promoter of international development. It exported industrial technology to friendly countries in the developing world. Throughout the years that followed, the US went from exporting automotive technology to exporting McDonalds- a low wage service industry. Cannon was shocked in 1994 after President Mandela was elected President of a "free" South Africa that one major carrot offered by the US was McDonalds. What ever happened to the US's export of industrial technology?

It is extremely difficult to keep abreast of what's taking place in Africa once one leaves the continent. The public media in the US has little or no coverage about Africa unless a disaster takes place. Even if there is a disaster, the coverage only lasts a few days. Fortunately, the internet has provided a medium to access public information via the BBC, Al Jazeera and other news agencies.

Since 2000, information provided by the World Bank, International Monetary Fund, and other similar bodies indicates a massive change is taking place economically in Africa. China's search for raw materials needed for its rapid industrial growth has played a key role in the changes taking place.

Some countries are doing better than others as a result of their raw materials trade with China if one believes the Bank? Yet, there is a lingering question that conflicts with the data. Does the average African have access to employment and capital which serves as the basis for the IMF reports? Does the economic trickledown effect work in Africa when it didn't work elsewhere?

Not according to the Afrobarometer Research Project. They questioned 51,605 respondents in 34 countries from October 2011 to June 2013. About one in five Africans questioned say they still often lack food, clean water or medical care as reported by the Guardian Weekly.

There is evidence of what capitalism provides in the form of consumer goods in any capital or major city in Africa. The well-to-do, as is the case in the West, has access to these goods and services. Yet side-by-side, there exists massive slums whose residents can barely survive daily. If slum areas are needed for development by local builders, who are frequently supported by their friends in government, they run the risk of getting bulldozed.

When asked about the success of capitalism, the late Joe Slovo supposedly said that some 90% of the worlds' poor lived under systems which were followers of the capitalistic market economies. Would the poor have a better chance to see their life improve under socialism? It is extremely difficult to compare capitalism and socialism while living in the USA.

Many Americans think socialism is communism. One is constantly being exposed to commercial advertisements promoting one product or another. There are few, if any, commercial advertisements promoting the welfare of the individual human being or the common good of citizens. All too often the products being advertised are consumed by people in debt since many, many products advertised are purchased with credit cards. Is debt a mechanism to placate the rich at the expense of the poor? How about keeping people's minds off of politics?

Cannon's union, the American Federation of Teachers endorsed Hilary Clinton for the Democratic nomination in the 2008 Primary. Cannon joined the Democratic Caucus in Calais and was the 1st to motivate for Barak Obama. Cannon thought it was time for a person of color to be President of the US. He had high hopes, as did many that Obama might be the one to take the country out of its foreign wars. The Obama delegates just beat the Clinton delegates by two or three votes for the nomination in the Calais caucus.

Edherue used to say that the elections in the USA were just as crooked as Nigeria. Cannon would laugh, but upon reflection, especially after the US 2000 elections, he wasn't sure. Ben repeated his view in 2004 and after what took place in Ohio (votes for Kerry not counted, etc.) it became clear Ben might be on to something.

Prior to Obama's election, the US economy tanked. Cannon's meager Individual Retirement Account took a major hit as did everyone else except the extremely rich. They could weather a 20% drop in value of their wealth without losing too much sleep. Unfortunately most Americans are not in a similar situation.

When candidate-elect Obama announced his chosen candidate for Treasury Secretary, a former Wall Street insider, Cannon had a gut feeling that not too much was going to change under Obama. Other friends of Cannon thought the appointment of a Treasury Secretary with Wall Street "cred" was required to ensure the whole economic system didn't fall apart.

Joy turned to disbelief when President Obama bailed out the Wall Street banks. How could one give tax payers monies to the very folks that caused the economy to dissolve in 2008 without demanding recipient financial requirements? Individual citizens throughout the entire country were losing their homes due to horrible bank practices and the bad loan decisions many of these homeowners made. This was another example of the dichotomy in capitalism. Help the rich while ignoring the poor.

After Obama was sworn in as President, Cannon still had a sense of hope things in the US may become a bit different. Here was a person with an African father from Kenya becoming President of the US. Cannon had spent many years in Kenya. He thought if Pius Odhiambo was still alive, he would have been thrilled. How ironic the US had a President of Luo ancestry whereas a Luo has never held the Presidency in Kenya.

When Cannon studied civics (are civics still taught in school?) in grammar school back in the 1950's, he was taught no one is above the law in the United States. Yet, as the years passed, it became apparent this was not 100% true. All too often the powerful are able to bend the law, especially tax law, to their advantage.

After WWII, the US established war time tribunals in Germany and Japan to bring individuals to trial from each country on charges of crimes against humanity. Decades later, the United Nations (UN) established the

International Criminal Court (ICC), whose purpose was to try individuals for their crimes committed against their fellow human beings. As of this writing, the US has yet to ratify the UN convention which established the ICC. Another example in the US of: Do what we say not what we do?

The US government (Republicans and Democrats) have accused individuals such as Saddam Hussein, of crimes against humanity. After the US invasion of Iraq, the US government stated Saddam should be tried at the ICC. That was before he was captured and tried in Iraq itself.

Throughout the past couple of decades, various US governments, democratic and republican, have made reference to the ICC. It was either for domestic political purposes or as justification for government action. An example being the 20 March 2003 invasion of Iraq calling Saddam Hussein a war criminal. Could one of the reasons for the US not ratifying the ICC conventions be, the fear that US officials might one day be charged by the ICC with war crimes such as torture, bombing of civilians, etc. How is it possible that the US could evoke use of the ICC or crimes against humanity only when it suits the US? US military interventions, coupled with US government support of dictators, are not viewed as being good by the rest of the world: some even think said actions are in themselves criminal. Unfortunately the US media presents a very different picture to the American people.

In many countries, the elected officials that make big mistakes while holding office are held accountable. They volunteer to resign or are forced to resign as a public sign of responsibility for their actions/decisions. In some cases, persons are brought to international courts to be tried for the wrongs committed while in office. Here in the US, there appears to be two sets of accountability: one for the lower class and little if any for the upper class. This also translates into different positions of power. Enlisted military personnel received jail terms for their behavior in Iraq's Abu Ghraib jail. However, the military officers responsible for the operation of the Abu Ghraib jail only received sanctions.

This dichotomy prevails even if bad decisions and alleged criminal behavior result in undeclared wars or questionable financial decisions. In the US, there are few if any consequences, except for the kids who die in the wars or the poor who suffer the most from Wall Street's poor and questionable legal economic decisions. There are by far more US military veterans who are homeless as a result of Wall Street illegal actions regarding home mortgages than there are fraudulent Wall Street brokers in jail. Especially those senior executives who set the table for maleficent systems at their firms: if there are any in jail?

In recent years, US Presidents concluded many of their speeches with the words "God Bless America". Some people overseas used to ask Cannon if he thought God only Blessed the US? Christianity isn't only reserved to the USA in the present world. Cannon had no answer to adequately address the question.

In his old age living in the USA, what boggles Cannon's mind, is the contempt shown by many wealthy and conservative Americans for the poor and downtrodden. Many elected public figures seek to eliminate programs that help the poor while seeking more tax breaks for the wealthy. References are too numerous to quote where Jesus connects with the poor throughout the Christian bible. How can you call yourself a Christian country when millions of children go to bed hungry nightly; when millions cannot read nor write; when millions have no jobs; when many thousand are homeless, including far too many military veterans? Is this a true reflection of a Christian country?

Many of these same wealthy and conservative Americans also are the most vocal cheerleaders and biggest supporters of the wars initiated by the USA. Yet, their children and grandchildren are not required to fight in these wars' ever since the US military became a volunteer one in the early 1970's. When blood has to be shed for the country, it should be shed equally by all regardless of economic standing. Where is the military draft to ensure a fairer distribution of hardship? This is another example where 1% of the population, often the poor, bears the burden of war and dies, while the very wealthy 1% of the population, prospers.

Conclusions

Africa is a vast continent blessed with intelligent, industrious and friendly people. As a whole it has an abundance of mineral resources. It has adequate fertile land to feed itself. As the influence and meddling of western countries in Africa continues to diminish, Africa will become more self-reliant. In the decades to come, Africa will become a major force in the world of geopolitics. Africa's days of being referred to as a basket case by westerners, will be a thing of the past. Unfortunately for Cannon, he will not still be on mother earth to witness Africa's rebirth.

As Cannon got older, it became more difficult to continue the routine first established overseas: a daily jog sometimes followed up by a swim. This routine afforded Cannon the opportunity to drink beer without gaining much weight. It became harder and harder to run in Calais especially during the winter due to the icy roads and a pain in the right hip that caused discomfort. Being old school, Cannon thought it was like a "cramp". Bear with it and eventually it disappears. It did not disappear. There was no cartilage only bone-on-bone.

During the summer of 2008, while "pulling" lobster traps, Cannon felt a sharp groin pain. After the summer was over, on one of his trips to Rhode Island, Gudrun convinced him to visit a specialist to have the groin checked. Cannon was informed he had developed a hernia that required fixing.

The hernia was repaired in late October followed by a right hip replacement in November. Gudrun was a terrific soldier putting up with Cannon who was initially immobile and required constant care while she was still teaching school. The holidays weren't the best. Yet, they still were able to break bread with Cannon's kids and grand-daughter. After completing physical therapy and getting doctor clearance to drive his shift auto, Cannon returned to Maine in February 2009. It became easier to get about, but Cannon's jogging days were over.

Cannon's Catholicism has been a cornerstone of his life, especially in later years, which helped him to cope with old age. The short comings of the Catholic Church, such as the pedophile issues in the US, illustrate the human imperfections in some ministers. God cannot be blamed for the short comings of human beings. The Catholic gospels do not promote a capitalistic world. Human beings are not on planet earth only to consume goods and receive services. If consumption is life's sole purpose, Cannon must have taken the wrong road in life. Cannon's hopes, dreams and enthusiasm for a more just and better world may have to wait until the next life.

While Cannon's physical body undergoes major changes associated with aging, his mental state gravitates more and more towards the injustice of consumer capitalism. The US promotes Free Trade agreements which benefit the wealthy far more than the average person. In many countries covered under US trade agreements, the workers are often paid a pittance while toiling in horrible working conditions i.e. Bangladesh garment workers. Cannon's past efforts internationally to promote workers justice seem part of a life long gone.

It took the death of Senator Ted Kennedy to get Cannon and Gudrun to begin a serious discussion about marriage. They both were getting old. Their long distance relationship was insane. While watching the funeral on television, they decided it was time to get married. A ten year courtship was long enough to get to know each other!

July 24, 2010 Cannon and Gudrun were married in St. Bernard's Church North Kingstown, Rhode Island. After the mass and marital ceremony, a small reception was held for family and a few friends. Just prior to the wedding, Cannon moved from Calais to North Kingstown. Ben Edherue wasn't able to attend the wedding, but he telephoned his best wishes. Ben always used to kid Cannon saying he was getting so old that he would soon forget what marriage entailed.

Out of the blue on 10 November 2011, Cannon received an email from Oke Edherue that Ben passed. Cannon had spoken with Ben a few weeks prior to his passing. During the conversation, Ben mentioned he was suffering from some minor aches and pains. Cannon just assumed these were the normal things men Go through in life. Cannon was shocked by the news and still finds it hard to believe Ben is no longer a member of the human race.

Ben's wife, Juliet, gave birth to Ben's only son on the 5th of November. Ben awoke from a coma on the 6th and was able to cradle his son before joining his ancestors on the 7th at 2: 15 AM. Ben went to meet the ancestors knowing his son would carry on the family heritage along with the three older girls. Ben passed due to an intestinal blockage. Cannon lost a brother.

National Geographic and IBM, with financial support from the Waitt Family Foundation, created the Genographic Project. The goal of this anthropological study was to use modern genetics to chart footsteps and migratory paths of distant ancestors as they moved out of Africa. The project hopes to collect some 100,000 DNA samples from a worldwide diversified participating group for this study.

Cannon's daughter, Chandra, enrolled him in this study as a birthday present. A DNA testing kit was provided. Cannon took swabs from the inside walls of his mouth. The swabs were placed in vials and mailed to the study in Houston, Texas.

According to the study, Cannon's DNA indicated he was a member of the Haplogroup R1b, M343 Sub clade R1b1c, M269. This group of ancestors is said to have originated in the region of the Rift Valley, in present day Ethiopia, Kenya or Tanzania. It moved over time from the Rift Valley to the Middle East and then to Central Asia. It then moved into Western Europe. Cannon's immediate ancestors moved from Ireland and Italy to the United States in the late 1800's.

If the aforementioned study can be believed, Cannon was Ben Edherue's brother. We were both members of one universal extended family, originating in the Rift Valley, Africa. Cannon will always wonder if Ben's death was preventable. Or was the call of the ancestors so demanding that

Ben couldn't do anything but accept the call? Cannon lost a colleague and dear friend who helped Cannon to move away from being a conservative. "**Africa, anything is possible**" as Ben always said.

Esemo, Udi oro'me obo, Eke rai ona! Uno anwa z'eho Wha gbe bru obe ruru omai ehru emeje ma emo ra je re emu Ododo ore kpo ho eha eso ha Esemo wha da! Hoooo! - The drinkers.

Appendages

1. BA Diploma Providence College 1963

COLLEGIUM PROVIDENTIENSE

Omnibus praesentes litteras inspecturis Salutem in Domino

Maiores nostri, inter alia multa, sapienter illud in primis instituerunt, eos omnes qui in publicis disciplinarum palaestris se dignos sapientiae amatores probaverint, Baccalaureos vel Magistros, vel etiam Doctores iubendos atque renuntiandos. Quod ut etiam in nostro Collegio legitime fieri posset, Rhodiensis Insulae Respublica per litteras nobis datas die XIV Februarii anno MCMXVII opportune instituit. Inter illos vero qui id honoris meriti sunt, accenseri iure optimo debet

Petrus Jacobus Cannon.

Is enim posteaquam legitimos annos disciplinis praescriptis dedisset, luculento doctrinae experimento iuxta constitutiones et scripto et orali prolato, Facultatis Doctorum Collegii antedicti suffragiis dignus est habitus qui Baccalaurei titulum ac iura consequeretur. Nos itaque, illorum sententia probata, laudatum virum

Baccalaureum Artium

iussimus ac renuntiavimus, et omnibus et singulis iuribus, privilegiis, praerogativis ornavimus quibus ii omnes fruuntur qui eundem gradum in quolibet alio Collegio fuerint adepti. Ne autem novae consecutae dignitatis monumentum desit, publicum hoc testimonium Nostra manu subsignatum eidem habendum dedimus.

Actum Providentiae die quarta mensis Junii anno MCMLXIII.

Praeses

Secretarius Generalis

2. U.S. Coast Guard Honorable Discharge 1963

from the Armed Forces of the United States of America

This is to certify that

PETER JAMES CANNON (2002-956) SN, USCGR

was Honorably Discharged from the

United States Coast Guard

on the 29TH *day of* JULY 1963 *This certificate is awarded as a testimonial of Honest and Faithful Service*

E. B. Sawtelle

E. B. SAWTELLE, CAPT, USCGR
DIRECTOR OF RESERVE
FIRST COAST GUARD DISTRICT

DD FORM 256 CG (REV. 5-60)

3. Municipality of Tigbauan, Iloilo Province Philippines 1965

REPUBLIC OF THE PHILIPPINES
PROVINCE OF ILOILO
MUNICIPALITY OF TIGBAUAN

Office of the Municipal Council

EXCERPT FROM THE MINUTES OF THE PROCEEDINGS OF THE MUNICIPAL COUNCIL, TIGBAUAN, ILOILO, PHILIPPINES, DURING ITS SPECIAL SESSION HELD AT THE MUNICIPAL SESSION HALL, TIGBAUAN, ILOILO, ON MAY 19, 1965, AT 6:00 P.M.

PRESENT:

Mr. Bonifacio M. Trivilegio. . . . . Municipal Mayor
Mr. Jose Torrefranca, Jr. . . . . Vice Mayor
Mr. Celso Ledesma . . . . Councilor
Mrs. Maria B. Tenefrancia . . . . "
Mr. Jesus Ledesma . . . . "
Mr. Jose Tuble . . . . "
Mr. Ramon Ledesma . . . . "
Mr. Leovigilde Diaz . . . . "
Mr. Jose Tilos . . . . "
Mr. David Alquisada . . . . "

ABSENT:
----None--------------------------------

RESOLUTION NO. 20, S. 1965

RESOLUTION ADOPTING MR. PETER J. CANNON, AN AMERICAN PEACE CORPS VOLUNTEER ASSIGNED IN THE MUNICIPALITY OF TIGBAUAN, PROVINCE OF ILOILO, PHILIPPINES, AS ITS SON.

WHEREAS, universal peace and understanding is the goal of man of all race, creed and color;

WHEREAS in the attainment of this goal, organizations are set up, maintained, and dispersed to diffuse the spirit of understanding, brotherly love and give and take all across the face of the globe;

WHEREAS, among these organizations, the PEACE CORPS, organized and maintained by the United States of America is one which is dedicated to this job and has substantially succeeded in its mission at least in this patch of the world;

WHEREAS, like a chain which could only be as strong as any of its link, this oranization will be as strong as its individual composition;

WHEREAS, this town has seen how this world organization works and can bear witness to the performance of an individual volunteer in the person of Mr. Peter J. Cannon, a native and resident of the City of Providence, Rhode Island, 02908;

WHEREAS, Mr. Peter J. Cannon has amply and convincingly demonstrated that mankind can and is one huge family, akin in spirit, reacting to the same stimuli and emotion and despite difference in color, race, creed, can work successfully together for the upliftment of man and the realization of the "one world" idea;

WHEREAS, Mr. Peter J. Cannon has amply and convincingly demonstrated that mankind can and is one huge family, akin in spirit, reacting to the same stimuli and emotion and despite difference in color, race, creed, can work successfully together for the upliftment of man and the realization of the "one world" idea;

WHEREAS, Mr. Peter J. Cannon, has and could be one of us and that the fact that he is not a native born of this town is due to the accident of birth an immutable law of nature that man cannot chose the place of his birth:

WHEREAS, while the fact of birth cannot be changed or altered yet an avenue is open to bypass this impediment and rightly call a man brother by way of adoption;

WHEREAS, this body has that power to do as without inpairment to the interest of the community;

RESOLUTION NO. 20, S. 1965
Tigbauan, Iloilo

Page -2-

BE IT RESOLVED AS IT IS HEREBY RESOLVED, to convey a message of appreciation to the Peace Corps organization of the United States of America, for its substantial contribution to world peace and understanding and the upliftment of mankind;

BE IT RESOLVED further as it is hereby resolved to adopt Mr. Peter J. Cannon as a son of this Municipality in order to authenticate and put down for posterity the fact of his adoption and to strengthen the bond of nearness which he was able to weave between him and the residents of this town, with the fond hope that this will be the tiny acorn to grow into a stately oak of American- Philippine brotherhood:

BE it resolved finally as it is hereby resolved to furnish Mr. Peter J. Cannon, Headquarters, Peace Corps Organization, care Philippine Desk, Washington D.C., the Council of the City of Providence Rhode Island, U.S.A. a copy each of this resolution for their corresponding information and cognizance.

UNANIMOUSLY APPROVED.

I hereby certify to the correctness of the above-quoted resolution.

RAYMUNDO TEMUEL
Municipal Secretary

ATTESTED:

BONIFACIO M. TRIVILEGIO
Municipal Mayor

4 Description of Peace Corps Services

PEACE CORPS

(PANGKAT PANGKAPAYAPAAN)

726 HERRAN STREET
MANILA, PHILIPPINES

TELEPHONE
5-24-21

DESCRIPTION OF PEACE CORPS VOLUNTEER SERVICE

Mr. Peter James Cannon
Peace Corps Volunteer
Philippines 63-01-06

Mr. Peter James Cannon has been serving satisfactorily as a Peace Corps Volunteer since June 15, 1963. Before leaving the United States, Peter satisfactorily completed an intensive eleven-week program at the University of Hawaii in Hilo, Hawaii. Upon arrival in the Philippines, he participated in a special training program for Peace Corps Volunteers at Philippine Women's College in Iloilo.

Peter is responsible to the Bureau of Public Schoos during his service in the Philippines. He serves as Co-teacher assigned to Tigbauan Central School in Tigbauan, Iloilo. As a Peace Corps Volunteer and Co-teacher, he co-teaches English as a Second Language.

Additionally, Peter acted as a counselor in a summer camp for indigent children.

This Volunteer will complete his tour of service with the Peace Corps in the Philippines on June 1, 1965.

MAURICE D. BEAN, Director
Peace Corps/Philippines

Satisfactorily completed service on JUN 1 1965

F. Kingston Berlew
Acting Associate Director
For Peace Corps Volunteers

PHILIPPINES TRAINING ABSTRACT

University of Hawaii June 15-August 28, 1963

TECHNICAL STUDIES: Theory and practice in the teaching of English and science, designed to meet the requirements of educational aides in elementary schools of the Philippines	100 hrs.
AREA STUDIES: History and contemporary culture of the Philippines.	100 hrs.
LINGUISTICS: Preparatory to technical study in teaching English as a second language and to the study of Philippine languages.	36 hrs.
AMERICAN STUDIES: Democratic traditions and institutions, contemporary American scene.	50 hrs.
WORLD AFFAIRS AND COMMUNISM: International problems; the Emergent nations of Southeast Asia and the U.S. relationships with these nations. Strategy, tactics, and menace of Communism.	25 hrs.
HEALTH AND MEDICAL TRAINING: First aid, preventive measures, tropical medicine.	40 hrs.
PHYSICAL EDUCATION AND RECREATION: Physical conditioning games and dances of the Philippines	40 hrs.
PEACE CORPS ORIENTATION: Aims, goals, and purposes of the Peace Corps and the Volunteers' role within it.	20 hrs.
LANGUAGE: Study of Tagalog, the national language, and the dialects of the areas where the Volunteers would be assigned.	85 hrs.

5. President of the U.S. Lyndon B. Johnson 1965

THE WHITE HOUSE

WASHINGTON

Dear Mr. Cannon:

I understand that you will soon complete your service as a Peace Corps Volunteer.

Today the Peace Corps is recognized throughout the world as an expression of the highest ideals of our nation. That judgment rests on the conduct and accomplishments of you and your fellow Volunteers. There can be no more fitting tribute than this to the memory of the man whose vision launched the Peace Corps, our late beloved President John F. Kennedy.

While the role of a single person may be small, it is only through a collective effort such as the Peace Corps that we can hope to build a world in which men and women may share more of the world's bounties and less of its sufferings, and in which nations will offer one another support and respect.

I am indeed proud of the contribution you have made as a Peace Corps Volunteer.

Sincerely,

6. U.S. Jobs Corps Certificate 1965

STAFF TRAINING CERTIFICATE

This is to certify that

Peter Cannon

has completed full Staff Orientation at the Job Corps Staff Training Center at

Santa Rosa, California

DATE December 17, 1965

CENTER DIRECTOR

7. Job Corps Staff Training Certificate University of California 1965

UNIVERSITY OF CALIFORNIA EXTENSION

This is to certify that

Peter Cannon

was a registered participant in the

JOB CORPS STAFF TRAINING

Paul H. Sheats
Dean, University Extension

8. WPRO Radio, Providence, Rhode Island Citizen of Week 1966

24 MASON STREET • PROVIDENCE, RHODE ISLAND 02902 • 521-4000 WPRO 630 KILOCYCLES

June 14, 1966

Mr. Peter J. Cannon,
73 Gentian Avenue,
Providence, Rhode Island.

Dear Mr. Cannon:

It is the custom of WPRO Radio to bring to the attention of our Southern New England listening audience every Sunday during our programming hours, the name of a person who has achieved a prominent place in his respective field. Therefore, it is our pleasure on Sunday, June 19, to honor you as our Citizen of the Week.

The message heard on WPRO aired at various intervals reads as follows:

WPRO salutes Mr. Peter J. Cannon of Providence, assigned recently to duty in Asia with the Catholic Relief Services of the National Catholic Welfare Council. Mr. Cannon served from 1963 to 1965 with the Peace Corps in the Philippines. He is a graduate of Providence College and served for two years with the Coast Guard. WPRO is proud to honor Peter J. Cannon, Citizen of the Week.

Our sincere congratulations.

Sincerely,

Leo R. LaPorte
Director of Public Relations

LRL:jm

A DIVISION OF CAPITAL CITIES BROADCASTING CORPORATION

9. Diocese of Lokoja, Nigeria 1968

Diocese of Lokoja
P. O. Box 31 – Lokoja, Nigeria – Tel. 47

16th August, 1968.

Mr. Peter Cannon,
Red Cross Representative,
c/o Catholic Church,
Idah.

Dear Mr. Cannon,

Thanks for your letter and the copy of the Report on the Idah Relief Programme. I can assure you that if things went well throughout it is mostly because you fitted in the group. We were very pleased to have you and any time you come back we will accept you again without difficulties.

Best wishes in your new appointment until we see you again.

Most sincerely yours,

A. Delisle,
Bishop of Lokoja.

10. International Committee of Red Cross 1968

RELIEF ACTION NIGERIA
1968/69

To Peter C A N N O N

in appreciation for service rendered.
INTERNATIONAL COMMITTEE
OF THE RED CROSS

PRESIDENT

SOCIÉTÉ
D'UTILITÉ PUBLIQUE
GENÈVE

1863

COMITÉ INTERNATIONAL
DE SECOURS
pour les
MILITAIRES BLESSÉS

1864

COMITÉ INTERNATIONAL-SECOURS AUX BLESSÉS-GENÈVE

1868

COMITÉ INTERNATIONAL·SECOURS AUX BLESSÉS·GENÈVE

1870

COMITÉ INTERNATIONAL
DE LA
CROIX ROUGE
(GENÈVE)

1880

COMITÉ INTERNATIONAL
DE LA
CROIX-ROUGE

1917

COMITÉ INTERNATIONAL
DE LA
CROIX-ROUGE

11. Cabinet Office, Kingdom of Lesotho 1971

Cabinet Office,
P.O. Box 527,
MASERU.

23rd June, 1971.

Dear Mr. Cannon,

I acknowledged with thanks receipt of your letter dated 21st June, 1971. I also noted that you will be in the near future leaving for South Korea. It had been always very nice to be with you and we enjoyed your stay with us in Lesotho. Moreover I, personally appreciated your services very much. I wish you could do the same in South Korea.

I am pleased to know your replacement by Mr Eugene Rosera and I hope he is going to be as co-operative as you were. I, and on behalf of the Government of Lesotho thank you very much and wish you and your family success wherever you go.

Once more I would like to extend my sincere gratitude for all the admirable work you did for our country - Lesotho.

Good Luck ! God bless you.

Yours faithfully,

CHIEF SELBOURNE LETSIE
MINISTER TO THE PRIME MINISTER

Mr Peter J. Cannon,
Catholic Relief Services,
P.O. Box 159,
MASERU.

12. Ministry of Justice, Kingdom of Lesotho 1971

LESOTHO

Ministry of Justice,
P.O. Box 402,
<u>MASERU</u>.

24th June, 1971.

(Dear Mr. Cannon),

Thank you for your letter of 21st June, 1971 by which Catholic Relief Services/Lesotho has informed me of your departure from Lesotho due on the 19th July.

I thank you most sincerely for the good work you have done during your stay in Lesotho. We are sad to lose your services and we shall miss you dearely. However, the excellent work you have left behind will help to sustain our courage for more difficult times that lie ahead.

On behalf of Mrs. 'Mota and on my own behalf I wish you luck and God's guidance at your new post.

With best wishes,

Yours Sincerely,

(P. 'MOTA)
<u>MINISTER OF JUSTICE</u>

Peter J. Cannon, Esq.,
Lesotho Program Director,
P.O. Box 159,
<u>MASERU</u>. Lesotho.

13. Apostolic Delegate to South Africa 1971

In Reply Please Quote

No. 6680.

APOSTOLIC DELEGATION
800 PRETORIUS STREET
PRETORIA

TEL. 74-2489 P.O. Box 522
TELEG. ADD. "VATICDEL"

28th June, 1971.

Dear Mr. Cannon,

From your letter of June 21st, 1971, I learn the sad news of your departure from Lesotho on transfer to the C.R.S. program in South Korea.

I take this occasion to express to you the sentiments of my warm gratitude for the services you have rendered to the progress and development of Lesotho during your period as Program Director of Catholic Relief Services/ Lesotho.

In wishing you well in your new assignment, I pray that God may keep you and Mrs. Cannon and your family in health and happiness in South Korea.

With my kind regards and good wishes, I remain,

Sincerely yours,

John Gordon

Apostolic Delegate.

Mr. Peter J. Cannon,
Director: C.R.S./Lesotho,

P.O. Box 159,
Maseru,

L e s o t h o.

14. Prime Minister of Lesotho, Leabua Jonathan 1971

OFFICE OF THE PRIME MINISTER
MASERU
LESOTHO

PM/PRIV/H/22/1 30 June 1971

My Dear Peter,

Please accept my thanks for your letter of 21 June 1971, in which you inform me that you will be departing Lesotho in the week of 19th July and that you will be replaced by Mr Eugene Rosera as Acting Director.

I very much regret that you are leaving us after our happy mutual association. The work of Catholic Relief Services in Lesotho, which has been of such successful benefit to our country, has been greatly extended during your administration due to your enthusiasm and desire to see our young nation prosper. Your own personal efforts and the friendly relationship which you have been able to establish with our people are greatly appreciated by myself and my Ministers. We are very grateful for all you have done for us.

I sincerely wish you and your wife and daughter a happy and interesting sojourn in South Korea. You will always be welcome visitors to Lesotho.

With our thanks and warm personal regards,

Yours sincerely

Leabua Jonathan
Prime Minister and Minister
of Foreign Affairs

Mr. Peter J. Cannon
Lesotho Program Director
Catholic Relief Services
P O Box 159
Maseru

15. Ministry of Agriculture, Kingdom of Lesotho 1971

LESOTHO

G. 8B

AG/FOOD/2/2

Ministry of Agriculture,

P.O. Box 24,

MASERU.

30th June, 1971.

Mr. Peter J. Cannon,
Lesotho Program Director,
Catholic Relief Services,
MASERU.

Dear Mr. Cannon,

Thank you very much for your kind letter of the 21st June, 1971 in which you informed me of your departure from Lesotho on the week of the 19th July, 1971 and that Mr. Eugene Rosera would take over from you.

There is no doubt that your going to South Korea will give you additional experience in your important work, but we in Lesotho will, indeed, miss you because we had learned to understand and appreciate your straightforwardness. South Korea's gain will be Lesotho's loss. I sincerely hope Mr. Eugene Rosera will be as effective in Lesotho as you have been.

Hope to see you this evening.

Yours sincerely,

A.S. Mohale

Permanent Secretary

16. MA, St. Francis Xavier University, Nova Scotia, Canada 1972

Sancti Francisci Xaverii Universitas

dicti illius Paulini Quaecumque sunt vera fide memor
dum alumnis merentibus lauream mercedem publice tribuit
quibus ducum deinde municipes inter munus constituit

Peter James Cannon

qui provinciae propriae providens ad normam institutis suis praescriptam studiorum curriculum rite perfecit ac pericula prospere devicit hoc academico cum omnibus iuribus privilegiis et honoribus ab eo profluentibus ex Facultatis consulto decorare decrevit gradu

Magistri in Disciplinae Adultorum Artibus

Cuius rei haec membrana sigillo eiusdem Universitatis munita et Praesidis Decanique subscripta manibus testimonio legentibus omnibus sit

Datum Antigonisciae in Nova Scotia

Decanus

SANCTI FRANCISCI XAVERII UNIVERSITAS 1853

Die V Novembris A. D. MCMLXXII

M. MacDonell

Praeses

17. University of Bergen, Norway 1974

UNIVERSITETET I BERGEN

The Faculty of Social Sciences hereby declares that

Mr. Peter J. Cannon

having passed satisfactorily academic and written requirements for mellomfag (3 semester full-time study), is awarded a

DIPLOMA IN SOCIAL ANTHROPOLOGY

the content of which, incorporated with relevant previous educational credits from St. Francis Xavier University, Canada and Providence College, USA, in quantity and quality is equivalent to the Candidatus Magisterii, the lower degree awarded by the Faculty of Social Sciences (9 semester full-time study).

Bergen, June 10, 1974

Tore Sandvik
Dean
Professor, Dr. Juris

Jan Johnsen
Faculty Secretary

18. Department of Education, State of Maine 1975

Department of
Educational and Cultural Services
Augusta, Maine

This is to certify that

Peter Cannon

has successfully completed the
Human Development Teacher Education Institute
held April 9 - 11, 19 75
Sponsored and conducted by The Division
of Human Development & Guidance Resources

Magic Circle
A Program of Primary Prevention

Carl D. Mowatt

Carl D. Mowatt, Director

19. Maine Indian Education, State of Maine 1975

Maine Indian Education

River Road, Box 291 -:- Calais, Maine 04619 -:- Tel. (207) 454-2126

July 11, 1975

Peter Cannon
South Street
Calais, Maine 04619

Dear Peter:

Please consider this in response to your letter of June 18, 1975.

Your contract for the coming year (1975-76) has no status because no one contract has status until the Council votes to award a contract. As you are well aware, the Maine Indian Education Council awarded no contracts for the coming year because of the unavailability of funds and had scheduled discussion and finalization of your job description at its July 14 meeting. You were, however, an employee in good standing who never received any disciplinary letters or action stating that your contract was to be terminated. Therefore, it is accurate for you to assume and tell anyone else that you would have been employed (subject to your agreement) for the coming year.

If you would like me to write anything more specific to be used for your records, let me know.

Sincerely,

Meredith Ring
Superintendent

cc: Maine Indian Education Council Members

20. AFL-CIO Labor Studies Center 1976

This certifies that

PETER CANNON

has satisfactorily completed the course of study in

NEW STAFF INSTITUTE, NOVEMBER 28 - DECEMBER 10, 1976

and is awarded this certificate of completion.

21. Asian-American Free Labor Institute, AFL-CIO 1978

Asian-American Free Labor Institute

815 16th STREET, N.W., WASHINGTON, D.C. 20006 • TELEPHONE: 202/737-3000 • CABLE: AAFLIN

GEORGE MEANY, *PRESIDENT* • HUNTER P. WHARTON, *SECRETARY-TREASURER* • MORRIS PALADINO, *EXECUTIVE DIRECTOR*

June 15, 1978

TO WHOM IT MAY CONCERN:

Mr. Peter J. Cannon was employed as a Program Officer by the Asian-American Free Labor Institute for approximately two years. The Asian-American Free Labor Institute, an auxiliary of the AFL-CIO, is a non-profit voluntary agency which develops programs with the free and democratic trade union movements throughout Asia.

During this period, Mr. Cannon was responsible for monitoring and backstopping the Institute's extensive labor education, cooperative and community development programs in the Philippines and Korea. His duties included program and budget analysis, drafting revisions to Country Labor Plans submitted from the field, as well as monitoring the Implementation Schedules derived from the Country Labor Plans. He was also responsible for the analysis of field reports, the preparation of correspondence to the field offices, preparing reports as well as special assignments as needed.

During his employment, Mr. Cannon was called upon to fulfill two Temporary Duty Assignments, TDY, one in Bangladesh and the other in Korea. In Bangladesh, he developed a program for a series of labor education seminars for industrial unions affiliated to the national trade union center. While in Korea, he prepared project proposals to be developed with local, regional, and national unions for the provision of medical services for union members, water supply, expansion of an animal husbandry cooperative and the establishment of a labor education classroom. During these TDY assignments he was also responsible for maintaining office activities and procedures, assisted in the preparation of project proposals as well as the preparation of the draft Country Labor Plans for the countries.

Mr. Cannon is reliable, dedicated and conscientious in the fulfillment of his job. We highly recommend him as a man of action, a person who can get to the core of a problem and find a practical solution.

Sincerely,

M Paladino

Morris Paladino
Executive Director

22. A. Philip Randolph Institute, President Bayard Rustin 1978

October 28, 1978

Mr. Patrick J. O'Farrel
African-American Labor Center
345 East 46th Street
New York, New York 10017

Dear Pat:

When you have a chance, please take a look at the enclosed resume from Peter Cannon, formerly with the Asian-American Free Labor Institute. Brother Cannon is presently doing some consultant work, but has expressed a keen interest in returning to the field, preferably in Africa.

As you can see from the resume, Brother Cannon has had a good deal of experience both in the United States as well as in Asia and Africa. I think his experience with the Catholic Relief Services in Lesotho demonstrates a special talent for administration and intelligent planning.

While I understand that you have relatively little staff turn-over, I would appreciate it very much if you would take a careful look at Brother Cannon. I think he would be an excellent addition to any international organization.

With warm regards,

Fraternally,

Bayard

BAYARD RUSTIN
President

BR/mk

23. US Coalition of Labor Union Women, AFL-CIO 1985

Officers Council
President
Joyce D. Miller
ACTWU
Executive Vice President
Addie Wyatt
UFCW
Treasurer
Gloria Johnson
IUE
Recording Secretary
Lela Foreman
CWA
Corresponding Secretary
Elinor Glenn
SEIU
Vice Presidents
Clara Day
IBT
Evelyn Dubrow
ILGWU
Odessa Komer
UAW
Georgia McGhee
AFSCME
Gwen Newton
OPEIU
Anna Padia
TNG
Patricia Stryker
AFT
President Emerita
Olga Madar
UAW
General Counsel
Winn Newman

August 21, 1985

Mr. Peter J. Cannon
African American Labor Center
AFL-CIO
P.O. Box 42316
Nairobi, Kenya

Dear Peter:

I cannot thank you enough for all your hospitality to myself and the rest of our CLUW delegation, during our stay in Kenya.

Without any hesitation, I can truly say that my trip to Africa was the most exciting and most interesting of all my travels throughout all the other countries of the world. I really fell in love with the warmth of its people and the beauty of its scenery.

Peter, I am anxiously looking forward to coming back to Kenya.

Again, thank you for all your help, and for making the trip that much more enjoyable. I really feel that we are close friends.

Best personal regards.

Very sincerely,

Joyce D. Miller
National President

JDM/dps

412

24. The Workers' University, Cairo, Egypt 1985

THE WORKERS EDUCATIONAL ASSOCIATION
THE WORKERS' UNIVERSITY
6 EL NASR Street, Cairo, Egypt.
Tel. 606715-608460-608241 (219-268)

المؤسسة الثقافية العمالية
الجامعة العمالية
مكتب : المدير العام

القاهرة في : / /

Cairo, 3 April 1985
ref.: L40301.085

To: Patrick O' Farrell,
Executive Director,
AALC.

copy to:
Mr. Peter Loebarth, Cairo.
Mr. Glenn Lezak, Zaire.
Mr. Peter Cannon, Zambic.

Dear friend,

On my return to Egypt after my visits to Zaire, Kenya, and Zambia, I take the opportunity to express my gratitude to you in particular, and to the AALC in general, for having arranged this very useful trip.

From my meetings with my colleagues I learned that the great importance of the AALC cooperation in the field of labor education is not limited to Egypt, but is true for the other countries as well.

Your representatives in Egypt, Zaire, and Kenya, Messrs. Peter Loebarth, Glenn Lesak, and Peter Cannon, have been extremely kind and helpful in arranging the trip, and in sorting out all problems.

Please accept on behalf of everybody my sincere thanks for your kind cooperation.

Yours fraternally,

A.M. Dimallawy

A.M.Dimallawy,
Director-General,
WEA/WU.

العنوان : ٦ شارع النصر – مدينة نصر – القاهرة – جمهورية مصر العربية
تليفون : ٦٠٦٧١٥ ، ٦٠٨٤٦٠ ، ٦٠٨٢٤١ (داخلى ٢٦٨ ، ٢١٩) مباشر : ٦٠٩٠٣٧

25. Brotherhood of Railway, Airline and Steamship Clerks Freight Handlers, Express and Station Employees, AFL-CIO 1986

BROTHERHOOD OF RAILWAY, AIRLINE AND STEAMSHIP CLERKS, FREIGHT HANDLERS, EXPRESS AND STATION EMPLOYES

AFL-CIO—CLC

J. F. OTERO
International Vice-President

File: 217-0
Subject: International Affairs -- Africa 1985 BRAC Team Activities

January 13, 1986

Mr. Peter Cannon
AALC Representative
Post Office Box 42316
Nairobi, Kenya

Dear Peter:

Somewhat belatedly, I hasten to convey our sincere appreciation for the hospitality and assistance you provided the BRAC team composed of Sister Shirley Robertson and Brother Jerry Hester during their recent tour of Africa.

They have returned to the United States with a more comprehensive understanding of the problems and aspirations of transport workers in the African countries they visited. Their report indicated that their meetings with all counterpart unions were fruitful, enriching and educational. They also reported that the success of their mission was greatly enhanced by the care and concern displayed by you at all times during their visit to your country of assignment.

On behalf of International President Kilroy and the BRAC Executive Council, I again thank you very sincerely for making the visit of our BRAC team to Africa a fruitful and unforgettable experience. The African-American Labor Center can be proud to be represented by you on these activities of great importance. Thanks for your help!

Wishing you and your family a healthy and happy new year, I remain,

Sincerely and fraternally,

Jack

J. F. Otero
International Vice President

acs

cc: R. I. Kilroy, IP
Irving Brown, AFL-CIO
Pat O'Farrell, AALC
BRAC Team

AFL-CIO BUILDING / 815 16th STREET, N.W. / 5th FLOOR / WASHINGTON, D.C. 20006 / (202) 783-3660

26. Federation of Kenya Employers, Nairobi, Kenya 1986

FEDERATION OF KENYA EMPLOYERS

(Affiliated to the International Organization of Employers)
Waajiri House
Argwings Kodhek Road Milimani, Nairobi.

Branch Office
P.O. Box 84115
Mombasa
Kenya
Telephone 311112
Ralli House Nyerere Avenue

P.O. Box 48311
NAIROBI
Kenya
Telephone 721929/721949/721952
Telegrams:
FEDERKEM, Nairobi

Branch Office
P.O. Box 1449
Kisumu
Kenya
Telephone 41504

Ref. No. TDO/Jo

19th February, 1986

Mr. Peter J. Cannon,
African - American Labor Center,
P.O. Box 42316,
NAIROBI.

Dear Peter,

This is to express my sincere thanks to you and to the African - American Labor Center for the positive role which you have played in promoting workers education in Kenya.

I am also pleased to note that your replacement is none other than Mr. John Gould whom I have had the privilege to meet when he was in Kenya. I am sure that with his knowledge of Kenyan Labour situation, he will continue with your good work. I am told by my trade union friends that a praise from me for them is suspect in that it may indicate that they may have been too soft on employers! But I take it that you will take my praise of your work in good faith and that you will find your future career fulfilling.

Yours sincerely,

Tom D. Owuor
EXECUTIVE DIRECTOR

27. The Dockworkers Union, Mombasa, Kenya 1986

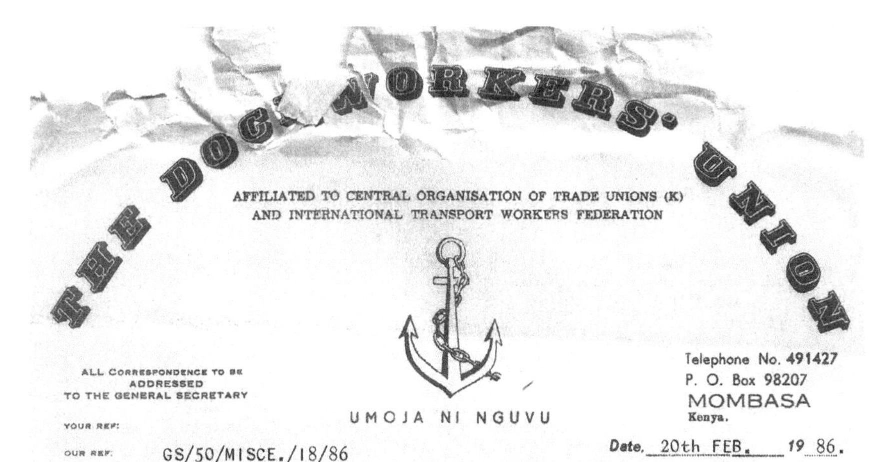

THE DOCKWORKERS' UNION

AFFILIATED TO CENTRAL ORGANISATION OF TRADE UNIONS (K)
AND INTERNATIONAL TRANSPORT WORKERS FEDERATION

ALL CORRESPONDENCE TO BE ADDRESSED TO THE GENERAL SECRETARY

UMOJA NI NGUVU

Telephone No. 491427
P. O. Box 98207
MOMBASA
Kenya.

YOUR REF:

OUR REF: GS/50/MISCE./18/86

Date. 20th FEB. 19 86.

Mr. Peter J. Cannon,
American Labour Center,
P. O. Box. 42316,
Nairobi.

Dear Brother,

TRANSFER TO WASHINGTON D.C.

I have learned from the circular letter dated 17th February, 1986, of your impending transfer to the United States of America.

I therefore, write to express our regrets on your departure and to express our appreciations on the excellent co-operation we have received during your term of office.

We would also like to welcome your successor Mr. John N. Gould, and assure him of our co-operation as well as to wish him every success in his new job.

Yours faithfully,

F. M. YUNIS,
GENERAL SECRETARY.

c.c. Mr. Lane Kirklan

c.c Mr. Frederick O'Neal

c.c Mr. Patrick J. O'Farrell.

28. Kenya National Housing Cooperative Union, Ltd. 1986

KENYA NATIONAL HOUSING COOPERATIVE UNION LTD.

P.O. Box 51693 — NAIROBI

Tel. .... Telex. ....

Date: 4th March 1986

Ref: NACHU/DEV/6/VOI.I/

Mr. Peter Cannon,
AALC Cooperative Representative,
P.O. Box 43216,
NAIROBI

Dear Sir,

I take this opportunity to thank African American Labour Center for the support it has given and continued to give to NACHU since its inception. I in particular thank you for all the support and advice you have rendered to NACHU while working as AALC Representative in NAIROBI.

On behalf of NACHU Management and Staff I wish you and your family a good stay in your new working station.

We all look forward to meeting the Regional Director for Africa Mr. John N. Gould when he arrives in Kenya to take up his new appointment.

Yours faithfully,

Ndeti J. Kattambo
General Manager

Copy to: Mr. L.M. Mugo
Treasurer
NACHU

Mr. Philip Mwangi
Chairman - NACHU
P.O. Box 1161
NAKURU

Mr. Justus Mulei
Secretary General - COTU(K)
P.O. Box 13000
NAIROBI

29. Tom Mboya Labour College, Kisumu, Kenya 1986

TOM MBOYA LABOUR COLLEGE

Telephone: 40491/40492
Telegrams: "Labour College"

Ring Road,
P. O. Box 754,
Kisumu,
Kenya.

Our Ref: TMLC/AALC/44

Your Ref: ________

Date 7th March, **19** 86

Mr. Peter Cannon,
AALC/Kenya Representative,
P. O. Box 42316,
NAIROBI

Dear Brother Cannon,

I have received a memo indicating that you will be leaving Kenya for other assignments in your Washington office.

I would like to take this opportunity, first on my own behalf, and on behalf of the College faculty members and all other College Staff to express our sincere appreciation for the co-operation we had while working with you.

I think it is fitting to state that your hard work during the COTU Workers Education Institute days and the task you undertook to develop College Plan of Operation together with other physical efforts you put while the College was being furnished through AALC assistance is something that shall be remembered by all colleagues in the Kenya Trade Union Movement for many years to come.

We wish you every success in your new assignment and hope that you will not forget to keep us informed of what you are doing either individually or as a College.

Be assured of our best trade union regards.

Yours fraternally,

HENRY KOWERU
Deputy Principal

30. Ministry of Labour, Minister P. Aringo, Nairobi, Kenya 1986

MINISTRY OF LABOUR

Telegrams: "LABCOM", Nairobi
Telephone: Nairobi 722200
When replying please quote
Ref. No ML/B/113 Vol.II(114)
and date

OFFICE OF THE MINISTER
P.O. Box 40326
NAIROBI

25th March, 1986

Mr. Peter J. Cannon,
Regional Representative,
African American Labour Centre,
P. O. Box 42316,
NAIROBI.

Dear Mr. Cannon,

As you prepare to leave Kenya, I want to thank you for all that you have done to assist the Labour movement in this country. You came to help launch the Tom Mboya Labour College and stayed to assist the workers of Kenya in all capacities.

Your assistance to the Labour College has been inestimable. In addition to your contributions at the design stage, you have helped guide its curriculum development and have taught many courses yourself. With COTU, itself, you have provided continual advice, assistance and solidarity. Large numbers of Kenyan trade unionists have benefited from training programmes in the United States through your good offices, while many American trade unionists have also visited here to conduct training programmes and to exchange ideas with their trade union brothers.

Above all, my Ministry has appreciated your valued contribution towards making the Kenyan trade union movement more responsible and able to better represent the workers of this constructively. At all times, you have been sensitive to the tripartite nature of industrial relations in Kenyan. Your enthusiastic co-operation with my Ministry and the employers group has certainly advanced the harmonious development of Labour relations here.

We will miss you. It is testimony to your character and concern that you have almost become one of us. It is equal evidence to your work, however, that your contributions will stand after you depart. In doing so, go with our best wishes and with a piece of Kenya in your heart.

Yours faithfully,

Peter Oloo Aringo, EGH, M.P.
MINISTER FOR LABOUR

c.c.

Mr. Patrick J. O'Farrell,
Executive Director,
African American Labour Centre,
144 K Street, N.W. Suite 700,
WASHINGTON, DC 20005,

31. Ambassador Gerald E. Thomas, US Embassy, Nairobi, Kenya 1986

EMBASSY OF THE
UNITED STATES OF AMERICA
NAIROBI, KENYA

March 27, 1986

Mr. Peter J. Cannon
Representative
African-American Labor Center
P.O. Box 42316
Nairobi

Dear Peter:

I am sad to hear that you are leaving Kenya. After six years in Nairobi, I can understand that your home office wants you back, but you will be missed. You have provided invaluable advice and support to this mission and to United States interests generally.

Over the years, we have looked to you to offer sensitive readouts of local labor issues and personalities, as well as to recommend which of the latter might benefit from visitor programs to the United States. You always have been ready to offer innovative solutions to thorny problems; but, more frequently, your "heads up" has been just enough to defuse them before they become serious.

Personally, I shall miss your good humor and unflagging high spirits. My very best to you and Kari upon your return to Washington.

Sincerely,

Gerald E. Thomas
Ambassador

32. Central Organization of Trade Unions (COTU) Kenya 1986

CENTRAL ORGANIZATION OF TRADE UNIONS (KENYA)

Chairman-General:
PHILIP M. KIBIRIBIRI.
Secretary-General:
JUSTUS MULEI VELE
Treasurer-General
WERE DIBO OGUTU

(C. O. T. U. (K)
All Correspondence to be Addressed to Secretary General
Telephone: X28565,X28566&X23X33 761375/6/7
Telegrams: "COTU"

SOLIDARITY BUILDING,
DIGO ROAD,
P. O. Box 13000,
NAIROBI.

Our Ref:..COTU/AALC/RO/85/2/1/142

Your Ref:.................. Date7.-.4.-.....1986....

Mr. Peter J. Cannon,
Representative,
African American Labor Centre (AFL-CIO),
P.O. Box 42316,
NAIROBI.

Dear Bro. Cannon,

I regret that you will be leaving us soon after our long mutual association. The work of AALC in Kenya has been of great aid to the Central Organisation of Trade Unions and our members over the years and has been extended during your time in Kenya. COTU has grown and prospered during this period due in no small part to your enthusiasm and hard work. Your own personal effort and the fraternal relationships which you have been able to foster on behalf of the American workers is deeply appreciated.

On behalf of COTU, its affiliated (29) unions and our Tom Mboya Labour College, I wish to thank you very sincerely for your indefatigable efforts in assisting our movement to gain strength. The AALC (AFL-CIO) can be proud of your unselfish service.

I sincerely wish you and your family well in your new assignment in Washington, D.C. at your Headquarters.

Our thanks and warm personal regards.

Fraternally,

Philip Mwangi
CHAIRMAN GENERAL

OUR MOTTO "EVER FORWARD WITH WORKERS"

Deputy Secretary General JOSEPH J. MUGALLA
Assistant Secretary General GEORGE ODIKO
1st Vice Chairman General JAMES AWICH
2nd Vice Chairman General JOSEPH NYABIYA
Deputy Treasurer General
JOHN MURUGU

33. International Institute for Development, Cooperation and Labour Studies, HISTADRUT, Israel 1988

INTERNATIONAL INSTITUTE FOR DEVELOPMENT, COOPERATION AND LABOUR STUDIES
(AFRO-ASIAN INSTITUTE) HISTADRUT — ISRAEL

INSTITUT INTERNATIONAL D'ETUDES DU DEVELOPPEMENT, DE LA COOPERATION ET DU TRAVAIL
(INSTITUT AFRO-ASIATIQUE) HISTADROUT — ISRAEL

המכון הבינלאומי ללמודי פיתוח, קואופרציה ועבודה
המכון האפריקני־אסייני של ההסתדרות

August 1, 1988

Mr. Peter J. Cannon
AALC Representative
P.O.Box 727
Maseru 100
Lesotho

Rece: 11/8/88
PJC

Dear Peter,

It was indeed a great pleasure to work with you on the SATUCC workshop and to renew our personal acquaintance. I found a great deal of common ground and interest and trust that we will have the opportunity to work together again in the future.

As requested, I enclose our Programme of Studies for 1989 and two sets of application forms. Please forward the completed forms as soon as possible so that we may give full consideration to the applications.

Please pass on my best regards to your wife. I look forward to be able to welcome you both to Israel in the not too distant future.

All the best,

Mark Levin
Head of Division, English Language Studies

ML/ee/9327

Enclosures

H-707 7 NEHARDEA STREET P.O.B. 16201 TEL-AVIV 64235, ISRAEL * TEL. 03-229195, 229196 * CABLES: AFROASIAN TEL-AVIV * TLX. 361480 AAI IL

34. Ambassador Robert M. Smalley, US Embassy, Maseru, Lesotho 1989

EMBASSY OF THE
UNITED STATES OF AMERICA

Maseru, Lesotho
May 16, 1989

Mr. Patrick O'Farrell
Executive Director
African-American Labor Center (AFL-CIO)
1400 K Street, N.W.
Washington, D. C. 20005

Dear Mr. O'Farrell:

I will soon be completing my assignment as U.S. Ambassador to the Kingdom of Lesotho. Before relinquishing this office, however, I want to commend the outstanding service and performance of your African-American Labor Center (AFL-CIO) Representative in Maseru, Peter Cannon.

During the past two years, Mr. Cannon has been a tremendous help to me and to my staff in our effort to understand and keep abreast of the complex labor developments here in Lesotho, in South Africa and in other countries in the southern African region. While still unable to visit South Africa, I believe that Peter is remarkably well versed in developments there. In our case, he has come to our aid on any number of occasions with deeply insightful analyses and interpretations of Lesotho-South Africa labor relations.

During my tenure, this Embassy has developed a small but serious assistance program in the labor field. This reflects my belief that labor unions, organizations and workers will play a leading role in the transformation of southern Africa, including the abolition of apartheid, and in the future political and economic evolution of the entire region. In Lesotho, we are taking a number of small steps now to ensure ourselves a role in that process. Recently, for example, we have provided resources to assist this country's Ministry of Labor conduct a national labor survey to match existing labor skills in Lesotho with the skilled and semi-skilled requirements of the Kingdom's mammoth water transfer scheme, the Highlands Water Project. Within the next few months, we will also begin a multi-year training program with the Ministry of Labor. This undertaking will utilize U.S. Department of Labor training resources to strengthen the technical capabilities and institutions of this critical Ministry.

We owe a great deal to Peter Cannon's expert advice on each of these and other initiatives, and this letter acknowledges our gratitude for the very large contribution he has made. Peter has maintained excellent relations with the Embassy and our Johannesburg-based Regional Labor Officer, as we have labored together in the pursuit of common objectives.

Sincerely,

Robert M. Smalley
Ambassador

cc: Mr. Peter Cannon
AALC, Maseru

35. Ministry of Employment, Social Welfare and Pensions, Maseru, Lesotho 1990

Ministry of Employment, Social,

Welfare and Pensions,

Private Bag A116,

Maseru 100.

ESP/TU/19 23rd May, 1990.

Mr. Peter J. Cannon,
Representative,
African-American
Labour Centre,
P.O. Box 727,
MASERU 100.

Dear Sir,

This is to acknowledge receipt of your letter dated 10th May, 1990.

It is with profound surprise that the African - American Labour Centre Headquarters has decided to close its offices in Lesotho. Your contribution to the trade union movement in Lesotho has been very much appreciated.

Permit me to take this opportunity to congratulate you on your selfless and relentless efforts in promoting a merger of our two labour federations; your support in the Skills Profile Survey and your involvement in bringing labour specialists from America to conduct workshops in Lesotho, to mention but a few.

It is my conviction that you have enjoyed your stay in Lesotho and, in a sense, you will be our Ambassador wherever you will be posted.

Please accept Sir, the assurances of my highest consideration.

Yours sincerely,

C.T. THAMAE
PRINCIPAL SECRETARY

36. Construction and Allied Workers Union of Lesotho 1990

C.A.W.U.L.E.,
P.O. Box 4055,
Maseru. 104.
LESOTHO.

28th May, 1990.

Mr. Peter J. Cannon,
Representative,
African American Labour Centre (AFL-CIO),
P.O. Box 727,
Maseru. 104.

Dear Brother Cannon,

I regret that you will be leaving us soon after our long mutual association. The work of the AALC in Lesotho has been of great aid to CAWULE in particular and, indeed, to Trade Unionism in Lesotho. The formation of the Construction and Allied Workers Union of Lesotho was an inspirational milestone which was due, largely, to your optimism, your enthusiasm, and your hard work. Your own personal effort and the fraternal relationships which you initiated to bring workers of both our countries together have made an indelible impression on us, and we do hope that these efforts will not appear to have been in vain.

On behalf of members of CAWULE and the interim Executive Committee, I wish to thank you most sincerely for your indefatigible efforts in assisting our movement to gain strength. I a m sure the AALC (AFL-CIO) and the American people will be proud of your unselfish dedication to duty.

I sincerely wish you and your family well in Washington, and hope that you will always remain mindful of ou r problems here.

I remain,
Yours in the struggle,

GENERAL SECRETARY.

37. Ministry of Foreign Affairs, Maseru, Lesotho 1990

Ministry of Foreign Affairs
P.O. Box 1387
MASERU
Lesotho

FR/CL/CTR/171

30th May, 1990

Mr. H. F. Jeter
Embassy of the United States of America
P.O. Box 333
MASERU

Dear Sir

The Lesotho Highlands Development Authority (LHDA) will commence construction of Phase IA of the Lesotho Highlands Water Project at the end of 1990. This Phase involves the employment of 3,000 to 6,000 persons of various nationalities.

Due to the envisaged complexity of the industrial relations, LHDA will require the services of an Industrial Relations Consultant for a period of twenty (20) weeks.

We have been informed that the local AFL-CIO Office will close in July and are eager to secure the services of Mr. Peter Cannon, AFL-CIO Representative as he is familiar with labour practices in Lesotho and South Africa.

We hereby request you use your good Offices with the competent authorities in order to assist us in securing his services for the LHDA.

Yours Sincerely

Ntlhakana N. A.

FIRST SECRETARY, EUROPE AND AMERICAS
for **P.S. FOREIGN AFFAIRS**

cc : Mr. Peter Cannon
AFL-CIO Office
P.O. Box 727
MASERU

: FR/CL/PROJ/2

38. Co-operative for Research and Education (CORE) South Africa 1990

CO-OPERATIVE FOR
RESEARCH AND EDUCATION
P O Box 42440 Fordsburg 2033
62 Marshall St Johannesburg 2001
Tel: (011) 836 9942/3 Fax: (011) 836 9944

Mr. Peter Cannon
AALC
P. O. Box 7583
MASERU
Lesotho

20 June 1990

Dear Peter,

On behalf of all the members of the CORE I wish to place on record our appreciation for the very difficult task you performed so admirably; patiently under circumstances which can only emphemistically be referred to as trying conditions.

In the time we came to know you we appreciated your cool and collected approach and the professionalism which you brought to the task.

We know that you will not be lost to the trade union struggle worldwide and that you will always hold and have a special place with all of us who came to know you and work with you.

With best wishes to you and Karic for the future.

Yours fraternally,

Phiroshaw Camay
PC/ft

39. African-American Labor Center, AFL-CIO 1990

African-American Labor Center

Centre Afro-Américain du Travail • المركز الأفريقي الأمريكي للعمل

Lane Kirkland
President
Thomas R. Donahue
Secretary-Treasurer
Patrick J. O'Farrell
Executive Director

1400 K Street, NW • Suite 700 • Washington, DC 20005

Tel.: (202) 789-1020 FAX: (202) 842-0730 TWX: 710-822-1115

August 10, 1990

To Whom It May Concern:

Mr. Peter J. Cannon has been employed as a Field Representative for the African-American Labor Center (AALC) for the past 11 years. The AALC is the international institute of the AFL-CIO responsible for carrying out the policies of the AFL-CIO as they relate to Africa and implementing programs of trade union development throughout the continent. Due to budget reductions and a reorganization of our programs in Africa, we have made the difficult decision to eliminate the position held by Mr. Cannon.

This decision in no way reflects on Peter's ability to perform the required tasks or commitment to the organization and its objectives. Over the past 11 years Peter has been responsible for two extremely important programs in Africa - Kenya and South Africa - and has been involved in numerous other trade union programs in other countries.

To elaborate, Mr. Cannon assumed the responsibility for our South Africa program in June 1986 under very difficult circumstances. Upon arrival Peter was immediately denied a visa to enter South Africa and was forced to conduct and coordinate all activities from Lesotho. From this disadvantage Peter was able to maintain close contact with the South African trade unions, implement programs, and conduct business in an orderly and professional manner. This office was pleased with Peter's analytical reporting, accounting procedures, evaluation and sound judgement. While in Lesotho Peter was also responsible for the trade union program there as well as our regional effort. From 1989 to 1990, in Lesotho, Peter was instrumental in a major, nation-wide skills survey project and efforts to draft new labor legislation for the country's workforce. Regionally, Peter initiated numerous programs which brought together unionists from the various countries to compare and coordinate their activities.

From 1979 to 1986 Mr. Cannon was responsible for our country labor program in Kenya. Of primary significance was his responsibility for the planning, building, and administering the Tom Mboya residential labor college. The college had a construction cost of 2.8 million U.S. dollars and, when completed, included 72 beds and classroom space for 120. In addition to his responsibilities in Kenya, Peter also provided specialized program assistance in Zaire, Uganda, and Mauritius.

\- 2 -

From the above it should be evident that Peter Cannon is willing to accept responsibility and execute those duties in a professional manner. We highly recommend Peter as a person of hard work, dependability, and dedication.

Sincerely,

Patrick J. O'Farrell
Executive Director

MTL:sw

40. United Food and Commercial Workers Union, AFL-CIO 1990

Gary R. Nebeker
International Vice President
Director
International and Foreign Affairs Department

June 6, 1990

Mr. Peter J. Cannon
Representative
African-American Labor Center
Centre Afro-American Du Travail
Post Office Box 727
Maseru 100 Lesotho
SOUTH AFRICA

Dear Peter:

I am sorry to hear that you will no longer be employed by AALC. I always felt that you were one of the best representatives that the AFL-CIO could have in Africa. I have observed your dedication and willingness to work in difficult areas, with difficult problems.

Please contact me when you arrive in Washington, D.C.

With my best wishes, I remain

Sincerely and fraternally,

International Vice President and Director
International and Foreign Affairs Department

William H. Wynn
International
President

Jerry Menapace
International
Secretary-Treasurer

United Food & Commercial Workers
International Union, AFL-CIO & CLC
1775 K Street, N.W.
Washington, D.C. 20006
(202) 223-3111 FAX (202) 466-1562

41. Lesotho Highlands Development Authority, Deputy Chief Executive 1994

Lesotho Highlands Development Authority

P.O. Box 7332, Maseru 100, Lesotho. Telephone: 311280 Fax: 310050 Telex 4523, LHDA LO

TO WHOM IT MAY CONCERN:

The Lesotho Highlands Water Project is one of the largest and most intricate tunnel and dam engineering projects under realization in the world today. It is expected to consume an estimated $ US 5.2 billion over some thirty years. Phase 1A includes the construction of two dams, excavation of 83km of 5m diameter tunnels and the construction of an underground power station of 72MW.

Its a pleasure to commend on the invaluable advice, outstanding service and innovative performance of Mr Peter J. Cannon to the LHWP during the past three years. Mr Cannon's role as the labour relations and safety facilitator between the Contractor's and their labour force has been admirably professionally performed so and that under circumstances which can only euphemistically be referred to as "trying conditions".

It is a testimony to his character, enthusiasm, and concern that his valued contribution within the Engineering and Construction Department of the Lesotho Highlands Development Authority has been inestimable. Above all his unstinting efforts to promote industrial peace and a safe working environment are reflected in the minuscule number of working hours lost to industrial unrest and the diminishing disabling injury frequency rate on the job sites.

Rest assured that Mr Cannon has earned over the past three years my professional and personal assurance of the highest consideration.

Yours sincerely

W. ROHRBÄCH
DEPUTY CHIEF EXECUTIVE
ENGINEERING & CONSTRUCTION

42. Lesotho Highlands Development Authority, Deputy Chief Executive 1997

Lesotho Highlands Development Authority

P.O. Box 7332, Maseru 100, Lesotho. Telephone: 311280 Fax: 310060 Telex 4523, LHDA LO

TO WHOM IT MAY CONCERN

The Lesotho Highlands Water Project is one of the largest and most intricate tunnel and dam engineering projects under realisation in the world today. Phase IA includes the construction of two dams, excavation of 83km of 5m diameter tunnels and the construction of an underground power station of 72MW costing approximately US$ 5.2 billion.

Mr P. Cannon has taken an active role during the execution of these works from 1st January 1991 to January 1997 employed by the Lesotho Highlands Development Authority. As Labour Relations and Safety facilitator he has conducted his duties in a professional manner throughout this period.

His diligent efforts to promote industrial peace and a safe working environment are reflected in the limited number of industrial unrest occurrences and the diminishing disabling injury frequency rate on the job sites, during the past six years.

Rest assured that Mr Cannon has earned my professional esteem.

Yours sincerely,

L. Fabian
DEPUTY CHIEF EXECUTIVE
ENGINEERING & CONSTRUCTION

LESOTHO HIGHLANDS
P O Box 7332
31 JAN 1997
Maseru 100 Lesotho
DEVELOPMENT AUTHORITY

43. US Wheat Associates, Cape Town, South Africa 1999

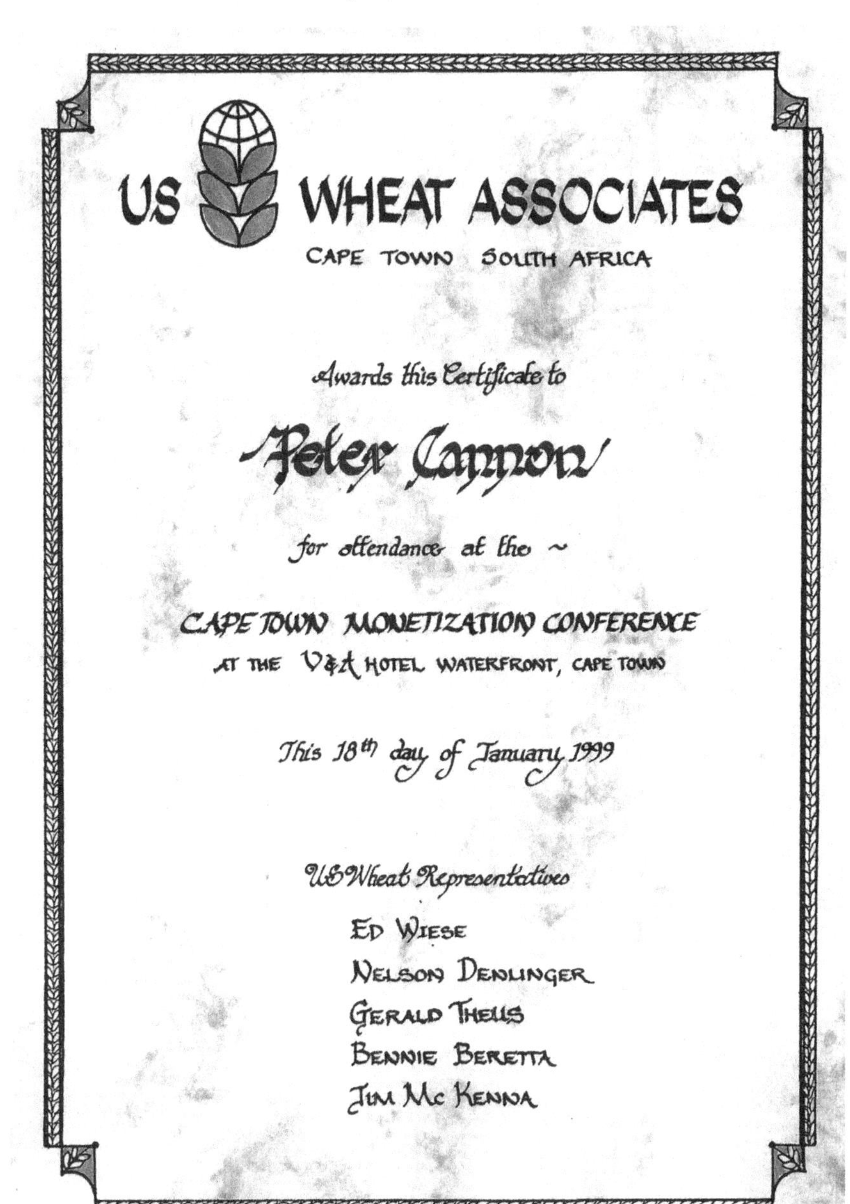

US WHEAT ASSOCIATES
CAPE TOWN SOUTH AFRICA

Awards this Certificate to

Peter Cannon

for attendance at the ~

CAPE TOWN MONETIZATION CONFERENCE
AT THE V&A HOTEL WATERFRONT, CAPE TOWN

This 18th day of January 1999

US Wheat Representatives

Ed Wiese
Nelson Denlinger
Gerald Theus
Bennie Beretta
Jim Mc Kenna

44. Solidarity Center, AFL-CIO 2001

AMERICAN CENTER FOR INTERNATIONAL LABOR SOLIDARITY

March 14, 2001

To whom it may concern:

Recently (July 15–September 15, 2001), Mr. Peter Cannon successfully completed a temporary assignment with the Solidarity Center Africa/Middle-East office in Nigeria, West Africa. This assignment was particularly difficult because Peter was facilitating a mandatory transfer of a long term SC field representative whom he worked with for many years. Peter's long years of experience in the international arena was important in successfully facilitating this transition, while at the same time maintaining program continuity in the region.

In conclusion, Peter and I have an excellent employment relationship for over 15 years and I would not only highly recommend him to prospective employers. I intend to employ him for other assignments if he is available when the need arises. Please feel free to contact me at the above address if you need additional information concerning this matter.

I have briefly outlined Peters scope of work on this assignment. (See attachment)

Sincerely,

Byron Charlton,
Coordinator for Africa/Middle East

BC/smt

Enclosure

HEADQUARTERS
1925 K STREET, NW
SUITE 300
WASHINGTON, DC
20006-1105
PHONE 202-778-4500
FAX 202-778-4525
E-MAIL acils@acils.org

45. Aurora Associates International, Inc. Washington, DC 2001

11-06-201 5:53PM FROM

November 6, 2001

TO: Mr. Peter Cannon
70 North Street
Calais, MN
04619

Dear Mr. Cannon,

On behalf of the Board of Directors of Aurora Associates International, Inc., I am pleased to offer you full time employment as Senior Project Director (Chief Technical Advisor) serving USDoL's Veterans Employment Service Project based in Lagos, Nigeria. The annual salary will be $71,000.

Your employment contract was sent to you November 2, 2001. It is contemplated that this contract represents an "at will" employment relationship. Nonetheless, it is the intent of Aurora and Peter Cannon to provide to the other reasonably prompt written advance notice of any known circumstances or changes that would affect continuation of the employment relationship. Therefore, written notice of intent to terminate employment (except for cause) should be given as far in advance as is practicable under the circumstances.

Once again, I welcome you to the Aurora team. I look forward to working with you and sustaining a productive professional relationship throughout your time as employee with Aurora.

Sincerely,

Robert C. Walker
President

46. Genographic DNA History Results 2009

Certificate of Y-chromosome DNA testing

In recognition of your participation in the Genographic Project, we hereby certify that

belongs to:

Haplogroup R1b, M343 (Subclade R1b1c, M269)

The designations for all twelve loci examined for this purpose are listed here,
along with the Short Tandem Repeats (STRs) outcome for each.

393	19	391	439	389-1	389-2	388	390	426	385a	385b	392
13	14	11	12	13	16	12	25	12	11	14	13

November 19, 2009

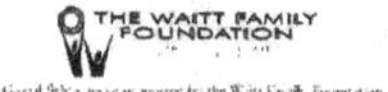

NATIONAL GEOGRAPHIC

About the Author

This is Peter Cannon's first book. He has extensive tripartite experience in basic human rights and organizational development. His decades long cross cultural ability to deliver services professionally under varied conditions took place in Angola, Bangladesh, Botswana, Canada, Congo, Egypt, Ghana, Kenya, Liberia, Lesotho, Madagascar, Malawi, Mauritius, Nigeria, Norway, Philippines, South Africa, South Korea, Sudan, Swaziland, Togo, Uganda, Vietnam, Zambia and Zimbabwe. He resides with his wife Gudrun, in North Kingstown, Rhode Island.